A SPIRITUAL PSYCHOLOGY

A SPIRITUAL PSYCHOLOGY
J.G. BENNETT

PUBLISHED BY
THE J.G. BENNETT FOUNDATION
PETERSHAM
MASSACHUSETTS

U.S.A.

Title: A Spiritual Psychology
Author: J.G. Bennett

Original edition: Hodder & Stoughton, London 1964
Revised editions: CSA Press, Lakemont GA et al. 1974
This edition published by the J.G. Bennett Foundation, Petersham
MA 01366, 2020

ISBN: 9798626375756

Publisher's note

"A Spiritual Psychology" was first published in 1964. The body of
the text is drawn from transcriptions of lectures and discussions taking
place at a special seminar at Coombe Springs in August 1962, with
commentary by John Bennett. Most of the participants in the seminar
were students of G.I. Gurdjieff of long standing, or practitioners of
Subud or both, and there were also a number of newcomers who were
from neither group. All sessions were led by John Bennett, and the
transcripts were formatted first by Dr. Isabel Turnadge, and then edited
and annotated by Bennett. "A Spiritual Psychology" was republished in
1974 in its present form after Mr. Bennett removed the original Prologue
and Appendix and inserted a new first chapter.

Visit: https://www.jgbennett.org

asp2ed v:20201203

Contents

PREFACE

Man's noblest quality is the will to discover an imperishable Reality beyond the changes and chances of this mortal world. This quality is what l mean by "spiritual". Man's spirit is his will. This is what St. Thomas Aquinas taught and it is the secret of understanding our human nature. The soul is an artifact, the result of our life experience. It may be transient and it may be immortal, depending upon whether or not our will, that is, our spirit, has taken possession of it. Those who deny the will in man deny the spirit. Those who affirm the will, affirm the spirit—whether they realize it or not.

Since will is commitment to action, it follows that A Spiritual Psychology must be a practical psychology. One can go further and say that it must be a "do-it-yourself psychology," by which I mean that we must find and live by our will and not look to anyone else to do the work for us. This is where A Spiritual Psychology differs from most clinical psychology.

The present book was therefore written with a practical aim in view. That is to help people to learn how to "work on themselves" in their search for the imperishable Real. At the present time, we have a school at Sherborne House, near Cheltenham, England that is applying the techniques developed at Coombe Springs. It is a method that owes the most to Gurdjieff but has been extended from other sources and tested over many years. It has proved successful not only under guidance at Sherborne, but also for people who have to work as well as they can on their own. For the benefit of readers of the present book, I shall describe the way in which I have advised people to work with it.

The procedure we followed was a talk in the morning introducing a program of work to enable us to verify for ourselves the validity of some part of the psychological structure. In the evening we pooled our observations and discussed them. We should have done better if we had had more time.

The program I suggest to the reader is to take the book chapter by chapter. Read carefully the first morning talk and close the book. Spend one week in carrying out the program and at the end of the week read the evening discussion and compare it with your own experience. Then repeat the experiment for one more week to see what more you can get from it. This should enable you to test the ideas both theoretically and practically.

After the second week, go on to the second chapter and so on through the book. You will find that the practical exercises will lead you towards a non-verbal awareness of depths of your own nature that you previously had no means of reaching.

If you wish to ask any questions or extend the program, you can write me at Sherborne House, Sherborne near Cheltenham, England and I will reply as well as I can.

1. A SPIRITUAL PSYCHOLOGY

If you are the reader I hope for, you are in search of a satisfying answer to the question: "What is the sense and purpose of my life and how am I to achieve it?" I am not so naïve as to suppose that this book will answer the question to everyone's satisfaction. I can only give the answer that has satisfied me. We are needed to maintain the balance of energies in the Solar System and to help its spiritual evolution. We exist to serve Nature rather than to make use of Her. If we serve consciously the purpose of our existence we become "real" beings. If we fail to serve we remain "ghosts" living only a dream life. Once this is understood our first aim must be to prepare ourselves to be able to live the life intended for us by Great Nature.

In the past, mankind has been enticed or driven into this path by the hope of heaven and the fear of eternal punishment, but the reason for it has not been revealed. So when the promises and threats ceased to work, people saw no more reason for effort and sacrifice, except for their own welfare and that of their nearest and dearest. For centuries, people almost universally accepted the injunction to be "content with that state of life to which it has pleased God to call us!" Today we hear this no longer. Since the eighteenth century, Western man has reversed the assurance that "God's in His heaven, all's right with the world" to read "Man's on the earth, all's right with the heavens." Seventy years ago, Swinburne wrote his *Hymn to Man* with the refrain "Glory to Man in the Highest for Man is the master of things." We have lost confidence in God and are fast losing confidence in man.

A new source of confidence has arisen: the great human institutions. In its crudest form this is the communist state. But we also have it in the belief that governments, churches, corporations, well-organized pressure groups are able to guarantee stability at least "in our day." Science, economics, computers and the weapons of power have taken over from Jove and his thunderbolts. In these strange gods, the silent majority places its faltering trust and looks with dismay on those who want to do away with its institutions. For thousands of years, mankind has looked to institutions to solve its problems. It has been assumed that man himself is a known fixed quantity whose life conditions depend upon the organization of society. In our day, this position has been overtly adopted by the Behaviorists. They hold that man is entirely the product of his culture. He is a plastic, shapeless creature at birth and is formed completely by the society in which he grows up. This extreme view is recent but it was implicit in the older view that the social order is essentially good. Up to the seventeenth century, the only institutions that seemed important were those of church and state and to a lesser extent the guilds of merchants and craftsmen. This was true not only for Christendom but also for the vast areas of Asia and Africa dominated by Islam. It was truest of all for China where the search for the ideal form of government was the business of philosophers and rulers alike.

It is true that the sacredness of the individual and the rights of man were accepted as axiomatic, but only within an accepted social order. The Old and New Testament, the Qur'an, the *Bhagavad Gita* and the Analects of Confucius all agree that Institutions are God-given and must be respected. New man-made institutions of various kinds appeared since the beginning of the nineteenth century. One was the joint stock company leading to the industrial and financial empires of our day. The other is the world organization starting with the International Postal Union in 1856 and leading to the United Nations with all its offshoots.

Few question that institutions are needed for the orderly working of human society, but many have begun to doubt if they do or ever will promote human welfare. The loss of faith in institutions is accompanied by a fear of their power, not as formerly to dominate by military, political and economic weapons but by direct action on the human psyche. Skinner, in his *Beyond Freedom and Dignity* and in *Power and Innocence*, together with scores of other psychologists and sociologists, though holding very different views as to man's nature and his prospects for the future, all agree that a new threat faces us: the use of power to deprive the individual of inner liberty. Behaviorism may have lost ground in recent years, but it still spells a threat that many regard as even more serious than the external hazards of war, pollution, exhaustion of resources and universal famine.

Against behaviorism is set the human potential movement with its promise of unlimited growth both for the individual and for the human race. This has been linked with the search for new forms of psychic and religious experience. Millions are experimenting with pentecostal religion and various brands of eastern spirituality. Millions also have tried drugs and other hallucinogenic agents. None of these experiments have given convincing results. Ideas and methods, teachers and writers have sprung into prominence and after a few years faded away. An interesting feature of all these movements is that they usually stabilize with a solid core of convinced believers and a flow of seekers who swell the numbers and give the illusion of growth, but sooner or later drift away.

We live in a society with deep contradictions and conflicts. Three main streams can be discerned. There are those who fear and oppose change, whose idea of progress is to have more and more of the same and to have it more and more securely. There are those who want change but see it in external achievements. They look to a new world created by science and technology and by the power of organization. This group ranges from behaviorists to science fiction addicts. Most of them would echo Swinburne's "Glory to Man in the Highest." The third stream includes the human potential movement; but this can be interpreted in so many, and often contradictory, ways that all that can safely be said is that its followers believe that the solution of human problems must be sought in man himself and not in his institutions. We can distinguish two branches. One can be called transformism. This term was adopted by Ouspensky in 1938 to describe his own teaching. The present book is all about transformism and I shall say no more here than to state its main claim: man as we know him is an incomplete being with limitless potential for development or transformation. Man's destiny is altogether bound up with his capacity for self-perfecting. The second branch takes a more negative view of man. He is nothing who becomes something by the mere process of living. The current version of this second branch is Existentialism. There is only the "human condition" which is what happens to us and not what we are born with. For the existentialist, "essence" is a meaningless word. There is no human nature, no human instincts, man is what he makes of himself. Sartre, the apostle of existentialism says: "man first of all exists, encounters himself, surges up in the world and defines himself afterwards... to begin with, he is nothing. He will not be anything until later and then he will be what he makes himself." Such a creed can lead to profound pessimism as it has done with Sartre and many others. This pessimism is one of the characteristics of our time: but until recently it was not shared by those who looked outward at man's achievements and ignored his inner emptiness.

Until the 1960's there was widespread optimism as to man's future. Those who belonged to each of the three mainstreams were confident that their way of life would prove successful and ultimately prevail. There has been a dramatic change in the last few years. Only professional optimists can pretend to see the way clear ahead. The political, economic and financial structure of the world no longer inspires any confidence. Formerly, there was always some enemy that we could blame. Now we see that all are equally helpless and equally alarmed about the future. No one seriously believes that we have seen the end of war and revolution. Social reform has failed to bring social well-being. Social engineering sprang up like a mushroom and its collapse has been one of the spectacular events of the last decade. Behavioral science, neighborhood studies, programmed learning, computerized welfare, compensatory social factoring—all these promising lines have proved to be dead ends. The young generation turned from drugs to political protest, from politics to pop and from that to the spiritual quest. Nothing works and no one can see why. This is strange in an age that prides itself on its pragmatic realism and can point to the achievements of science and technology to support the claim that man can achieve whatever he sets his hand to.

Evidently, the problem is much deeper and subtler than people suppose. Man's outer world has changed out of recognition in the past thousand years, but his nature has remained as enigmatic and recalcitrant as ever. While we in the West have been achieving mastery over inanimate objects, the East has kept its attention on the human predicament. As a result, they know far more about man and his nature than we do. We are an "undeveloped country" so far as man is concerned and we are trying to catch up by borrowing psychological methods from the East as they are borrowing technology from us. We are making the same mistake of trying to use unfamiliar techniques without acquiring the know-how. We are attempting to mount large-scale human engineering operations without understanding man.

We do not take account of the full range of human potential. It has been said that man is like an iceberg: only one eighth is visible above the surface. Even those who believe in human perfectibility do so in naïve superficial terms. The unseen man is not only the source of his potential, it also acts constantly and unpredictably upon the visible man. If we use the word "spiritual" to mean that part of man's nature which is beyond the reach of ordinary observation and analysis, then by "Spiritual Psychology" we understand the study of man as a whole: the potential man and the actual man taken together. Using this concept, I would say that human engineering in the West has failed because it has neglected the spiritual man.

This does not explain why the various "spiritual" movements are also failing. This book attempts to answer this question and to offer a way that corresponds to the needs of our time. It is based upon more than fifty years of research and experimentation since I first became aware that I could exist outside my body. This happened when I was nearly killed at the Western Front on the 21st of March 1918. I then understood once and for all that there is something in man that is neither mind nor body and which is not subject to the conditions of space and time. Since then I have pursued this trail through many countries and with the help of many teachers and wise men. I have been exceptionally fortunate in the spiritual men and women I have met. I have seen for myself that access to the spiritual world is not the prerogative of any one religion or any one teaching. Even among obscure sects like the Druzes, the Yezidis and the Ahl-i-Haqq, I have met men who were unmistakably spiritually advanced. The same is true of more recent movements like Subud. The strongest influence in my life has been George Gurdjieff and much of the spiritual psychology developed in this book has been learned from him.

I want to start by making an important distinction between psychic experiences and spiritual development. Our state of consciousness usually alternates between sleep and waking.

Very seldom we have moments or even periods of enhanced or expanded consciousness when we and the world appear quite different from what we are accustomed to. These states are very exciting and they give us hope of getting beyond the limitations of our ordinary life. Such moments come spontaneously in times of severe stress or illness near death. They come by means of drugs and other artificial agents. They can also be reached by exercises such as fasting, meditation, privation of sleep. They can be shared by many people under the influence of emotional excitement providing their attention is directed towards the "other world" as in revivalist meetings. All these changes of consciousness are attributable to changes in the nervous system and the chemistry of the blood. In themselves they have no spiritual significance. This does not mean that similar states do not arise in genuinely spiritual conditions, but the important thing is that they are merely symptoms that can be produced by a variety of causes. The truly spiritual development of man takes place beyond his consciousness. It is "supramental" to use the admirable term introduced by Sri Aurobindo Ghose, the great Indian nationalist and yogi. Cosmic consciousness has captivated the minds of western seekers since Bucke wrote his immortal but naïve work. "God-realization" is another catch phrase to be used with caution. There are states that are indications of spiritual progress, but they are not the goal of our striving. There is a serious error in equating a *state* with a *station*—in Sufi terminology a *hal* with a *makam*. We can enter high states of and yet remain ourselves just as we were before. There have been serious consequences of the error of mistaking a state of consciousness for a transformation of being. It has been assumed, often unwittingly, that since experience of higher states of consciousness is what we seek, we can judge the merits of a movement by its ability to produce higher states of consciousness in its followers. Another consequence has been the assumption that all ways of attaining higher states—including the use of psychedelic drugs—are equally valid. Such assumptions betray our ignorance of the spiritual life. Spirituality is primarily the domain of will and being. It is not concerned with unlocking the *Doors of Perception* as Aldous Huxley and many others have supposed. Aldous was a tragic figure. I first met him in 1933, when he was coming regularly to Ouspensky's meetings in London. Our last meeting was not long before his death when he had lost his wife, his eyesight, his home, library and hardest of all, his hope of understanding the meaning of life. He stands for the human predicament at a very high and subtle level. In *Brave New World*, he was one of the first to tell us that "experience" alone can be a dead end. In *Island* he showed that life has more to offer than glimpses of the world of the *Perennial Philosophy*, but he could not bring himself to make the sacrifice demanded of those who wish to become citizens of that world. This is the intellectualist hazard. Very intelligent people find it hard to accept the doctrine of the "supramental" literally. They will plunge into the hardest conceptions such as the monism of the Vedanta, as Aldous did for many years, but they cannot give up the belief that the truth is more accessible to the intelligent than the simple-minded. They cannot see the depth of Christ's saying: "Father, I thank Thee that Thou has hidden these things from the wise and prudent and hast revealed them unto babes." The "babe" can recognize "being", but the prudent tend to be attracted by knowledge!

The real quest of man is for substantial being. We are shadows or ghosts that have the potential of becoming real beings. Few in any age have the steadfastness of purpose and the sensitivity of perception to reach the highest goal. They are the spiritual giants. Those with lesser potential are nevertheless capable of attaining real being, if they feel the need strongly enough and if they can discover or be shown the way.

So far, the development of our ideas follows orthodox lines. All religions and all spiritual teachings agree that man is capable of transformation and that his transformation depends upon his own faith and determination. There they generally leave it. In reply to the question: "Why should we seek transformation and why is it made possible?", the answers hitherto proposed are no longer satisfying. The Hindu-Buddhist doctrine of liberation from the pain of existence means little to those who cling to existence because they can imagine no other state. The Christian-Moslem doctrine of resurrection in a state of bliss or torment has lost its credibility. We laugh at the Russian propaganda which tells the peasants that the astronauts did not find God when they went beyond the sky; but we are still so conditioned by time and space concepts that we think that nirvana, or heaven, or indeed any kind of real existence must be "somewhere". We are not helped by the pseudoscience which says that since matter and energy are interconvertible, it follows that there is no matter but only a "spiritual energy". Modern physics can help us, but in a very different way, by liberating us from the idea that space and time are a receptacle and that whatever exists does so "in" space and time.

The realization that we must go beyond space and time to understand anything, including the physical world, came to me more than fifty years ago at about the time I met Gurdjieff in Constantinople. I was able to understand that existence in space and time with its dream-like character is only a shadow of what our being can transform into. I had no difficulty in making the step from mathematical physics to Gurdjieff's cosmology. In my first talk with him in the palace of Prince Sabaheddin at Kuru Cheshme on the Bosphorus, I told him of my conclusion that the dimension of eternity was no less real than time and space. His reply changed the entire direction of my life: "What is the use of *knowing* that if you cannot *be* it? Of course there are higher dimensions, but they are useless to us unless we can live in them." I naturally asked how this was to be done. His reply opened my mind to the idea of transformation of being. I saw clearly that though I might extend my knowledge of the world as much as I pleased, I would remain the same man unless I could change myself. I already knew myself well enough to find the thought of "knowing without being" quite intolerable.

This is how my search for reality began. It has led me from country to country, from one teacher to another. It has taken me into various movements, groups and communities, all of which had something valuable to give me. But the thread which has guided me consistently through all these years has been the "system" or teaching of Gurdjieff. I have learned from it, the greater part of what I now regard as valid for understanding the "sense and meaning of our lives".

Gurdjieff himself searched from the age of eleven and

travelled far and wide in Africa, Europe and Asia. He found schools of wisdom in Turkestan and Tibet and in several instances was permitted to stay for long periods of time in order to assimilate the teaching. I have followed his teaching back to its sources and have become convinced that he brought to the West the material required for creating a new world.

For twenty years, I studied with Gurdjieff and Ouspensky and then for another twenty years I experimented with large and small groups of seekers at Coombe Springs, a large house near London. One of these experiments provides the subject matter of the present book. The Coombe Springs period lasted from 1944 to 1966. In 1948 and 1949 I spent all my available time with Gurdjieff in Paris and New York. He appointed me his "representative for England" and entrusted me with a variety of missions. The largest and most important part of my own spiritual psychology has come from Gurdjieff, but I am convinced that we all have to create our own picture of "Man, the World and God". The fragments from which the mosaic is constructed reach us from various sources and they are put together by our own search and cemented by our own spiritual travail. Even if we are unable to create a new world-picture, the one that we finally accept must be our own, tested in our experience and lived in our lives.

The spiritual life is much harder than the material life for we are working in a medium nine-tenths of which is beyond the reach of our ordinary experience. That is why spiritual people need all the help they can get. In our time, it is not easy to find true spiritual guides who understand the needs of modern man and his terrible predicament.

In her own account of her life, St. Teresa of Jesus, the Carmelite reformer and great mystic, refers more than once to "these directors, who, knowing nothing of the spiritual life, exhaust both soul and body and impede progress." She says elsewhere that "Those who go by the way of prayer, have more need of guidance than others, and the more spiritual they are, the more they need it!"

These words, by one of the most spiritual of saints, have often made me ask myself where spiritual guidance can be found in our time. There have been great directors, like St. John of the Cross, who have left behind them inspired instructions for those who follow the spiritual life. But these books are written for monks and nuns, whose way is different from that of the layman living in the world. And yet there always have been, and certainly are today, many who are drawn strongly by spiritual influences and are, therefore, as St. Teresa says, much in need of guidance. There is an abundance of devotional literature; but devotion is not necessarily the same as spirituality. There are books on the psychology of religious experience, pastoral psychology, but I have not found many that deal with the special problems that arise for those whose nature drives them to find the Reality behind the form; who, even in their outward life, cannot be satisfied with successful action; but who must be convinced also that what they do is directed toward values that are imperishable—beyond success or failure.

Such people are what I understand by "spiritual" people. They may be religious, or they may expect to find what they want without religion. Spirituality is not identical with religion. The artist, who looks for a quality in his art that this world cannot give, is a spiritual man even if he denies religion. A religious man who is content to do what he has been taught to the best of his ability may be a much better man than the other, but he is not, as such, spiritual.

Before going any further, I had best attempt to explain what I mean by the word "Spiritual." This is really impossible, because the very nature of spirituality is that it cannot be reduced to knowledge or to any kind of verbal formula. The nearest I can come to it is to say that spirit is the essential quality of anything or any being. In a sense, it can be called the "ideal" behind the actual; but the word "essential" is more appropriate by the sense it conveys of the opposite of "existential," of the measurable and the knowable elements of our experience. The same thing can be said in another way, by making the distinction between spirit and matter. We do make mistakes about matter, being accustomed to thinking of it as "what things are made of". This does not mean that we "know" matter; but we certainly know a great deal "about matter." We understand matter nowadays in quite a different way from, say, a hundred years ago. In the nineteenth century, matter meant combinations of the chemical atoms, and scientists imagined that they knew nearly all there was to know about it. In our days, matter has come to mean energy for most people; but for scientists—especially physicists—it has become a mystery. Neither matter nor energy mean the same to a theoretical physicist as they did thirty or forty years ago.

So we can console ourselves that, if "spirit" is hard to define, matter is not much easier. It has become evident to physicists that materiality is relative; and it is probable that many properties that used to be regarded as "spiritual"—such as sensation, thought, and even consciousness—are only different states or forms of matter in some form or state of combination.

You may think that I have included so much of our experience within the material world that spirit has little place left to occupy. This is very far from being the case. The non-material is as rich in content as the material. It is the realm of quality and value. Values have distinctions of their own: beauty is distinct from goodness, elegance from enonomy, truth from rightness; and, in general, every value from all other values. There are endless combinations of the primary and the derived values that make in their totality what I have called "The Domain of Value".

The content of the Domain of Value is "spirit" and so spirit is the totality of all forms of value, that is, of all possible qualities.

Just as I think that materiality is relative, so also do I believe that spirituality is relative. The song of birds in the spring, the fleeting glory of an autumn sunset, a charitable deed generously done, a picture that we recognize as an authentic work of art, any ordinary job of work properly carried through and finished, the "trembling of the soul at the very gates of Paradise"—all these are bearers of spiritual quality, but they are neither of the same kind nor of the same order of spirituality.

You may object to the distinction of spirit and matter, and say that all things I have described are, after all, only the properties of matter. A picture by a great master and a miserable daub are both no more than paint and canvas arranged in a visible form. The difference is only in our thoughts and feelings about them, and I have said that thoughts and feelings are probably nothing but states of matter. So it all reduces to materialism after all.

My answer is that it seems so from the standpoint of

"knowledge" but knowledge is not all. We do not "know" which is the true work of art, we "judge" its quality by some power in us that is quite different from knowing. We know about matter, but spiritual qualities are recognized by judgment.

If this is not clear, let us at least agree that we are able to recognize qualities when we see them. I will only ask you to accept one more idea and that is that "qualities have a reality of their own", whether they are connected with material forms or not. For example, I would ask you to accept the idea that "goodness" is real and would still be real if there were not one good person or thing in the whole world. Obviously, you can find this absurd and reject it as sheer nonsense; all I ask you to agree to, is that there is nothing absurd or illogical in the "idea" that spiritual qualities have a reality of their own, quite different from the reality of matter. With this idea, I want you also to suppose that spiritual qualities are relative in the sense that one can talk of a "higher" spiritual quality and a "lower" one.

Now we only have to say one thing more and we can go ahead. All spiritual qualities form a world or worlds of their own that we shall call just "spirit" for short.

Now, you can ask me what all this has to do with St. Teresa and the "spiritual life." You would understand "very easily", if you were to read her life and her own writings. By spiritual life, she means the search for the perfection of quality that transforms a duty into an "interior act". This search is not compulsory; we can fulfill our obligations without the peculiar scrupulosity that looks for something more than doing what we are commanded or required to do. This does not quite express what I mean. Suppose you speak to a friend about spirituality and he says: "I have no time for all that nonsense. I try to do my duty as a father and as a good citizen. I go to church because I think it is right, and as far as is reasonable in our present age, I keep the command-ments. If I tried to do anything else, I should be neglecting my plain and obvious duties which take up all my time and energy." Now, you could not tell your friend that he is all wrong; that there is something finer behind all these duties that he might be looking for. It would not be fair; and, in his case, it might not even be true. At the same time, it might be quite different for you, and you would be most acutely aware that you have problems that he knows nothing about. Those problems—if they are genuine—are spiritual problems and they are the same problems that troubled St. Teresa until she found, or was shown, their solution.

The point is that people who are troubled by these problems of "quality for its own sake", do need guidance. It is not enough that they should know "what" they ought to be doing. They are troubled about "how" they should do it. That is why ordinary psychology will not help them. I will come to this later. It is enough to say now that by "spiritual psychology", I mean the study of man on the assumption that spirit is "real", and that the spiritual life is a reality. It is possible to study people who are troubled by spiritual questions as if there were something wrong with them and they needed to be "cured". It is possible to do this even from the standpoint of religion; then it is called "pastoral psychology". You will see later why I separate pastoral psychology and spiritual psychology, as two quite different ways of approaching the human problem. Eric Fromm, whom I met in Mexico fifteen years ago, drew my attention to the distinction between soul-sickness and world-sickness. The one calls for the assurance that there is hope for oneself, but the other demands hope for the sick world. There is the psychology of adjustment and there is the psychology of perfection. The true spiritual psychology seeks for a providential solution of all problems personal, social and cosmic.

The need for a spiritual psychology has appeared at a time when many students of man are turning away from human psychology to study animal behavior as the best way to know man. Ethology, one of the latest born scientific disciplines, has in a decade transformed our understanding of animal life. We can no longer use words like "brutal", "bestial", "animal instincts" as though they distinguished man from his fellow animals. The wonderful researches of men like Farley Mowat and Adolph Murie have shown that the life of the wolf pack is in many ways more orderly and more "human" than our societies. Nikolaas Tinbergen and Wolfgang Kohler have shown how different the mentality of apes is from our old ideas of "monkey behavior". Some ethologists and especially Konrad Lorenz have emphasized the animal origin of human aggression and other characteristics of man and his societies. But in emphasizing quite rightly the animal component in human nature, the ethologists have lost sight of the spiritual component, which we do not share with other animals. This does not mean that we must go along with Kant when he said: "the end is man. We can ask why do animals exist? but to ask why man exists is a meaningless question" (in lectures on Ethics.) Gurdjieff took precisely the opposite view and said that the one meaningful question is "Why do I exist?" If this question is valid, then clearly the answer must come from a place that is beyond ourselves. This "place" is the spiritual region. It is "beyond" us in the sense of being inaccessible to our senses and our ordinary means of investigation and reasoning. The paradox of man is that he has a spiritual nature but does not and cannot know it. A spiritual psychology is an account of man that takes full measure of his spiritual nature without overlooking or neglecting his animal nature. It studies man as a complete whole, partly knowable but partly unknowable by ordinary processes of observation and reasoning.

You will ask me next whether I think that I am competent to write a "spiritual psychology". Heaven forbid! It is not lack of experience that would prevent me from writing: on the contrary, it is that I have seen so much that I have really come to accept my ignorance of the subject. I have had a very long experience of spiritual questions; my interest in them goes back at least sixty years. It is nearly half a century since I began to study spiritual questions with groups of students, and I have continued ever since. During that time, I have known thousands of men and women, who had a real or imagined spiritual search, and many of them have talked to me about their problems. This experience has taught me one thing and that is that the mystery of man remains a mystery. We can help to some extent by experience and more by kindness, but the mystery remains. Little by little, as the years have passed, I have reached certain conclusions, mainly as a result of my studies of Gurdjieff's method. I have seen that there is a well-defined structure that connects the material and the spiritual sides of man's nature and takes account of the relativity of both matter and spirit. Matter can exist in coarser or finer states of aggregation. The coarsest states include visible matter and the finer include sensations, thoughts and consciousness. Spiritual relativity implies a hierarchy of values. If there were no "levels" in the spiritual world there would be nothing to strive for, no success or failure in the spiritual life. I think that this notion of a twofold relativity is new in this field, and I have found that it has been a real help in dealing with my own problems and those of other people. I have also seen how misleading psychology can be that does not recognize that "will" is a reality quite different from either matter or spirit, that cannot be spoken about in the same language. Because I have found spiritual guidance for myself in these ideas, I am making this attempt to write a "spiritual psychology".

Before I go further, I would like to make a clear distinction between spiritual questions and theological questions. Theology is concerned with the supernatural. Any psychology, spiritual or not, is concerned with the natural. Spirit and matter are equally natural; that is to say, they are not God, though of course we may believe they are God's creation. Supernatural action is the direct intervention of God in the Creation in such a manner that no creature can understand its working. It is as different from "spiritual" action, as it is from "material" action. It may take place in and through nature, but it differs from natural action by the fact that it is wholly mysterious and cannot be explained in terms of the laws of nature or the qualities of spirit. If, from time to time, we shall come up against an action that we believe to be supernatural, I shall try to remember to make it clear that this is properly outside the scope of any psychology. The point is that if supernatural action is performed directly by God, only God can know what it is, and therefore that we can know it only if God reveals it. In other words, everything connected with the supernatural can be known only and exclusively by Revelation. As I make no claim to any such Revelation, this book can only be about natural matters, unless I find it necessary and possible to draw upon revealed sources.

If the anatomy of my spiritual psychology owes almost everything to Gurdjieff, much of the content has been derived from other sources. Since 1924, I have been convinced of the value of Buddhist psychology as developed in the Pali Pitakas. I learned Pali with Mrs. Rhys Davids who with her husband introduced these ancient texts to the English speaking world. The central document is the Samana Phala Suttanta: The Great Discourse on the Fruits of the Life of a Sramana. When I first studied this in the original, I was convinced that it gives an objective account of the spiritual development by way of discipline and meditation. The four Jhanas or states of higher consciousness have become an integral part of my own understanding of the spiritual path. I also studied Sanskrit in order to enter into the spirit of the Vedas and Upanishads including the *Bhagavad Gita*. Many years later, I was able to meet a very great Yogi, the Shivapuri Baba who was one hundred thirty-five years old when I first saw him. His three disciplines of body, mind and spirit are the epitome of the practical psychology of the Upanishads and I have made use of them in completing some of the missing links in Gurdjieff's system.

I have learned even more from Islam than from the Vedic religion and Buddhism. Having lived many years in Moslem countries and having met many Sufis or dervishes, I am convinced on the one hand that Sufism was the principal source of Gurdjieff's teaching and on the other that Sufism today is very much alive and can give much that the world needs at this time. I have learned most from an unorthodox Sufi Hasan Shushud, a descendent of the great Konevi who was a companion of Jellaluddin Rumi. Hasan Shushud first introduced me to the Khwajagan, that extraordinary Sufi school that existed in Central Asia from the eleventh to the sixteenth century of our era and has as its present day successor the greatest of all Sufi orders, the Naqshbandiyye founded by Bahauddin of Bokhara in the fourteenth century. Hasan himself is an exponent of Absolute Liberation; that links him to Buddhism rather than the orthodox mystical Sufism of teachers like Ibn al-Arabi and Jellaluddin Rumi. I have learned practical exercises including the use of breath control and of fasting, from Hasan that go beyond anything I received from Gurdjieff.

I have also been privileged to meet and see a great deal of Sayed Idries Shah who is already making his mark on the Western world both as a writer and as practical psychologist. Shah is so well-known from his own books that I need add nothing except to emphasize the importance of his contribution to understanding the menace to the future of mankind that is latent in "human engineering".

Between 1957 and 1961, I was immersed in Subud. This spiritual movement has a Sanskrit name—for Subud is the contraction of *Susila Budhi Dharma* which means "good spiritual discipline." Nevertheless, Subud is essentially a derivative of Sufism. Its founder, Bapak Muhammad Subuh came to England in 1957 at the invitation of a small group of pupils of Gurdjieff who were interested in what they had heard of his teaching which seemed to have much in common with Gurdjieff's system.

Subud consists, for all practical purposes, of one single element: the "latihan". This is a spiritual exercise, in the sense that it comes from, and is directed by, a power or influence that cannot be expressed in material terms. It is not something that can be "known" in the way that we can know—theoretically at least—energy transformations.

The latihan consists of two parts: the opening or contact and the regular practice. The opening or contact is accomplished once and for all by the simple act of "asking and receiving". Anyone who wishes to receive the contact—unless there are some impediments such as mental disturbances—can do so after a three months' probationary period. The contact is given by someone who has already received it and it is therefore a kind of transmission of influences. The exercise of the latihan is to be done without directing thoughts, desires or effort in any way. It is the act of will made in the intention alone. The intention is directed towards acceptance of a submission to "Dharma" which can be interpreted as meaning that which is objectively right.

In 1962 I came to the conclusion that the latihan is too limited in its action to provide a complete way of life. This was confirmed by the observation that those who practiced it with enthusiasm and conviction tended to become narrow in outlook and loyalty. Subud was becoming a new cult or at best a Moslem sect. I was not interested in dogma but in method. As a method the latihan works, but it does so in a very specific manner by unblocking the channel that leads from the outer to the inner parts of the self. This action cannot take more than one to two years. In fact, I think it can be completed within six to ten months and to continue longer is non-productive and finally counter-productive. I can recommend the latihan especially to those who are overactive intellectually and emotionally shut in.

Another movement that I have followed with great and sympathetic interest is the Transcendental Meditation brought to the West by Maharishi Mahesh Yogi. I first met him in 1959, but was then so immersed in Subud that I did not attempt his meditation. Many of my own pupils were initiated and I could observe the benefit, especially to those who were nervous, overactive and impatient. They became calm and much more efficient in their daily lives. There was also an unmistakable benefit to health.

I finally decided to seek initiation myself and practiced the Maharishi's meditation as part of my own discipline. It consists in the use of a mantra repeated silently in the breast in much the same way as the prayer of the heart of the Russian orthodox monks. It is a condition of initiation one undertakes not to disclose the mantra. The method of Transcendental Meditation is much gentler and more controlled than Subud. It is now very well known throughout the world and its value as a natural and effective means for removing psychological tensions and for awakening the meditator to the reality of a spiritual world is accepted even by those whose profession would make them skeptical. One great beauty of Transcendental Meditation is that it can be practiced alone or in groups and that it can be transmitted without long preparation. It lends itself to wide dissemination.

On the other hand, it appears to me to be another limited action that does not normally reach all parts of man's nature. In particular, I see no evidence that it strengthens the will or that it is outstandingly effectual in promoting understanding between its practitioners. It is of great value within the context of the modern world. We are over organized, tense and lacking in faith. Few are prepared to submit themselves to the rigorous demands of total transformation. Millions feel the need for a spiritual action that is within their capacity. Transcendental Meditation is genuine action. Its primary effects are physiological. The Maharishi himself describes it as a reconstruction of the nervous system. This is admirable, for it underlines the essential unity of man: our nervous system carries within it the depth of our own being. The reality of man is one and indivisible. In my talks with the Maharishi, for whom I have the greatest of admiration, he showed me how well aware he is of the distinction between natural and spiritual operations in human nature.

If we regard Subud and Transcendental Meditation as natural actions that prepare the way for spiritual actions, what are we to make of movements that claim explicitly to be the direct action of God Himself in the soul of man? This is the claim of the Pentecostal movement which is said to be expanding more rapidly than any other in all parts of the world. Having observed this and similar actions in myself and others, 1 have become convinced that there is a serious though innocent self-deception. All spiritual action originates "beyond the mind" and it is by no means easy to recognize the level from which a particular action comes. It almost always happens that people either fail to recognize that an action is supramental or else ascribe it to a level far higher than could possibly be the case. Nearly all spiritual action originates in our own supramental regions. It can occasionally and accidentally happen that a spiritual power beyond man acts upon an individual. A direct Divine action would be beyond human strength to bear.

One result of misunderstanding these things is that people quite sincerely and honestly make for some teacher, movement or method, claims that cannot be valid. In this way contradictions and conflicts arise. Exaggerated hopes give place to unjustified pessimism or even rejection. Spiritual people get the reputation of being unrealistic and unreliable. This is particularly tragic at such a time as the present when mankind is in desperate need of spiritual guidance and help.

These are sufficient reasons for the study of spiritual psychology, but they are no guarantee that such study can give reliable and reproducible results. Only material phenomena repeat themselves with the regularity for scientific investigation. All spiritual action is unique and when it comes from a high level it is always unpredictable and unrepeatable. This elementary principle should be impressed upon everyone concerned in the study of man. Failure to grasp it has been responsible for a vast amount of fruitless "research" in the field of psychic and spiritual phenomena.

If we want to understand spiritual action we must develop the power to experience and recognize it in ourselves. Observed from within, it follows laws that are as certain as gravitation and entropy. Observed from without it is arbitrary and irrational. This does not mean that the human mind is totally helpless in front of spiritual action. We can gain considerable insight if we have a working model to help our thinking and if we know how to make experiments and observations without expecting to arrive at reproducible results. The purpose of the present book is not to teach the reader but to help him to learn for himself by making his own experiments.

My observations of the work of spiritual teachers in many countries for more than half a century have led me to the conclusion that several kinds of action must be distinguished.

1. There is the brief encounter. In India, this is called *Darshan*. Men and women who have gained the reputation of saint or sage usually allow strangers to visit them for a few moments or even to spend hours or days in their presence. The action is sometimes overwhelming. Many have reported that their lives were permanently changed by one visit to Sri Ramana Maharshi of Tiruvanna. In my own case, my life took an entirely new direction at the end of one evening with Gurdjieff in October 1920. The effect can be instantaneous by one look or touch. It can also come by question and answer. The result is only rarely powerful and lasting; the great majority of visitors to saints and sages feel uplifted and encouraged, but their lives remain unchanged.

2. There is the *Institution* which has its own force of ideas and of fellowship. The action is often by some ritual, religious or nonreligious. Great numbers of people come under the influence of some institution that claims to transmit grace, or as the Sufis say: *baraka*. The action goes beyond mere teaching or discipline. It requires faith on the part of those that give and of those that receive. It is a real action, but not in itself sufficient to transform people. We must do the work ourselves and for that we need human help. Generally, institutions fail to make the necessary demand and cannot give the required help. These, combined with the decline of faith, are the chief reasons why churches and other religious institutions are no longer attracting those who are

searching for guidance and support.

3. There are teachers: priests, gurus, sheikhs, spiritual guides. They possess knowledge that ordinary people have been too lazy or lacking in opportunity to gain for themselves. Teachers work both with individuals and groups. The contact between pupil and teacher is close only where the teacher refuses to take more than a very small number of pupils. For the most part, teachers spread themselves too thin and individual students are little better off than the followers of institutional religion. In some respects— particularly the transfer of grace—they may be worse off. The "personality" of the teacher gives an apparent substitute for the "baraka" that is transmitted from beyond the individual. Sooner or later, the inadequacy of the source becomes evident and the pupil is left high and dry. In these days it is very hard to find a teacher. I am often asked how a seeker is to recognize his teacher. First, one must never make an impulsive decision. If one feels "this is it; he is my teacher," one should wait and test. If the impulse was right nothing will be lost. Then one must remember that the first requirement of a teacher is the freedom from self-seeking. No one should "mount the seat of guidance" so long as he has the desire or need for personal benefit either in the form of power or money. He must have knowledge both theoretical and practical, but these alone do not make a teacher. He must have reached a stage of self-knowledge and humility that allow higher energies to flow through him with little distortion. This can be tested by looking at his pupils. The true teacher gets out of the way and lets the energies act directly on the pupils so that they are free from him. The false teacher makes his pupils dependent on him.

4. There is the so-called "Fourth Way" in which the primary aim is to accomplish a task for the good of mankind. Here teaching is secondary and it can even be said that there are no teachers. The requirements of the fourth way are very exacting. They can be expressed in the words Service, Sacrifice and Understanding. These are my rendering of Gurdjieff's formula "Conscious Labor and Intentional Suffering". A true fourth way school must have contact with a Higher Source from which it draws its strength and its guidance. Those who enter it must be prepared to commit themselves to be "in the world but not of the world." They are

seldom required to *appear* as different from other people, but they must *be* different. The director of such a school must know the task before him and his place in the working of the spiritual action of his time. He must be able to train his pupils in such a way that they can first fulfill their part in the task of the school and afterwards be able, to the measure of their capacity, to initiate their own fourth way work. Gurdjieff, so far as I know, was the first to introduce the term "Fourth Way" to designate the tradition of non-institutional service to humanity and the methods of training that go with it. According to him, the fourth way alternates between concentration and expansion according to the needs of the world. The history of mankind shows a very slow evolution proceeding in cycles of varying length. We can trace epochs of two to three thousand years back to the end of the ice age ten to twelve thousand years ago. Each such epoch is characterized by a system of values that is almost universally accepted in all parts of the earth. There are still greater cycles of ten to twelve thousand years, each of which has been marked by a major catastrophe in which a great part of mankind has perished, but which has led to an extraordinary step forward in human evolution. Such an event occurred about twelve thousand years ago and there are many indications that such an event is due to occur again. If this is so, there is an immense task of preparation to be undertaken. At such times the fourth way becomes most active and the opportunities for personal transformation increase enormously compared with ordinary periods.

My own personal interest has always been attracted by the fourth way. At first, I understood very little beyond the need to serve a teacher. For more than forty years, I served my teachers Gurdjieff, Ouspensky and then again Gurdjieff. After Gurdjieff died, I served Subud and next the Shivapuri Baba. Then I met Idries Shah, and becoming convinced of the importance of his mission, set myself to help it forward. Then finally, I met a man who neither asked for nor needed the service of others. Though a man of very high attainment, he insisted on serving me. This was Hasan Shushud who is more than a dervish or Sufi, for his way is beyond all paths. It is the way that leads to Absolute Liberation from all conditioning. With his help I found my own task and was given the means of accomplishing it.

Thus it came about that, at the age of seventy-four, I founded a school here at Sherborne House where I am writing this Introduction. The aim of my work is clear. The world needs prepared people, able to act from their own initiative and capable of conscious labor and intentional suffering. I have set myself to transmit all that I have received to those who are able to take it.

The present book describes an experiment made at Coombe Springs which helped me very much in my preparation for Sherborne. The method has proved successful not only at Sherborne, but also for people who have to work as well as they can on their own.

Before leaving this introduction, I want to place the spiritual psychology in the wider context of human destiny. Kant's non-question "Why does man exist?" becomes for us the central question. Gurdjieff formulated it in the words "What is the sense and purpose of life on the earth and, in particular, of human life?" It is strange that we do not see that this must be the most important of all questions. If we see any complicated piece of machinery we naturally ask "What is it for? What work does it do?" We look at human instructions and ask what is their aim and purpose. Life on the earth is a mechanism of unique beauty and complexity. We no longer argue that it must have had a "Maker" because we have seen not only that the argument is fallacious (as Kant showed) but that it is otiose (as Darwin unintentionally demonstrated). This is probably the reason that we have failed to notice that the question "What is the sense of all this?" remains even if we no longer put it in the form "Why did God create life on earth and man in particular?"

If we have to answer that there is no sense and purpose in life, we fall back into existentialism. If we say that the sense and purpose of life is to survive and enjoy ourselves, we separate ourselves from the rest of nature which we are in process of destroying by pollution and the exhaustion of resources. We may not like the ethological view that man is wholly an animal and to be understood as such, but we can no longer deny the unity of nature. Life on the earth is one indivisible whole and if any part suffers, all suffer.

We look at the situation through human eyes and are concerned only with human survival, human welfare and human progress. There are even people who suggest that space travel may make such advances that one day we shall be able to leave this planet derelict and uninhabitable and start a new career for the human race in some other solar system. Such callous rejection of any duty towards our Mother Earth should shock us as unspeakable blasphemy, but it fails to do so, because we are blind to the reality. It does not cross our minds that it is not Nature that exists to serve us, but we exist to serve Nature.

Gurdjieff's great discovery, message, revelation—call it what you will—was the Law of Reciprocal Maintenance. He formulates this in the words: "Everything that exists is maintained by other forms of existence and must itself in its turn maintain other forms. We men cannot be exempt from this law and therefore our lives must also serve to maintain the existence of something other than ourselves." The Law of Reciprocal Maintenance is obviously true for this solar system. Life on earth is maintained by the sun's radiant energy, by the atmosphere, oceans and crust of the earth. Vegetable life by fixing carbon and releasing oxygen maintains itself and all other forms of life. Ecological science has demonstrated how closely every form of life depends on other forms. We men alone destroy both life and the basis of life. Gurdjieff says that in doing so we are destroying ourselves. We must produce energies needed for the conscious evolution of life on the earth and of the solar system, including the Moon. Hence the famous saying "Man exists to feed the Moon."

It is very hard to convey what this really means. One has to grasp the idea that there are Intelligences of a higher order than man who are responsible for the orderly existence and progress of the earth and the solar system. Gurdjieff refers to them as "Sacred Individuals" and I have used the term Demiurges, which is the Greek name for the Powers that keep the world in good order. These powers need energies for their work and we men have the capacity to produce these energies, by our own voluntary efforts. All that lives produces such energies, but vegetable and animal life produce them unconsciously and automatically. We men differ because of our capacity for conscious and intentional action. This capacity comes from our spiritual nature. By exercising it in the right way, we not only fulfill our obligation towards Nature, but also transform our own being. This "right way" is called by the Shivapuri Baba: *Swadharma*; by Pak Subuh: *Susila Budhi Dharma* and by Gurdjieff *Being-Partkdolgduty* which he translates as "conscious labor and intentional suffering." It is also the "death and resurrection" of Christian doctrine.

All teaching and all religions agree that there is something that man is required to do in this life: but no one has hitherto explained why and for what purpose. Gurdjieff has given an answer that is very ancient, for it goes back at least to Zoroaster, but it is also very much up-to-date for it touches on all the questions that disturb mankind today. The preservation of our planet is a sacred duty and the reward is a better future for our descendants and the attainment for ourselves of imperishable being.

In this book I have shown some of the first steps on the way of Swadharma or Being-Partkdolgduty. Once you begin to see how this works and realize how it can transform your life, you will acquire the taste for it. You will see that what is demanded of us is not only possible, but the only way in which life can be made worth living.

J.G. Bennett
Sherborne House
April 25th, 1973

2. THE MATERIAL SELF—OR MAN-MACHINE

Every day during the summer school, an introductory talk was given to prepare the minds of the students for better understanding of the theme to be discussed in the evening. The first began with an explanation of the distinction between 'I' and 'me'.

J.G.B. 'I' and 'me' are two realities so different that there is no way of combining them into a single conception. We can find out a lot about 'me'. Some parts of 'me' we can study directly, other parts of 'me' we cannot reach because they are deep down, but they are still 'me'. 'I' am not like that. The truth is that we cannot know 'I', because 'I' is 'I', the Knower and never the Known. Therefore, we shall separate our study of 'me' from the search for an understanding of 'I', and we shall talk about 'I' only on the very last day, when we have prepared the ground.

So, we begin with 'me'. 'Me' is not simple. There are many different kinds of 'me', and it can even be said there are different worlds to which 'me' belongs. There is one part of 'me' which belongs to this earth. This is my body and it is just like this earth and everything else that is formed from earthly materials. There is another part of 'me' that is upon a different level, and a third part upon still another level. The best way to study 'me' is to take each kind of me or self separately.

There are seven distinct elements that go to make up the whole of me, therefore we need to understand these seven different elements one by one. We shall find that when we have studied them, they are immensely different in their nature and in their importance. There is however not one of them which can be called 'I', or even can tell us where 'I' is to be found. 'I' is different in its very nature from 'me'; for one thing, it cannot be said that there are kinds of 'I'.

We must therefore accept that there is a difference between 'I' and 'me'. Certainly 'I' is not the same as my body. My body is part of 'me'. It is not the same as my thoughts and feelings and so on; they are part of 'me'. I am not what I see or hear, or think, or anything like that; all that is part of 'me'. 'I' am not what I want, what I hope for, the various urges and drives that work in me; all those are still part of 'me'. However coarse or however fine, all the things that we can study or know about are a part of 'me', not 'I'.

The next thing is to come to an understanding about kinds of 'me'. I am not going to make a scheme in advance, but work directly from the outermost because it is the easiest kind to study, and go on to the innermost which is quite beyond our understanding. I shall go from the outside to the inside, from that which is perfectly easy to see and touch to that which is quite beyond seeing and touching. Now, what is it that is easy to see and touch? It is this body. This is the first part of me, this physical body. This physical body is made out of the same material as the earth is made; all its elements are taken from the substance of the earth. The same elements, the same physical and chemical processes hold it together, and in the end will destroy it, as they hold together and destroy everything else which exists on the earth. This body is therefore a physical or material object; it is the same as tables and chairs, things that we make, or trees or mountains, as everything in nature. Everything on this earth has a body like our body; that is, everything that exists on the earth has a material form with which to exist. This is true for the sea and the winds no less than for solid objects. The feeling we men have that our reality is connected with our body is not an illusion but an important truth.

We must learn to distinguish between this material object, this physical body of ours and the life that is in it. This body will still be here when the life goes out of it. At first, it will not be visibly changed very much; it is only later, when various physical and chemical processes continue on their own, that it will gradually be destroyed. As the various chemical substances break down there will remain only those that are most resistant: the material of the bony skeleton. Under favourable circumstances, this may be fossilized and may last for millions of years. All that we know about the anatomy of early man comes from these fossil remains and yet we know for certain that they came from men. In some cases we can even be confident that fossils several hundreds of thousands of years old are the remains of men very like ourselves and entitled to the same proud name *Homo sapiens* that we give to ourselves today. All this is possible because the skeleton is a solid body. Even a fresh corpse is solid enough—especially in *rigor mortis*, and a living body in spite of its suppleness and mobility, is more like a solid material object than, say, a pool of water, a breath of wind, a note of music or a sunbeam. So we had better ask ourselves what it means to be solid.

A more or less solid body, such as a material object, is a special kind of existence in the universe. A solid body means something which keeps its shape, and so is different, say, from liquids, which do not keep their shape. It more or less keeps its size, and that makes it different from gases which do not keep their size. It is in one place, and that makes it different from sound or light radiation, which spread everywhere. Although there are various conditions of matter like solids, liquids, gases and radiant energy, they all have different properties. Among the properties of a solid body are: that it is more or less fixed in shape, more or less fixed in size and more or less fixed in position. Matter exists in other forms, liquids, gases, radiant energy, which do not have these particular properties.

Now, what is usually forgotten, because we are so accustomed to living in the midst of solid objects, is that they are exceedingly rare in this universe of ours. The more we know about the universe, about the insides of planets, about the way suns are made, about galaxies, the way in which matter is distributed in space and all the different forms of radiant energy there are, the more we realize that the solid state is something exceedingly rare. In fact, not one thousand millionth part of all the matter in the universe is in this solid state. The suns have nothing solid, the insides of the planets are mainly in a fluid condition, all that is present in the inter-stellar and inter-galactic space, except for small aggregations like meteorites and the small planets, is not solid.[1] All the solid things are very highly localized, mostly on the surfaces of planets like ours. Therefore, having a solid body, or being connected with a solid body, must be regarded as a very special condition of existence. It allows one to keep one's own

---

1   Since these lectures were given evidence has come to light that the central core of the earth probably consists of iron in a genuinely solid state. For this reason, I have increased the estimated proportion of solid matter from 1 in 10^{10} to 1 in 10^9 which probably does not affect the argument.

shape, and to be more or less impenetrable. One solid body cannot pass through another, but liquids can pass through one another, gases can mix indefinitely, radiation can penetrate through space, through liquids, sometimes through solids also. Because solid bodies keep separate, and because their shapes are more or less permanent, we can distinguish between chairs and tables, houses, mountains and so on, and between one human body and another. This separateness, this possibility of recognizing the same body today, tomorrow, next year and so on is due to the fact that it is a more or less solid body. No solid bodies that we know are perfectly rigid. All can be deformed by powerful stresses, but few can move and change in shape as can our bodies with their partially plastic bony skeleton and wholly plastic tissue structure.

What does having this kind of body mean? Supposing our bodies were not of this sort; suppose that we were made of water, or of air. Then our perceptions would be completely different; all our abilities to experience space and time would be quite different. We would not be concerned with measuring things, with objects, and naming objects; we would not have the kind of language that we have. Practically all our language is built up from seeing and naming different kinds of solid bodies, describing how they act upon one another and what they are doing. Supposing we were wholly liquid beings, we would not be at all like this. If we were gaseous beings, we would have no notions of space, or even of size. If one could imagine that a gaseous being was somehow able to be conscious, it would have quite different notions from us men. If we were beings made of radiant energy, again everything would be quite different; we should not even occupy a place, because, as you know, radiation spreads everywhere. If our bodies were made of something still finer than that, our conditions of existence would again be totally different from anything we know.

We forget all this, and therefore we do not understand what advantages and limitations are imposed upon us by living in a solid body. An exercise that I sometimes try to carry out for myself is to put away all the pictures and images that arise from the fact that I have a solid body. It is a very difficult thing to do, but if you try it, you begin to experience a most strange sense of freedom and transformation; you are set free from all sorts of fixed ideas about things that come from the fact that we have solid bodies, and that we see everything in terms of solid bodies. But at the same time you are deprived of the power to do anything whatever.

This may seem very remote from psychology, but you must remember that the status of the body in relation to *man* as a being has been a vexed question for thousands of years. Aristotle thought that the soul is just the form of the body. If this were true, we should have to say that we have a 'solid soul'. We shall see in a few minutes that this is not quite so strange as it sounds. When as Christians we speak of the Resurrection of the Body we picture a solid body like our present one, because it seems to us that a man without a body would be a mere shadow—a ghost that did not 'really' exist. One of the objections to ghosts is that they can pass through walls, and we are all inclined to share the feelings of St. Thomas who would not believe in the Resurrection until he had satisfied himself that the body of the Risen Lord satisfied the conditions of impenetrability that distinguishes a solid from a ghost.[1]

I have insisted upon this first characteristic of *me*, that is, my body as a solid object, because we are too much accustomed, when talking of our physical body, to think of it as a living body, as if that were the whole story. It is not. The fact that ours is a living body is enormously important, but it is different from the fact that it is a solid body, an earthly body. It is quite possible to conceive that there should be a person without a physical body of this particular kind, without the limitations which our physical body imposes on us in the way of being fixed in size and shape, in form and perception, in time and space and so on.

Since there are different states of matter, there is nothing illogical or absurd in supposing that these could be organized to produce some kind of body. Theosophists refer to an 'etheric' body and to an 'astral' body, which are said to be made of matter in a finer state. There are difficulties, that are not logical or metaphysical, in the idea of non-solid bodies, but practical, for they are connected

---

1   The concreteness of Jewish thought which regarded the body as an integral part of the whole man as compared with the dualism of Greek thought is well demonstrated in an *Essai sur la Pensée Hébraïque* by Claude Tresmontant (Editions du Cerf, Paris, 1953).

with permanence and the differentiation of functions. A watery or gaseous body would

be very mobile; but it is hard to see that it would be very much use for any purposes we can conceive a body being put to. The body we have—even without taking account of its properties of vitality and sensitivity—is an extraordinarily versatile instrument. It is hard to see how a totally different kind of body existing under different conditions could provide the conditions necessary for what we know as *human experience.*

This physical body of ours is also an engine, a mechanism able to do very complicated things. Every physical object is a mechanism of some kind; but our body is a particularly specialised and complicated kind of mechanism, that is provided not only with engines connected with the muscles and bones, but also with a nervous system for the transformation of energies of seeing and hearing, and the rest of it. It is a limitation of our possible experience that we are bound up with this kind of nervous system, belonging to this earthly body. The nerves of our body are made of just the same chemical elements, and are subject to just the same physical laws, as everything else that there is on the earth.

There is, of course, much more in this body of ours than just so much solid matter with a quantity of associated plastic and liquid matter. There is life; there is intelligence; there is consciousness and so on; but the first plane on which we can know ourselves is the plane of matter, the plane of material objects. There is no doubt at all that this physical body is part of 'me'. All the different ways in which it is able to work are part of the ways in which this 'me' is able to work.

Before we stop this morning, I want to say something about energies. We can say that all that we can know of 'me' (for there is an unknowable 'me' also) is composed of energy in different states. That which gives my human body its powers of moving, seeing, hearing, touching, thinking and so on, is what I have called the *Automatic Energy.*[1] This has the power of regulating itself We can imitate it in very simple ways in what are called feed-back or cybernetic devices. In man it is highly organized and efficient. Nearly all the activity of our daily lives is regulated by

---

1   In *The Dramatic Universe,* Vol. II, pp. 228-9.

this energy—*without our being aware of it*. This is very important, because one characteristic of the automatic energy is that it works without consciousness. The first part of me, or the first 'self', is kept going by automatic energy.

Now, in preparation for the explanations which I will give this evening, I would like you to remember that you are present within a material object. Try to look upon yourselves as having this level of earthly existence within this more or less solid body. Set yourselves to see how this solid body is related to the other solid bodies round it in a kind of complex changing geometry. If you will do this, you bring yourself to become more aware of what earthly existence is. Only do not let your attention go on to look at your body as a living animal.

· · · · ·

The evening session that followed this introductory talk began with a series of observations and questions put forward by those who had been working together at Coombe Springs during the day. The work had been varied: some had done cooking and housework, others had worked in the garden or the workshops, others again had been sewing and mending. The evening discussion showed how unaccustomed we are to looking at our own bodies as material objects among other material objects, as things among things. The questions were recorded and transcribed verbatim. Some of the answers have been shortened and others amplified.

· · · · ·

Trying to put aside the thought of all other levels, it seemed that everything is the transference of material objects, or material forces: matter, thought, communications. All are material forces moving from one place to another.

J.G.B. Yes, both we and these material objects are, all the time, taking part in energy exchanges. There are always exchanges of chemical substances, of energies of various kinds, and these exchanges are constantly producing movements. This is very important for what I have to say about this part of 'me', for it will help you to see how 'me' works on this level.

Q. When you remember your body is a material object and stop, it feels like lump of lead.

J.G.B. At the same time it is a complicated mechanism. I said that every material object is a kind of mechanism; but you may ask in what sense is a stool a mechanism? The stool is transmitting various thrusts of its own weight on the floor. It is also a mechanism for reflecting light waves so that we see it in that particular colour, because it is so constructed that we see those colours and not other colours. It is a conductor of heat and electricity, it is even breathing and it is gradually wearing out. So you see that such a simple thing as a stool is a very complicated piece of machinery. Every material object has its own intricate combination of functions; but, however intricate they may be, it is nothing compared to that of the human body; which, in spite of its complexity, is still of the same kind as they are. Our body is transmitting thrusts through the skeletal system in exactly the same way as the stool is. When I stand on *my* feet, I am standing in exactly the same way as the stool is standing on *its* feet. When you look at me and see the colour of my body, I am reflecting colours in just the same way as the stool is. When I see things, I am responding to various impulses from light waves in just the same way as other material objects do. Although I respond in a much more complicated way, exchanges of energy are still working in me as in everything else.

Q. I am quite certain that 'me', my body, knows how to stand, but I noticed how it is acted on by my clothes, and also by the work I am doing. It is forced into wrong attitudes which result in tensions.

J.G.B. This shows you how this kind of existence must always be a particular kind of compromise. We depend upon our environment to be what we are, yet at the same time our environment is interfering with what we are trying to be.

Q. I think I have been even more clumsy today since I have been trying to be aware of my body; thinking about it makes me clumsy and I drop things.

J.G.B. That is possible, because for the most part, this body and all the other objects that we come in contact with are regulated automatically, and we do not have to think about it. But we must remember that in this automatic regulation, there is something missing; that is, we are not noticing enough what we are doing with other bodies. One effect of trying to remember about your body, is that you notice more how you do things, you notice more how many things you are careless about, which ordinarily perhaps do not matter, but which you now begin to notice. If you were to continue this exercise you would become much less clumsy and you would understand that the automatic energy is a very versatile and 'high-grade' energy compared with that which works in man-made machines.

Q. Looking back, I see that today I had a great affection for things which I use: the bed I was lying on, the things I was using while I was cooking, holding a cup and saucer. It is the first time that has happened to me. They were not just things to be used, but something in themselves.

J.G.B. That is not just imagination, it is an awakening to reality. Everything that exists has the right to exist, everything deserves respect. Also, because it is what it is, we can have a connection with it, a feeling of being more than connected, a *relationship* to things. This feeling, that you describe as affection, certainly comes from something deeper than the level of material things, but it is only made possible because you began to see things for what they are. When you actually see them for what they are, it is different, because then a relationship is made and you see there is something in you, something in 'me' which actually *corresponds to what is in them*.

Q. One becomes conscious of material objects as things. I was much more conscious today of the space they occupy and the space between me and them.

J.G.B. That is a valuable observation. It is almost impossible to grasp the extent to which our notions and perceptions of space and time are dependent upon the fact that we have this kind of body. It seems to us that if we had quite a different sort of body, let us say one made of air—and therefore without either size or shape—that space and time would still be space and time; but they would not be at all as we know them. They would be completely different. Not only would there be no means of measuring size or distance or duration or anything of that sort, but time and space themselves would turn into something quite different from what they *appear to be to us*. What you have perceived today is a realization of how the very notion of place is a subsidiary notion that arises only when there are material bodies. Because we have a body and something else is also a body, we are able to talk about place and position. We have this false notion that there would still be place and position if there were not this kind of body. If, let us say, we were transferred to some region of the universe where solid bodies were very far away—billions of miles away—and there was nothing there except clouds of gas, any kind of consciousness that could be present there would have no notions of place or position or size or duration, or anything like that. It does not mean that it could not have some sort of experience, but the experience would be totally different from anything that we know.

We ought to remember that, because we should see that this bodily life on the earth imposes quite severe restrictions and limitations on the way we are able to experience. But there is another, more positive side to it. The experience associated with a physical body is much richer than anything we could imagine associated with other states of matter. We are surrounded by all manner of things. These things are very wonderful, and it is perhaps one of the most extraordinary and ingenious features of the entire Creation that there should be such conditions of existence. Maybe one of the hardest and most subtle tasks that had to be performed in the whole process of creation of the universe was to produce planets where it would be possible to have this kind of existence. What is known about this in science shows that this sort of a planet with many different elements on it—some heavy, some light, with so much water and so on, is a very difficult thing to produce, probably beyond the power even of our own sun.

Some astronomers believe that the elements we have on the earth—most of which do not exist in the sun—could have been produced only by the destruction of a star: a super-nova, which is one of the rarest events in the universe. In spite of its comparative rarity, there may be many millions of planets where there can be this sort of existence. We can scarcely suppose that our embodied existence would be as important as it seems to us to be unless it were a cosmic phenomenon that occurs throughout the universe.

I do not mean by this that there must be human beings in every solar system; but that something like the association of with a material body can hardly be restricted to this planet. For some reason, we men have been put into this condition, that we live connected with a material object—our body. There are, behind these bodies, other things that we have to speak about, but this is the first plane of existence, so far as we are concerned. There are indeed other planes of existence, where the possibility of experience is very different from anything we know. But, so far as our human experience is concerned, this body is the basis, the foundation upon which all the rest is built.

Q. I often have a feeling about material objects, especially about the things I own; not possessiveness, but a very special relationship. There is a need to understand their nature, and to care for them as far as we can, and they will then serve us faithfully for as long as we are in contact with them.

J.G.B. Yes; this sense of belonging can be genuine. These objects that we own are really an extension of 'me'. It is not possible to say for certain where 'me' ends. Does 'me' end at my skin? In a way, my clothes are also part of 'me', and so is my house and the various things that I use regularly. So 'me' somehow goes out into the world, there is no very clear line of demarcation where 'me' ends and 'not me' has been reached. What you say about the things that we own, is really very much the same as with our body. We have a duty towards this body to keep it in a good condition. If we do, it will serve us. It is an instrument, and these things also are instruments.

Q. So when a child is saying 'my' toy, it is not so much a feeling of possessiveness as a feeling of relationship?

J.G.B. There is so much to be studied in the field of child psychology that I prefer not to speak about it here. I have found the works of Piaget, who has been working on this for more than forty years, most enlightening. I am inclined to agree that the child has a less complicated sense of 'me' than most adults.

Q. Does love or care alter the object, or does a part of the person remain with the object? Sometimes a beautiful object or one that has been loved, has an atmosphere that it shares with its owner.

J.G.B. These last three or four observations may help us to make the step from the notion of 'me' to the notion of 'self'. Instead of saying 'this is part of me', we can say 'this is part of myself'; we can say 'something' of myself has entered into this object, it is no longer wholly alien, outside, other than myself. This is true not only for me, but for others also. Something that has been possessed, cherished by someone with whom we have had some strong relationship, has something of that person in it; something of that 'self' has entered into it. This can be possible only if there is a material part of the self. If my self is so intimately concerned with this material body that people call it by my name, if its form is 'my' form, if its movements are 'my' movements, then certainly there must be something of 'my' self in it. When I observe that I speak of 'my' clothes and 'my' possessions and when I recognize that even when they are separated from me something of 'me' remains in them, then surely I am bound to admit that in some real sense they must be a material part of me.

This is so important that I must make sure it is clear to you. There can be an *action* between two completely different natures, but there cannot be any kind of *union* between them. Only things of the same nature can be united. Therefore, if my self is united with my body, and can even be united with my possessions, it follows that there must be a *material self*. We have now reached the central theme that I want to put before you tonight. It is that in a real, concrete—not a figurative or allegorical—sense, there is in every man one part of 'him' or 'me' which is material in its nature and subject to the same laws as other material objects. This is what I have just called the *material self*. This could also be called the 'thing-like self'. Indeed, Pak Subuh calls it the *roh kebendaan* or the 'thing-soul'. It is not hard to accept that there is 'something' material in 'me', but it is hard to agree that this can be called a self or, worse still, a soul. The names may be misleading, but the facts are there to be verified. So that you can do this if you like, I will describe some of the characteristics of the material self. It is by its very nature a *machine* though a very complex and versatile one. It is connected not only with this body as a visible thing, but also with parts of it that are not visible, such as our nervous system and the supremely complex mechanism of the brain. It is stimulated by what we hear, and see, and touch; also by what we think and feel. It has means of responding, dealing with these various stimuli, and its behaviour can appear to be that of a complete human being.

Q. I don't quite see how this can be called a self and still less a 'soul'. It seems to me to be like a dead thing.

J.G.B. You are quite right to object, because I have not said one necessary thing, and that is that our 'I' or our 'will' can enter into this material self and then it becomes a source of initiative. When our 'I' is joined with the material self it loses consciousness: because the energy of this self—the automatic energy I spoke of this morning—is neither conscious or even sensitive. That is why Gurdjieff says that when in this state man is 'asleep' and 'cannot remember himself'. 'Man is a machine': but a special kind of machine that sees and hears and thinks and moves about on its own initiative. That is because its ruler is made out of the 'automatic energy'. But still it is also true that the machine is a man. Why? Because a human will has got involved in it. This is obviously a 'fallen' condition, for man was not intended to be asleep and a machine.

Therefore, the material self is a bad place for the will. But this does not mean that the material self is undesirable: on the contrary, we could not be what we are without it. I want to make the distinction clear.

One may even meet people whose self is altogether of this kind, on this level. Such a person has a human body with all the various other human powers, but the material self is the dominating factor in the way that particular body behaves. In the ordinary condition of people, there is always something else behind; there is something which feels, which is sensitive. There are however people in whom there is practically nothing behind, nothing sensitive. But all of us, whether there is something or whether there is very little behind, each one of us has this first or material self. It is the first, or the outward, part of 'me'. This is also called the earth self, because it is associated with this particular kind of body and is subject, with the exception of the automatic energy itself, to the same physical and chemical laws as those of the material of which the earth is made.

Now, as we should expect, the material self is capable of

regulating the physical and chemical transformation of the body itself. Nowadays, the idea of material regulators with uncanny powers of adaptation is not strange to science. We have, on the one hand, the amazing development of man-made regulators, electronic computers and the rest. On the other hand, biologists have discovered that complex molecules, such as those of deoxyribonucleic acid (DNA), are able to regulate the synthesis of proteins and even transmit the hereditary pattern located in the genes of living animals and plants. We can well imagine a hidden regulator within the human organism that presides over its physico-chemical equilibria, its nutrition, defence, reproduction and life processes generally.

When I speak of a material self I do not refer to something ready-made that is formed automatically by the organizing powers of the living cells; but of a genuine centre of initiative and action that comes into being as a result of the power that is given to every man to act upon his own initiative.

We can watch the formation of the material self almost from birth. This does not mean that, before the material self is formed, the child has no conscious experience—on the contrary, it has full, conscious experience, but it is then free from the restrictions of the physical body. Even before it is born, there is a human being able to experience and to enjoy. There is plenty of evidence that pre-natal experiences leave their traces upon the 'me'. Unfortunately, this evidence is mainly of a sad kind. For example, if a mother does not love her child while she is bearing it in her womb, or if a father acts with violence or cruelty, the unborn child will be marked with a psychic injury that can be cured later in life only by very much care and love. This is because there is a sensitive part of the self that is not formed in the same way as the body, by a process of differentiation and growth, but in some way that we do not yet understand. I shall return to this later. I have only mentioned it at this stage so that you should not run away with the idea that, when I speak of the material self of the young child, I mean that there is nothing else present in his psyche.

Let us return to our observation of very young babies. They do not for some time distinguish between living and non-living objects. They notice things before they notice people—even their mother is an object with which they associate sensations. Everything that moves attracts them. They do not distinguish between movement and life. If you will reflect a moment, you will see that this is what we should expect from the material self. When babies do begin to recognize distinct and recurrent features in their experience, these are material objects, not actions that indicate life or consciousness. The most important observations are those of the way in which the child becomes aware of its own body. It is obviously aware of sensations of hunger and pain; but not of their source in its own body. We can accept—though we cannot verify—the assertion that the new-born child lives 'in a world of its own' until it has learned to recognize material objects and relate itself to its own body. You will note that its development always comes in that order: outside objects first, hands, feet and other parts of the body later. The awareness of the great fact that its body is 'me' comes quite late. At first, the child's body is a material object, like any other, and it is quite easy to see that he does not associate movement, life or consciousness with it in the early months. Several months are needed to be aware that the limbs can be moved intentionally and much longer to recognize the distinctions of life and consciousness.

It seems probable—and this should be capable of being investigated by an experimental psychologist or an acute observer like Piaget—that the will of the child does not enter the material self except by suggestion from its elders. I think it is unconscious of its automatism, and notices only its sensitive reactions about which we have to speak tomorrow. There is always, of course, sensitivity behind the material self but not *in* it.

I think I have said enough to show you what I mean when I said that the material self has to be developed. Another way of putting it would be to describe the self as starting empty and gradually being filled up with the results of living in a body. The first results will obviously be those most directly connected with the awareness of material objects.

When the child begins to speak, it starts by naming material objects. It does not find words for acts until later. Much later still come expressions of life and of consciousness. The late arrival of the word 'I' has been noticed by observers of all races and tongues.

It is inevitable that language should be material in nature since it is built up from our experience of material things. You will not be surprised if I say that language is an expression of the material self.[1] It would be more accurate to say that our language, being derived from our contact with material objects, is most suited for saying things about them. When we use language for talking about those parts of our experience which are not reached through the senses, we soon get into difficulties.

One example of the close connection between language and the material self can be found in the way we think and speak of time and place. We constantly tend to take the limitations of the material self for laws of nature.

For example, we are accustomed to treat separateness as an idea that is always the same. But this notion of separateness is rightly characteristic only of solids. Gases and liquids can be kept separately only by solid walls. But, just because we have derived our language from solid objects and because our thought depends upon our language, we treat separateness as if it always had the same meaning. For example, it colours, or rather creates, our notions of space and time. In reality, there are in us men, other layers of the self where our perceptions of time and space are quite different. Strangely enough, although these other perceptions of time and place are much richer and more important, we have the habit of taking for granted that the time and place experience belonging to the material self is the true one, and that the others are illusions, or, at best, 'subjective'. The truth is that non-successive time is just as 'objective' as clock-time.

I spoke about this same subject the other day at a lecture and afterwards a young man came up to me and said: "But after all, surely, a clock cannot lie; all this talk about other kinds of time may be self-deception; the clock is telling you the truth about time". That was said very sincerely by this young man, who, in spite of my having tried very hard for an hour and a half to explain these things that I am explaining to you now, still could not see

---

1   This is an important observation, because it is the material self that learns to speak, but cannot remember itself or know that it is 'I' except by being told. The child's true consciousness of 'I' is much deeper and cannot be expressed. Very few people even when they grow up know what *consciousness of 'I'* really means.

that the notions we have of time and place are notions that arise only because we have this sort of material body. They arise in us because we are connected with it, and have 'something' built up in us, in our nervous system, that comes from these sort of exchanges—sight, sound, touch, particularly sight and touch. That 'something' is the material self.

I must return for a few minutes to the subject of language, because it is most important to understand that language is almost entirely constructed from the same experiences as go to fill up the material self. This is true, as I tried to show you, of young children; but it is also true of the formation of the languages that men have constructed for themselves. According to pre-historians and anthropologists, man began to use language almost as soon as he became man. Who taught him and how is a mystery; I do not believe that primitive man learned to speak by himself any more than a child does. But the point is that he learned to name things, material objects, in order to deal with them and that is how it has been ever since. Man started as children do today with names and he went on to find words for actions. But it is certain that the actions that interested him and that he wished to communicate were actions connected with material objects, with coming and going, the making and using of material things; with eating and rejecting food and so on. Though our language becomes more and more refined and we deal with more elaborate things, it still remains anchored to the experience of what we can see and touch. We begin to name other things, our feelings, our passions, our likes and dislikes and so on, because to some extent we can recognize them, but only to some extent. We are pretty certain that if we say something is yellow, everyone else can see and recognize what is meant by yellow, and it seems to us that if we say somebody is sad, everyone who can feel can recognize and know what it is to be sad. But do I know, really, that my sadness is the same as your sadness? We have not the same way of knowing this as we have of knowing that my yellow is the same as your yellow—unless I am colour-blind.

I am saying all this because I want you to grasp this truth: that our language comes from the same source as our physical existence, it is based upon our knowledge of and contact with material objects. It is because of the way our language has grown, that we develop the forms of thought called logic. Logical thinking makes us say, for instance: "This is a stool, but this is a carpet. If this is a stool, it is not a carpet; if that is a carpet, it is not a stool," because that is how material objects are. But when we say about inner states: "This is sadness, this is happiness. If this is sadness, it is not happiness; if this is happiness, it is not sadness," then we are not talking about the same sort of things, because it is quite possible for people to be sad and happy at the same time, but it is not possible for things to be stools and carpets at the same time. It is just because our language is based upon contact with things, with material objects, that we suppose that our inner states are also like that. Therefore, we get the idea that it is not possible to be sad and happy at the same time. Sadness and happiness belong to our inner world where experience does not at all fit the language suited for talking about things. Our communications, our thinking—the two main uses that we have for language—are dominated by the fact that it has grown out of our material object life. For anything else it is very inadequate, and nearly always breaks down as soon as we begin to get at all far away from the material object life.

This is one reason why it is that by means of thought and communications of language, people can only have limited understanding of one another. They can have extremely accurate and reliable understanding of one another so long as they are dealing with material things. Someone can say "I have calculated that an eclipse of the moon will begin at three seconds past two o'clock on June 16th, 1995", and the other person will say "Well, I find it will be four seconds past", and then they go back and calculate again and they will agree that one of them is right and be perfectly happy about it. But when it comes to things of another kind, the inner things, there is nothing of the sort; there are no means of calculating and verifying inner states.

Pak Subuh has made a very important and remarkable contribution, thanks to his direct perception of the reality of things, namely, that human thought is of the same nature as material objects, and that this is why there is such a close affinity between man's thinking and the material world. The same thing has been said by other people in different ways, but the way in which he has said it is particularly striking, and, as you know, it has made a deep impression upon people who have never been interested in philosophy. It has been an eye-opener to many to be told that man has gained such a degree of mastery over the material world because of the affinity between 'thoughts' and 'things'.

We should be able to see for ourselves that man's thinking works well in the world of material objects, but has very little success outside of this world. There is, I remember, a passage in Whitehead's *Process and Reality* where he says that very thing about language. Indeed, this has been seen by philosophers, and also by people who have direct insight, like Pak Subuh; but we forget and suppose that our thought and our language are going to be adequate for going beyond material things. That is one of the many lessons we have to learn from understanding, and from studying the relationship of our physical body to the material world in which we live.

You may know that not all languages are so tied to the properties of material objects as are Indo-European ones. Some peoples— wrongly called primitive—who have a closer contact with the life of nature have developed and kept languages which spontaneously express the properties of life rather than those of things.

Now we must return to the subject of the material self and remember that I said earlier that it is not merely a chemical or electronic regulator of our body, but a genuine 'self' in the sense that we ordinarily use the word. I chose the name 'material self' to describe it in *The Dramatic Universe*.[1] It still seems to me the most appropriate name; but the idea is not by any means a new one.

Those of you who have studied Pak Subuh's book *Susila Budhi Dharma*, will see that he uses for this self the word '*roh*', which is translated as 'soul'. I think we probably made a mistake in taking this rather obvious translation of the word '*roh*' and would have done better if we had spoken about 'self', because the idea of a material soul is perhaps more confusing than the idea of a material self. The early chapters of *Susila Budhi Dharma* are concerned with this material self in man, with the part it plays in human life, and how it relates us to different sorts of objects.

---

1   For another way of reaching the notion of a material self, starting from the idea of 'Will', you can read *The Dramatic Universe*, Vol. II, chs. 26-30.

Those of you who studied the Gurdjieff system, particularly as it was presented by Ouspensky, know that he uses the notion of centres, within each of which there are different levels, and the lowest level of the centre is called the mechanical level or the automatic part. One of the most striking of Gurdjieff's psychological notions is that of the *formatory apparatus* which can be looked upon as the mind of the material self. The formatory apparatus is developed in just the way I have described, and in most people, especially of our western culture, has become the principal instrument of thought and action. This apparatus uses words as if everything consisted of material objects. It has no capacity for feeling or discrimination; but it can remember and associate ideas with prodigious skill. I am sure that Gurdjieff's 'formatory apparatus' refers to the same part of man as the material Self of which we are speaking tonight. It is a machine and yet it is a self of a kind. Its activity is mechanical, but unless we look closely it can deceive us into thinking that it is a conscious being. This is where the power of the automatic energy shows itself. There is 'something not quite right', as Gurdjieff puts it, about the material self. Its proper role is to provide the instruments by which we perceive, remember and act upon the material world of which our bodies form a part. And yet it can have a 'will of its own', which makes it a self. Many people have realized that there is something not quite right about this, though through not knowing about 'energies', they could not easily define the situation.

Schiller realized that something not his own is formed in man by the simple process of entering into his body. Jung quotes him in connection with the 'instinct of sensation' as saying that by this instinct man is "inserted into the limitations of time and space and transformed into a material object". He adds that "man in this state is no more than a numerical unit, the content of a moment, fixed in the world of matter."[1]

The study of the different parts of man in this mechanical state illustrates the same properties as I have said are connected with the material self. Whatever language we choose to use, it is quite certain that there is one part of 'me' which is connected

---

1   Schiller's Letters quoted in C.G. Jung's *Psychological Types* (Kegan Paul, Trench & Trubner, London, 1946)

with my material existence. This 'me' is able to think and to speak, because thinking and speaking are material activities, done by our vocal apparatus, by the mechanism connected with the brain and nervous system that controls speech. This 'me' uses the storehouse of images and names, language and so on, which is in my head brain, which is also a material thing.

This material self has many powers; it has power because of the wonderfully constructed mechanism it has at its disposal; that is, the mechanism of the human body, through which it has power over all sorts of other material things. It is really the Lord of all that exists on the earth. It is god-like; it can make and unmake; it can bring into existence new kinds of things that were perhaps not in the scheme of creation at all. But it is only a 'thing-god', a god of things, or the ruler of a thing-world. It has no feelings, no power to understand other natures different from its own. Therefore, some people—there are people whose material self is very much stronger than all the rest of them and dominates their lives—can have a very great deal of power, but they have no feelings, no pity. They may imitate such qualities, because this material self has an extraordinary power to simulate what it is not. This comes from the power it has of using language and communication. It can know about a whole lot of things that are really outside of its own world. It can imitate things that do not belong to itself or to its world.

The first stage of self-knowledge is to know oneself as a machine, to see where and how this material self of ours is rightly and appropriately engaged. For example, when we are dealing with material things, this is the right self to work, because it is the self that is connected with seeing, hearing and touching. It is able to speak and to think, to combine and to build up; but it is only the underground part of the house, one might say the basement. But, if people insist upon living in the basement, they do not see all that belongs to the whole of man.

Putting it in another way, this is an *instrument* which should be used by something else behind it. We will see as we go on what these 'parts behind' are, and how it is different when instruments are used by one self or by another self, but it is perfectly possible for this material self to disregard everything that is behind and to usurp the place of the master of the human being, of the human body and the human presence.

Anyone who treats the material self as the true man is bound to take a non-spiritual view of the aim of our existence. When Freud speaks of the *id* or thing-like self, he does not seem to mean quite the same, but he does recognize that there should be something behind. It seems to me that Jung does sometimes tend to regard the material self as the 'conscious mind'. His descriptions of the way it is formed seem to imply this. But if so his idea of Individuation would be unspiritual. We shall see more of this later on. For the moment, I want to draw your attention to the distinction between 'thinking' and 'intelligence'. By thought we usually mean the mental activity of the material self. Since this can be very successful, we suppose that this is the work of the true human intelligence. This is far from being the case: intelligence belongs to quite a different part of the self which is formed and works quite differently from the material self. It is probably best to use the word 'thought' for the power of the material self to know and act upon the material world.

People have different attitudes towards the power of thought. Sometimes it is said that the power of thought is the great glory of man, that it is his distinguishing mark that puts him at the head of all the rest of creation. People also say that thought is the enemy of all deep feeling, deep understanding and consciousness of reality. Both these sayings are true, because the material self is destined to be the lord of the material world, and in the material world it is a great and glorious thing. As everyone can see, in the form of science and technology, it is in the process of transforming the surface of our planet. But from another point of view, it is really nothing but a thing; one should be able to look upon it as one looks upon any other material object.

It is not easy to distinguish this material self from the rest; and so we are mostly in a state of confusion about 'me'. Because of this, we cannot understand either ourselves or other people. We do not understand the extraordinary shifts in our feelings, in our behaviour. We do not understand how it is that one minute we can be acting in one way and in another minute acting in a way totally impossible for the self that was there a few minutes before. That is because we constantly shift from one plane of existence to another, from one self to another. If the initiative passes to the material self, then when we have to deal with planes of existence that are higher, more subtle and more sensitive than the material world, we can make terrible blunders. It is very important therefore for us to know our material self, to know where is its right place and what work it should do. We must also learn to recognize what work it cannot do and should not attempt.

We should try to understand the character of everything that comes from the material self. The character of the material self is first of all indifference, lack of sensitiveness, and the tendency to externalize, to separate. All these qualities can be recognized if we look at any sort of material object. A material object is not sensitive: if a stone falls on my head and breaks it open, the stone does not care. The material self is the same. There is also what I would call externalizing, or separating, seeing things in compartments, the inability to penetrate. That also belongs to material things, and is carried over into this material self.

You may see a work of art and you may recognize great technique, and also perhaps a force, but you also see there is no participation; the artist has not entered into what he seeks to express in that work of art. Then also you can see that it was produced by the material self, in spite of the technique, in spite of the power because after all the material world has plenty of power in it.

You can sometimes see someone who is very much dominated by the material self, but is of a very high intellectual quality; he can produce a scheme for dealing with a particular situation and when you look at this scheme you see the defects in it; because feeling has not been taken into account. Then you can realize that that work was done by the material self.

When you see people behaving unaccountably towards one another, not feeling what they are doing to another person and clearly unable to feel it, then you can be pretty sure they are acting from the material self. When you see people unable to make compromises, unable to see more than one point of view about a given situation, that is the way of the material self. Nothing is able to enter, it is closed as material objects are closed to one another.

Of course, all of us must know and recognize that in every

one of us there is this material self. What matters is that it should be outside us and not inside us. It should be as much outside of us as our clothes are. When it gets inside us then it begins to produce inner results, and we shall find ourselves behaving in a heartless way. The material self is the proper and rightful lord of the material world, that is where it has its rightful place. But as soon as it comes out of that world then it is a mere thing, not to be treated with any more respect than other things.

One difficulty for us is that this body of ours is much more than a material object. Tomorrow we shall come to something deeper though still associated with this body. We know that within this body there is life, and that life is something more wonderful than the material world, and we tend therefore to think that this body of ours belongs to the world of life. It does, but not the material part of the body. It is the *life* within that belongs to the world of life. What is strange, really hard to understand, is that *thought* does not belong to the world of life.

Q. But do not people sometimes have thoughts that go beyond the words used?

J.G.B. Yes, we do have 'thoughts too deep for words', but they are not 'thinking'. You remember that I made a distinction between thought and intelligence. There are many kinds and degrees of intelligence. There can be 'seeing', there can be something we call by such names as 'intuition'; that is not what I mean by thought. Intelligence can go right out of the material world; and, certainly, even words can be transmuted, but unless they are transmuted, unless they are brought to life, they remain objects of the material world. It is possible to see something more than material things, but that must actually happen; it is not enough to say 'seeing can actually go beyond material objects'. One can see richer and more extraordinary sights behind the material world. When one does, it is different, but we must not forget that this only happens when it *does* happen. When not, then words come back again to their origin, which is always taken from experience of this material world.

Q. Could you clarify the problem of bodily inertia and mental inertia? In other words, we have to force ourselves to some extent to work. Has this something to do with the material self?

J.G.B. Inertia is in the nature of *things*. They can influence the way things happen, but they have no initiative, they have no drive. So long as we remain on the level of the material world, then we have to be stimulated to action. Some attraction or compulsion, hope or fear, something or other has to stimulate us or we remain passive. It is the same with thinking. Everyone knows that our thinking activity is very difficult to keep going if we are not interested. On the other hand, if we are interested, it is equally difficult to stop it. In other words, there is something behind thought which decides whether thoughts will move or not. If that something is not there, then the thinking mind is just an inert machine. We think 'Oh, a very active thing, the mind; thought is such a mobile and extraordinary thing in man!'. But it is not thought that is mobile, it is the man himself who is mobile and active. Let the man not be stimulated and then you see the difficulty of thinking.

No human being is solely composed of a material self; every human being has something behind, because a human being is alive. As long as he has his body as we have ours now, it is not only a material object, it is also a living body, and it is something else besides all that. That is what I call 'behind'—all that you do not see when you look at him. You cannot tell for certain, when you look at a body lying motionless whether it is alive or dead, because what your senses tell you is simply that there is a material object in front of you. Other tests have to be applied to see whether it is alive or not.

This body of ours exists here on the surface of the earth. It is made out of the materials of the surface of the earth and it participates in the physical and chemical changes proceeding incessantly on the earth's surface. In a word, this body is a *mechanism for the exchange of energies*. It exchanges energy through its senses, through seeing, hearing and the rest of it; through food and breath, through its metabolism. All this is possible because this body is very specially and extraordinarily devised and designed and constructed. Thanks to this wonderful construction of the body there comes our knowing, and this knowledge can translate itself into language, thinking, and bodily activities all of which can remain on the level of earthly existence. What takes man out of the level of the earthly existence is all that is or should be *behind* that, but what is behind has to be found out in a different way. It is very probable that people will one day devise machines that will be able to do pretty well everything that the material self of man can do; but that is, I am quite sure, just how far they will ever go. However clever they may be in producing an artificial man, that artificial man will never have anything more than a material self. Strangely enough, people have had the feeling that whatever man may construct, it will never be a human self. In all the different fables and stories and fantasies of science fiction about producing artificial men, it has somehow been realized that these artificial men, these robots, would only work up to a certain point. This means that you could conceivably, with very great deployment of constructive genius, produce something which would *work like* the material self of man. It would learn to talk, would learn to think, would be able to make and construct all sorts of ingenious devices, perhaps even to get rich. But it would have no heart. This helps you to see what this first self of man is. We can also see that this same cleverly constructed instrument could be a very valuable servant of man, and man's life on earth could be set free to do many things for which at present we have neither time nor energy. This is probably the clue, the key, to finding what this material self is for. Its proper role in our lives is to take over certain kinds of jobs that need not be performed by the higher and finer selves we shall be studying later.

Q. You mentioned this possibility of man constructing something that would be equivalent to a material self. Could not this creature one day ask itself "Who am I?"

J.G.B. Not equivalent, but having similar powers. Such a machine might ask your question and it would answer it by saying "I am the most wonderful thing in the world!" Or, it might even find out that there is something else a little more wonderful. It might even go as far as learning how to make itself as wonderful as that other one. All that is conceivable for such a machine. But still the machine would not become a *self,* unless the will were to enter into it. That is the point of the fables of the machines that *steal the will of their makers.*

Q. What happens when this material self dies? Does it die

completely? What happens to the motivating force, the animating force which makes it move and think? The material self perishes, but presumably there is something behind which animates it.

J.G.B. One thing we can say with confidence, and that is that at death, the will leaves the machine, and so it ceases to be a man. We cannot say what is left behind until we come to the question of the soul. But so far as the material self is concerned, we can be sure that it is helpless in the face of death. Let us try to understand why. It is a little like this: you have a motor-car; for that motor-car to go, it has to have gasoline in it and it also has to have a driver. If the driver gets out and walks away, that is one condition for the motor-car. If it runs out of gasoline, that is another. If the driver has no way of getting gasoline, he is not quite stuck, he can get out and walk away and find himself another car, or find some other way of travel. But the car is doubly dependent, it has to have a driver that cares about driving it, and it has to have gasoline to make it go. Our material self has that double dependence. It is dependent upon energy exchanges and this corresponds to the gasoline; it has to eat and drink and so on, it has to see and hear and touch. All of that is its motive power in the material sense. There is something else besides that, like the driver. That is another story. One way of looking at it is that the driver gets fed up with the car when there is no gasoline and goes off home. But it can also happen that the driver goes off even when there is gasoline, and that is another way in which things can die, then what will happen to the car is not so much a question of gasoline as what the driver is going to do about it. It is the same with us. Certainly food, energy exchanges and so on are the immediate support for the activity of the body, but there is something else besides that. None of us doubts that there is something else than a machine for exchanging energies here, sitting on these chairs.

But to answer your question: what happens to the material self when this partnership breaks up? I do not think that the material self has any possibility of an independent existence. I think that it is so completely linked up with the physical object that is our body that it does not exist apart from it. So I would say it seems likely that it dies when the body dies, or not long after. We can only make conjectures about the mystery of dying, one would have to go through it, and not only go through it, but study and watch what is happening at the same time. It is not given to us to have this kind of scientific attitude towards our own death. My own belief about this is that this material self immediately lapses into a state of un consciousness and soon dissolves. Different fates are in store for the other selves we shall talk about later.

Q. This of course means that it is a very terrible situation to base one's whole trust for existence on one's material self? On the other hand, can this material self not be a protection against the awareness one gets in the latihan of the sorrow and suffering in the world? If one were all the time in that state of awareness, one could not stand it.

J.G.B. It is true that the material self does not suffer sympathetically: but it can suffer antipathetically, that is by hating all that it cannot understand. But that is only when our will is caught into it. When we are separate from it, as does happen in the latihan, we feel it as a lump of lead or stone inside. Nevertheless, we must never forget that the material self is a necessary part of man, it is not to be despised or discarded as unimportant. It is not something we should wish to destroy in ourselves, any more than we should destroy our clothes. We need the protection of the material self, but it has to be outside us, not inside. It can sometimes happen to people that they are on the wrong side of the material self. It is as if they were turned inside out, the sensitive part being outside and the hard part inside, and this can produce a very undesirable situation. What you say is true; just as our body protects our nervous system, which is kept inside the less sensitive parts, so also the material self is a necessary sheath, or coating, for the inner or more sensitive parts of the self. There can be a premature peeling off or removal of this protective coating which is rather dangerous for people. They get into serious trouble if this happens before they are ready for it, before things can be put in their right order. It should not be destroyed, only it must be in its right place, serving its rightful purpose. If it gets temporarily put out of action, a kind of crisis occurs. This is described by Pak Subuh as *Zadab* or punishment. A man who has put his whole trust in the material self—as you well put it—is in a bad way. You know that Pak Subuh uses the word Satanic Soul as equivalent of

Material Self. The man who has let his will enter into the material self has sold himself to Satan. We should learn to recognize it and make sure that we keep it on the outside in its proper place. There it is not Satanical but serviceable.

Q. As we can make words for things which are not material, should we not be able to think about them?

J.G.B. We can and do think about them, only we have to realize the difference in the reliability of meanings. We talk about things which are tangible, and things which are intangible, and we tend to think that the meanings in both cases are equally reliable. The truth is that the meaning of words which are used for describing something so near the surface as our states of feeling cannot be verified with any certainty. Two people may say 'I am happy' and it may seem as if these words are just as clear as 'I am tall', or 'I am fat'. In reality, even such an apparently straightforward word as 'happy' means different things to different people; or, even to the same person, at different times. If you try to find out what the word 'happy' means to a person who has very little in him except the material self, you might have a terrible shock. Then you would see that the use of words for inner states is something that requires a different discipline of language from that which is sufficient for dealing with material things. We are prepared, in our scientific work, to accept a very severe discipline about the exact way in which we use words for material objects. But that discipline is child's play compared to what is needed for inner states, but we have no corresponding kind of discipline about words that belong to these inner and more subtle things.

Q. Bapak says that with testing and continued practice of the latihan, we might start being able to know these things naturally?

J.G.B. That is connected with purification, one effect of which is to set us free from the domination of the material self.

Q. What is the place of the poet, for instance? He can express ideas, feelings, abstract things, and it means a lot to people who are reading it, if they are sensitive to it. How does that tie up with materiality? He is expressing certain ideas, certain feelings. Is it somehow a little deeper than materiality?

J.G.B. Not merely a little deeper, it can be infinitely deeper. This is his job, and why he is important in the world. He has to search for ways of saying things that language cannot say. T.S. Eliot says, for example, that we grope for words to say things that cannot be spoken of and when we find them we want to say something else. This stretching of language to contrive somehow or other to say what cannot be said is a part of our task. We all of us have to do this, but it is the special profession of the poet to do it. Of course, there are also other ways of doing this.

Q. Are we not trying in poetry, to crack the associations of words which link them to the expression of material things by creating a new association away from these material things.

J.G.B. Not always. A poet could not do it if there were not something behind. He neither would be able to speak nor would we be able to hear what he says. If there were nothing else, if we were robots, it would be improbable that there would be any poets among us. If there were, it would only be because they had heard it from some other planet, let us say, which went in for that sort of thing, and they copied it. The point is that human experience goes beyond the material, it is going beyond it all the time. We plunge more or less deeply into the world behind the material world and we bring back something with us from this elevation, something that can be recognized. What the poet has to do is to contrive to say things in such a way that we can recognize what he has seen. It does not seem very likely that anyone would be able to read poetry and receive something from it that is beyond the material world, if he himself had not had experience from beyond that world in some way. In other words, the poet only reminds him, or helps him perhaps not only to remember, but to bring into better focus that which he himself has already glimpsed.

. . . . .

The discussion came to an end here. J.G.B. made some suggestions for putting into practice the ideas which had been explained about the material self.

J.G.B. The first thing to remember is that when we see and feel and touch things, our sight, feeling and sensation are not 'I'—they are something that is happening to 'me'. The thoughts that are present in my inner awareness—in my mind as we usually call it—are not 'I'. They are all part of me, but they must be looked upon as the materials with which I have to work. I must never allow them to capture my attention so completely that I forget myself. One way of safeguarding ourselves against being swallowed up by the material self is to develop a sense of responsibility towards material objects whether they belong to me or not. We have a tendency to take care of all that adds something to the content of the material self. 'My possessions make me what I am.' This is completely false: on the contrary, they prevent me from being what I am if I allow them to dominate me. But if I take care of other people's possessions exactly as I would care for my own, then I am no longer feeding the desire of my material self. If we look at things in the way that several of you reported earlier this evening; that is, if you recognize that they have the right to be what they are—in a word, if you respect them—you will find that you are more free in front of the material world and you will be in a little less danger of falling under the domination of your material self.

The real difficulty is to see the material self for what it really is. Ouspensky introduced us to the idea of the Man-Machine in 1921. We spent years in his groups making observations and experiments to enable us to decide *for ourselves* if we accepted this devastating theory that man for the greater part of the time— indeed for most people 99.9 per cent of the time—is in a state of slavery to his own machine. We found out very much about the working of this material self. But, so far as I personally am concerned, it was not until 1932 that I could say that I really saw it for what it is. I do not say this to discourage you, but so that you will not be disappointed if at first you find it difficult to see it for yourselves. But before we leave this first stage of our voyage of self-discovery, let me assure you of its importance. You may think that the material self has little to do with our spiritual quest. It has. It is the dragon that St. George has to vanquish; after which it then becomes his willing steed able to bear him far on his journey. To vanquish it we must first know it and then keep an eye on it. There is an intimate and wonderful relationship between St. George and the Dragon shown in mediaeval pictures. The Dragon is watching the saint to see if he can catch him off his guard. So long as the Saint is watchful, the dragon is helpless. This is the key-note of our relationship to the material world. It is there to serve us, but woe betide us if it catches us off our guard.

Tomorrow we shall go beneath the material surface to look at life and its meaning. But before we separate, I want to remind you that all that we have spoken about today refers to 'me' and not to 'I'. This does not mean that 'I' have no part in it. On the contrary, everything depends upon where 'I' stand. If 'I' identify myself with any material object, then I am that material object. The Man-Machine is only a self because 'I' enter into it. When I do, I lose my birthright; that is my consciousness of who and what I am. This will, I hope, become clearer as we go along. In order to understand a very complicated structure, we must first learn how to distinguish its different parts and their nature and function. This will be our task for the next two days of this study.

3. THE REACTIONAL SELF—LIKE AND DISLIKE

The second day began with a talk about life and the properties that all living things of whatsoever nature have in common. I spoke of the peculiar difficulty that biologists and philosophers have in giving an exact definition of what it means to be alive. We all know what it means: but what are we to pick out and say by *that* character we can always distinguish living from dead? Of a man, we say he is dead when his heart stops. But hundreds of people have been resuscitated after that kind of 'dying'. Formerly life was connected with breath, and the words for life and breath were often the same, and both were taken to mean the same as soul or spirit. Although certainly breathing, in the sense of taking in oxygen from the air, is common to nearly all forms of life, it is not completely universal. There are organisms that die as soon as air reaches them. Again, plants breathe, but apparently quite differently from us: they also need oxygen, but their main concern with air is just the opposite to ours: we take in oxygen and give out carbon dioxide, they do the reverse. There are other life activities such as feeding or metabolism, reproduction, self-renewal—but none of them are universal to all living things: nor can any of them be defined without some ambiguity.

There is another feature of life that I pointed out, and that is that it seems most improbable that life exists on the earth alone out of countless millions of planets in hundreds of millions of galaxies in this stupendous universe to which we belong. Whatever life may or may not be, it is certainly enormously important and even human impudence could scarcely suggest—in this twentieth century—that this planet earth is the only important place in the whole universe, all the rest being so much 'dead matter'.

But if life is universal, then it is certain to take all sorts of strange forms appropriate to the physical and chemical conditions on other planets. So a definition of life in terms of what living things *do* on the earth—*as we know it today*—that seems peculiar and special, is likely to be misleading.

From this, I went on to speak about the energy that is characteristic of all life.

J.G.B. Today, we shall seek to understand how one part of my selfhood is built upon the fact that I am a living being.

The second characteristic of 'me' is that it is the self of a living being. To sight and touch I am a material object, but to my inner sense I am a living creature.

For this I shall ask you to think about *life* as having a quality that is shared by all living things; simple cells, plants, animals and by us men. It can also be looked upon as a universal energy or state of matter. We can speak of the 'energy of life'. Yesterday we were talking about another kind of energy or energies, manifested in things. The automatic energy is certainly present in all higher organisms since it controls their instinctive activity, but it is not the finest kind of energy that is common to all life.[1]

I believe that the property that characterizes all life is to be sensitive. The very simplest living things have a sensitiveness that no non-living things possess. Sensitiveness is far more highly organized in animals and in men than it is in very simple things, like viruses and cells, but it is always there. The organization of sensitiveness, and the way it works, is different in beings of different kinds, but as we are studying on a very big scale, a whole world at a time, we shall take sensitiveness in all its forms and then try to understand how it enters into our own lives as men and women.

The property of sensitiveness, if you look at it carefully, is concerned with accepting and rejecting. Sensitive living matter draws back from what is harmful, closes to what hurts it and opens itself to what is good and gives it pleasure. You can see in the simplest organism under the microscope that turning towards and turning away, which is called 'tropism', which means having a direction towards or away from, turning towards the light and away from darkness if light-loving, or towards darkness and away from light if darkness-loving. There are various other

---

[1]   I did not go into the distinction of the energies associated with life: constructive, vital and automatic in detail as I did in *The Dramatic Universe*, Vol. II, Ch. 32. Those interested in studying the whole range of energies must refer to that chapter.

properties of living matter, such as self-preservation, nutrition, transformation and so on, but all of these are incidental, whereas sensitiveness is invariably present. It enters into everything; it is a universal power, or universal energy. All the other powers of life can be regarded as the organization of sensitivity. There is the sensitiveness of my body, the sensitiveness of my inner state, all organized in different ways.[1]

Yet, although sensitiveness is a property that can be present in every function of ours, it can also be absent. For example, one can have dead thoughts and one can have living thoughts. One can have dead emotions—although they may be strong—and one can have sensitive emotions. For example, a man may be in a 'cold fury' at not getting what he wants: but not 'feel' anything about what it really means to him and others. There can be dead seeing and living seeing; you can see and not be sensitive to what you see, or you can be sensitive to it. When things come to life for us then we enter into the world of life, and then life meets life. It is not sufficient to stop at the sensitiveness that is common to everything, as for example, when I draw back if I touch a hot coal. With us men, it is far more highly organized. If I know the way my sensitivity is *organized*, then I know that part of 'me'. When matter passes over the threshold from the insensitive to the sensitive, life begins. When it goes back over the threshold from sensitiveness to insensitiveness, then life ends.

From what we said yesterday, you will easily see that insensitiveness is associated with automatic energy and sensitiveness with sensitive energy. This is simple and straightforward once you see it: but it has taken me forty years to understand why the 'Man-Machine' is less sensitive than a toad.

So, I will ask you, today, to turn your attention from mechanicalness to sensitiveness. Observe how you experience it, remembering that with us it has a high degree of organization. You will remember that yesterday, I showed you how versatile

[1]   I should here again acknowledge my indebtedness to Dr. Maurice Vernet for making me see that organic sensitivity is the one invariable characteristic of all life. His paper: "Something New in the Philosophy of Life" in *Systematics* (Journal of the Institute for the Comparative Study of History, Philosophy and the Sciences, April 1963) is the only reference I can give in English. He has written many books in French.

the automatic energy can be, how when it manifests in thought, speech and action it can dominate the material world and make man its master. So here also we have an energy of sensitivity, that takes many forms, and when organized as it is in man enables him to have and to exercise many powers. Quite new and strange experiences, different from those of the material world, arise in us when we become aware of the working of the sensitive energies. As an example of what I mean by 'strange', you may observe that we can be sensitive when there is nothing to be sensitive about. We can be sensitive to imaginary stimuli, which certainly does not hold for the simpler forms of life. We can be sensitive to a very wide range of stimuli, from the same stimuli of light and darkness, of cold and warmth as influence the simplest living things; sensitive also to the conditions of our animal body, and, finally sensitive to all sorts of human likes and dislikes, pleasures and pains. We have to learn how to distinguish sensitiveness—highly organized or less highly organized—from the deeper qualities that lie beneath and which we have to study later in the week.

There is in man a sensitive nature as there is a material nature. What we shall speak about today are the properties of this nature and the place it occupies in our lives. You can probably see from the observations you made last night that, at first, it is not easy to assign things to the right world, or assign our behaviour to the right part of the self. We may suppose that something manifested through the body is a purely material effect, when, in reality, it may come from something which is behind. Today, you may well observe things that do not belong so much to the body as a living thing, as to the body as 'something more'. We are feeling our way towards the 'withinness' of man, and we must go in the right order if we are to understand. There is this second 'me' that is founded on sensitivity. It has the other various properties associated with it, but this is the key to understanding it.

You can try to notice and remember examples of sensitiveness, firstly, from your own direct experience during the day. Secondly, from memory, which is not quite so good, because we invariably distort things in memory. In memory it is almost inevitable that we lose something and we add something. Thirdly, it is possible to realize this working of sensitivity by thought; that is, just by knowledge, which is still less satisfactory. Try to see how well you can get a general picture of what sensitivity means in our lives. Remember what I said at the beginning about this 'towards and away from'. You can compare the sensitivity to a helmsman. He only has two instructions: Port or Starboard, like or dislike, yes or no, do this or don't do it, right or wrong. However they may be labelled, his instructions can only tell him to put the wheel over this way or that way. Your sensitivity works like that; or more exactly as if there were in you a fleet of boats each with its own helmsman, each with its own 'Port and Starboard'. I say this because each function has its own sensitivity distinct from the rest. There are instinctive pleasure-pain reactions, emotional like-dislike reactions, motor want to-don't want to reactions, mental yes-no reactions, sexual attraction-aversion reactions, and many more besides.

In every situation that we find ourselves—or, before every complex of influences that acts upon us—there is always something that our sensitivity shrinks from, and there is something our sensitivity turns towards. According to the way in which the actual instrument -the boat in which we happen to be sailing— through which the sensitivity works is organized, the things that we are drawn towards and those we shrink away from will be different. We are drawn towards some physical sensations, we shrink away from others. We are drawn towards some kind of emotional experiences, we shrink away from others. We are drawn towards some ideas, we shrink away from others. We are drawn towards certain kinds of activity, and from others we shrink away and try to avoid doing them.

There is natural sensitivity and there is unnatural or abnormal sensitivity. It is natural to be drawn towards life, to be open to experience; but there can be a sensitivity in man that rejects life and denies experience. Again there is the sensitivity that draws us outwards towards the great world outside, and there is the sensitivity that draws us inwards towards the equally great world inside. There is the sensitivity that makes us seek for the greater and that which makes us content with the less.

In other words, there is something which draws us towards a different level, and something which makes us shrink away in a certain part of us and draws us back to this world of material things. So you can see that this drawing towards and this shrinking away from can be very varied in its action. The property of sensitivity goes through it all, and we should see for ourselves—you should be able to see during the day—how through this we have a general part in this process of life that is going on, because everything that lives shares in this. I think it is probably true that all the differences existing among living things depend upon the organization of their sensitivity. What all have in common is participation in this universal cosmic quality of sensitivity which is life.

.   .   .   .   .

During the day following this preliminary talk, a number of the students took part in the repainting of the outer walls of the house at Coombe Springs. This involved scraping off the old paint and scrubbing the brickwork. Scaffolding was erected and several men and women, who had not tried such a thing before, climbed the tall ladders and worked on precariously balanced planks. Others were working in the garden below, so that most were in sight and earshot of each other. Whether it was because their attention had been turned towards sensitivity, or whether it was due to the excitement of undertaking new and unaccustomed tasks—maybe it was simply the glorious weather and the beauty of the gardens in full summer flower—the school became very gay and talkative. There was an immense expenditure of energy and many animated discussions. When the time came, in the evening, to meet and share experiences, it became evident that the school had been much more successful in recognizing the character of sensitive energy than in its approach to automatic energy on the previous day.

.   .   .   .   .

Q. I noticed in scraping the wall that it became rather monotonous and dreary, and I feel that some of us up there on the scaffolding were, as you say, shrinking away from this and became gayer and gayer and more excited. And probably because I am really rather frightened of heights, I forced myself to do a gymnastic on the top bar. Afterwards I was in a quivering electric state, but also had the joy of having done it, and the fear of having gone through that experience.

J.G.B. You have correctly observed one of the properties of sensitivity and that is that it gives us the feeling of being alive. Usually this energy is so weak in us that it is all used up in our instinctive reactions; but when we do some act that concentrates it—as for example, your gymnastics on the top bar of the scaffolding—you feel yourself alive. This is, no doubt, the chief reason why bodily danger attracts us. Certainly, fear is also a manifestation of sensitivity; but, as you will see as we go further, sensitivity is always two-edged.

Q. Is not fear a peculiarly human thing, which tries to overcome sensitiveness all the time? Thereby, I imagine, it gets slowly stronger and stronger, till it turns into doing this on the top bar, which is very typical of something a great many do, but I am sure it must be a peculiarly human quality. There are people, for example, who will not put on an extra coat when it is cold. This peculiar human quality includes even relationships with people, such as daring to say something unusual.

J.G.B. I would not say that it is fear that tries to overcome sensitivity, but another property of man that belongs to the next level of his self-hood. The 'building-up' you speak of is a need of our character—the need to prove that we are something. But the word character itself will not be clear to you until we come to it tomorrow. Let us stick to sensitivity for the moment.

I said this morning that one way we can look at sensitivity is to think of it as an energy, or a state of matter which has the property of being sensitive. I distinguished it from the properties of solidity and visibility which belong to material objects. There is, very probably, a universal energy that has this sensitive property. There are energies we shall be speaking about in the next two or three days that have mastery over the sensitive energy, and when they are deployed, then the sensitive energy is *used* instead of just *flowing of itself.* That produces just the kind of experiences that you have described. This sense of excitement and enhanced vitality is a desire to experience the release of the energy of sensitivity, and the peculiar quality it has of being two-edged. It is very likely that sensitive energy is such that it always has two poles. One cannot have pleasure without pain, one cannot have excitement without tedium and so on, and when these come together instead of alternating as they usually do, then it gives that sense of enhanced life. When both sides of this energy are working together, then one feels really alive.

Q. I saw two things today, the first was that without sensitive energy one could not do this job of scraping, because it was the sensitive energy that really connected you with the job. If there were not this sensitive energy, the arm and the implement would still be connected, but there would not be anything behind it. It is that which is behind the arm that actually makes one able to do the job of the scraping over the rough surface which requires changes in the position of one's implements, and so forth. The other thing was in relation to the scaffolding; it was possible to go up and down the scaffolding so that you would not have time to be afraid, because your sensitivity would be directed to the scaffolding itself, rather than to what you were afraid of, which is height.

J.G.B. Your first observation is undoubtedly right; the sensitive energy activates the mechanism. If it is withdrawn or lacking, then the mechanism will not work and that is why we say 'life', and 'a living body' and 'a dead body'; to be full of life, or to be very lifeless, inert. The other observations are different, and it brings out another aspect of sensitivity. That is, every kind of energy has some power of connecting things. The way things are connected materially is by their power of cohesion. That is one kind of connectedness. But the kind of energy we are now talking about enables us to touch things; there is a contact, not just a connection. This contact can be directed, and according to its direction our experience changes. For example, if it is connected to some imagination or some inner state that I am in, then I feel it in that way, but if it is connected to an outward tangible situation, then I am no longer so much affected by my inner state.

Q. It seemed to me that sensitivity is connected with quality. The idea seems to be connected with the beginnings of the possibilities of value, of discrimination between higher and lower quality.

J.G.B. Sensitiveness is not *in itself* discriminatory. When we act from sensitivity alone, we react to the immediate stimulus that is there, not to anything more that may be implied. For example, from sensitiveness alone we will draw back from a burning fire, but from something more than sensitiveness, something deeper in man, a man may go through fire because he knows that he will save his life if he goes through the burning instead of waiting for it to overtake him; or he may go into the fire to rescue a child. Sensitiveness alone will not make him do this sort of thing.

The word sensitiveness may have been misleading for some of you, because you may have thought sensitiveness is something like discrimination. We may say 'a sensitive artist' or 'this person is very sensitive'. I used the word in a much simpler meaning than that. That is why I emphasized that it is something we share with everything that lives.

Q. It is true, I did think of this as something like discrimination. It seems to me now that if this had not come before, we could not reach the point where discrimination is possible.

J.G.B. You are right. Although discrimination belongs to a different level than sensitivity, sensitivity must be developed first; we cannot discriminate where we do not feel.

Q. I thought perhaps sensitivity started with the instinct for self-preservation.

J.G.B. It certainly does not *start* with it, because many living things do not have this instinct at all. Some insects certainly do not seem to have it. I once drove for several miles through the middle of a swarm of locusts, countless millions of them, in the vineyards of Attica, in Greece. The peasants tried to stop them by making great flames of fire, but the locusts put the fires out by falling into them. They seemed devoid of any instinct of self-preservation. They went on and on, dying in millions. I have seen territories in Africa. Termites have a perfectly terrifying indifference to individual life in spite of the tremendous development of the automatic energy which gives a territory such power over the material world round it.

Anyone who has observed such forms of life must admit that the instinct of self-preservation certainly is not present in the *individuals* of the species. This is true not only of insects but of all colonizing animals. When man behaves like a herd-animal he loses it too. In reality, the instinct of self-preservation belongs to something higher than simple livingness. It is very often possible to see, even in our own experience, that when our own actions are dominated by some part of our sensitivity, we can do things that are destructive to ourselves without discrimination or even realization of what we are doing. No, one conclusion I have come to about this—and it interested me very much when I first began to see it—is that this level of sensitivity does not include the instincts that we associate with our animal nature, the instincts of self-preservation, of self-assertion, self-renewal or such like. These do not come from sensitivity, even from highly organized sensitivity; they come from something else, an energy of a different quality, which we shall speak about tomorrow.

Q. If I look at a person and I think he is intelligent, or stupid, or when I attach some quality to his appearance, or the sound of his voice, is this a function of sensitivity?

J.G.B. There is more than one way of passing such judgments. One may judge people mechanically. One could devise a machine that could do precisely that; that is, analyse, by means of a computer, the vibrations of the voice, and say that this person is like this or like that; the machine might be able to do it better than we could, but it would not be aware of what it was doing. If we ourselves are aware that there is a difference in the impact of this voice on us, rather than another, or this face rather than the other face, then that is where we become aware that sensitivity is present, and in this awareness lies the difference between a dead action and a live one. I can see in the same way as a computer would see, or I see in the same way as a living thing can see, and I can recognize the difference between the two. If I am seeing in the first way, I shall not be aware of it at the same time, because *to be aware one has to be sensitive*. But I can look back and see that I was looking at something in much the same way as a complicated electronic machine would have looked at it.

Q. I was looking at sensitivity rather in the way that plants are sensitive to light and water and air, and it reminded me how, when the sun shines one feels a lifting of spirits, and when it is stormy and dull it depresses one. It seems that we react to weather conditions just as the plants do.

J.G.B. There are two points of importance in what you have just observed. First of all, there is that push and pull, that attraction or repulsion, that pleasure and displeasure quality about sensitiveness. Light, warmth, air and the rest attract; damp, cold, darkness, repel. As we open to one, we close to the other. That opening and closing is typical of the work of sensitivity. I am sure that is one of the steps that will help us to understand this part of our nature. You also use the word 'react', and that I think is equally important in understanding sensitivity. The sensitive mechanism is a mechanism of reaction.

Q. Would you say that the reactions of the conditioned reflex are an outgrowth of sensitivity?

J.G.B. Yes, certainly. It uses precisely that quality of the sensitive mechanism; that is, the yes-no quality. The way that reflexes are conditioned in animals is by exposing them to unpleasant and pleasant stimuli; associating certain actions with a pleasant stimulus and other actions with an unpleasant one. By this means, certain 'associations of sensitivity' are established. This is possible because the nature of sensitive energy is such that it is capable of being organized. A reflex is a channel of sensitivity. A conditioned reflex is the organization of two or more channels in such a way that a stimulus in one will produce a reaction in the other. It amounts to nothing more than that.

One can say that such experiments are made on the sensitive parts of a living being. That is why such a very wide range of beings can be conditioned, even beings without a nervous system, which you might expect could not be done. It can be done, because of the nature of sensitivity. Sensitivity is a 'yes-no' mechanism, but it is a yes-no mechanism that is not experienced in the same way as is the yes-no mechanism of a machine, because there is in all living matter a tendency to open to certain stimulations and to contract in the face of others, to respond to some and to withdraw from others. At the bottom of all this, is opening and closing, which is something more primitive than instinct, while instinct itself is more primitive than intention. There is no intention in the working of the sensitive mechanism, but it is different from a material machine.

Q. Is appreciation more than a sensitive reaction of like and dislike?

J.G.B. Sometimes; but it may be only a reaction. The reaction may be sophisticated; that is, it may be the result of some elaborate piece of conditioning, but still it is a reaction. When we work on this level there is nothing behind our reactions.

Q. There is a quality in people that is known as *taste*. People have taste in cars, in behaviour, in speech, etc., and it occurred to me that this might be a function of sensitivity in people. Is there a connection here?

J.G.B. I think that perhaps what we mean by taste, is a consistent pattern of like and dislike in front of certain situations, such as works of art, social behaviour and so on. This consistent pattern can be on quite different levels, it can be nothing else but an automatic set piece, in which there is no feeling at all, but it may be on the level where we react sensitively. The sensitive reaction must be conditioned in some way or it would not come from 'me'. If I react merely as a living organism, I am not producing anything from 'myself'.

A work of art has—or ought to have—a sensitive life of its own, but we cannot recognize it as such unless we have some corresponding form of sensitivity in ourselves. A cow is sensitive to grass but she might not react to the grass in a painted landscape. We can see how, meeting with new and unaccustomed art forms, it takes time for us to build up a pattern of sensitivity that enables us to react to them—either positively or negatively—in a way that is not false or artificial. To be sensitive to any human artefact, there has to be something artificial formed in us. This can be quite genuine in the sense that there will be a feeling of liking and disliking, of pleasure in front of some situations and dislike in front of others, which is quite different from the first. There are higher forms of taste that we have not come to yet, because we have not come to those parts of the self. People who have taste of the first kind may have learnt to recognize the work of a certain master and they will say they like it because it is by 'so and so'. If it is not by 'so and so', they will not have any idea if they like it or not. That is quite common. Yet such people, because they have a good mechanical repertoire, will be considered to have an informed taste. That is entirely on the level of the electronic computer. It is the taste of the material self which has no feeling in it. You can test this by asking yourself if 'that work is by so and so' could be asserted on the basis of exclusively material criteria.

You could take the pigments used, the brush work, the age of the canvas, various tricks of composition and lighting—all of which could be measured or counted—and feed them into a computer and receive an answer whether a given painting was by Giotto or Cimabue, by Pissaro or Renoir.

There can, however, be a really genuine response of liking or disliking, based on a reaction mechanism that has been conditioned and prepared. There can also be something more than that, there can be real participation in the situation and a valuation that comes from understanding of true quality. It is only at that point that one can really talk of taste, and it is very remarkable how very rare people are who have this third kind of taste; that is, unconditioned taste, not reactional.

Q. It seems to me that sensitivity may have very deep moral implications?

J.G.B. When you use such words as 'very deep', you must make a reservation; because conscience is deeper than sensitivity. That which can appear as conscience on the level of sensitivity may be no more than formed habits of reaction; one can call this moral sensitivity. That is, sensitivity conditioned to a system of morals. A system of morals can be valid and socially significant, or privately significant. This kind of sensitivity can be very useful, but there is in man something deeper than this, which is truly his conscience, which we will come to later.

Q. Does this moral conditioning belong to the peripheral part of the human being you call 'me', and what you speak about as true conscience is a feature of 'I'?

J.G.B. All that we can say at this stage is that conscience is deeper than anything we have reached yet. It is important when you use the word peripheral to remember that, although we are speaking of something behind the material object—that is, this physical body and the energy exchanges that keep this physical body in action—we are still speaking of something very near the surface. In us men, the structure of sensitivity is associated with the nature of our nervous system and our blood chemistry. That is why there are the possibilities of conditioning and so on, but it is not the same thing as the nervous system. Sensitivity is finer than electrical or chemical energy.

In several of your questions, you have used the word *reaction* and that is a word we need to understand. The word reaction, as I would understand it, is the *immediate response to an immediate stimulus*. There is something in man which is constantly responding to the various stimulations that come to him. This something I have called—using the terminology of *The Dramatic Universe*— the Reactional Self of man. As I have pointed out several times, reactions are basically simple—opening and shutting, advancing and withdrawing, pleasure and pain, activity and inhibition, yes and no, like and dislike and so on, through all the possible pairs of opposites we can use for describing all the variety of reactions we have. The whole of this extremely complicated structure of reactions in man is somehow welded together into something I call his reactional self. It is not, in most people, very well put together, it is not very coherent, and we have different parts of this reactional self which are conditioned to react in one way, and other parts of that same reactional self which are conditioned to respond quite differently to the same stimulation. Thus we can have quite inconsistent reactions because in most people the reactional self is a loosely knit, rather formless structure, though very complicated. The reactional self is not a very high part of 'me', but it is very much nearer to my real nature than the material self we were discussing yesterday. Above all, the reactional self has the property of being alive. You will remember I spoke about 'dead' seeing and 'live' seeing. Whenever we have the experience of being *alive in the act of seeing*, we can safely say that we are seeing with our reactional self. Dead seeing is a mark of the Man-machine.

Q. Your saying that seeing or hearing can be alive, or seeing or hearing can be dead, I took to mean a sense of 'myself' at the same time as I saw all the trees, grass, etc., and a sense of 'myself' while I was working. Was my hearing alive in that sense because I sensed myself at the same time?

J.G.B. Yes, that is a fair description. The important thing is to realize that there is a difference between being like that and being in a state where all the sights, sounds and actions are all there and you are not there even in your material self, because your 'I' has lost consciousness.

Q. I think I got a glimpse of something this afternoon, mostly associated with smells. Walking through the woods, I got one or two or three different sorts of smells, and I caught a glimpse of how I reacted to these smells. It seemed to me that there were certain associations connected with a particular smell. This is frightening, because one fears that one can only experience a certain sensitivity if one gets a certain association. All this seems to be something I started in childhood. My first association with a certain smell is always there; when I get that smell, it brings back a particular association.

J.G.B. Yes, that is very important, because it will lead to the very theme I want to speak of tonight, so I will not say anything about it yet in case anyone else has something more to say about what they have observed during the day.

Q. I suppose this is really similar. When I was digging in the garden today, I dug up a newt. First of all, I had a reaction away from this thing, a reaction which I did not want to recognize, and I shut it off, but I was just aware of it. Then a reaction to 'nice animal' took over. I took it up on my hand, and, again the reaction was slight aversion towards it, as though it had something to do with my childhood, some association or other. And then, after a while, I let it scamper over my hand, I could feel it and became more conscious of my hand until I felt quite at ease with the thing, which caused some sort of feeling or emotion in me.

J.G.B. Yes, that is also in line with what I want to speak about. Let us try to put all of this together. There is a simple quality, power or energy—I have to use several words to avoid fixing the meaning too closely—that has the property of being pleased by some kind of stimulations and displeased by others. That is what I call opening and shutting. This is something very universal; everything that lives has this. Everything that lives is between these forces of attraction and repulsion, liking and disliking and so on. I have to say 'and so on' because it has so many varieties and it is the entirety that gives us this impression. Now, we want to see what there is in us men that is on the level of this particular kind of action, and that is what I call the '*Reactional Self*'. It is a part of 'me'. It is not yet certainly 'I'; it is not even in the fullest sense myself; for obviously there is something behind it.

You will remember that I said yesterday that the 'machine' becomes the 'Man-machine', the material self, when the will enters it. With that comes the ascription to it of 'I'. When the material self thinks, it says 'I think'. Now we have come to the sensitive part—the alive part—of our nature. When the will gets into this part, we say 'I like' or 'I don't like' and the rest. Then we call it the *reactional self*. The reactions are always there; even worms and plants have them but worms and plants are not selves. It is the condition in which our will—which is properly a human will—gets involved in 'like and dislike' that it forms the reactional self. When the habit of 'identifying ourselves' with our likes and dislikes is very strong, then we say that the person is dominated by his or her reactional self. Now, in the language that Pak Subuh uses to describe our experiences in Subud, he calls this the vegetable soul, and he speaks on his book *Susila Budhi Dharma* and elsewhere about this second level. In Arabic it is called the *Rukh Nahari*, or the vegetable force or soul. The Indonesian equivalent is the *Roh Tumbuh-tumbuhan*. You remember that I said the word '*roh*' is rather awkwardly translated as 'soul', and that it might be better to translate it as 'self', or rather a self. Bapak himself, I have noticed, uses in conversation the words '*roh*' and '*djiwa*' as if they were more or less the same. '*Djiwa*' means spirit, and he talks of the *djiwa* or spiritual quality of plants. It is possible that the word *Djiwa* means self in the way I am using it: that is a seat of the will.

The fact that he uses those two words shows that we ought to look beyond the limitations of the words to something else. That is why I have found it necessary, when we try to talk about these things, sometimes to use the word *energy*, sometimes the word *quality*, sometimes the word *self*. But then comes the question: Why vegetable? This throws us at once into the study of the different kingdoms of life.

What is it that characterizes the vegetable or plant life? Certainly, the vegetable life is sensitive. Its life cycles are built upon accepting and rejecting. It reaches out into the air for light, air and moisture; and it reaches down into the earth for humus and minerals which it requires for its growth. But how does it exist? There is no active pursuit in plants; what might appear to be searching, is only the working of their sensitivity, that enables them to feel and stretch this way or that way. But we know quite well how little power plants have to go in search of what they need. A plant may die from drought within a few feet of water; it has no means of reaching that water, or even of knowing the water is there. But it may, with its root sensitivity, be able to go down very deep in order to find water. Obviously, one great difference between plants and animals is that the plant has to take or reject what comes to it, whereas most animals can, to a certain extent, go in search of what they want. I think you will agree that a plant is typically a 'reactional being'. In its fertilization (the way it receives the seed), in its development, growth and diffusion, the plant works by a very complicated, beautifully adapted set of reactions, of yes's and no's, of accepting and refusing. This is what enables a plant to be itself. There is not, in individual plants, anything behind all this; because if there were, plants would behave differently, they would not live as they do live. As reactional beings the plants are wonderfully adapted in the way they are able to arrange for their own pollination, the spreading of their seeds, for migrating from one place to another and selecting the habitat that exactly suits each particular variety of species. You will understand why I say 'being' and not 'self': the plant has no 'I'.

The migrations of plants from continent to continent require hundreds of thousands of years, whereas the migrations of animals may take only hundreds. Why is this? It is because the plant lives by its reactions. It is able to spread reactively over a certain area and if conditions are favourable it becomes established; where they are unfavourable it dies out. So it moves on, by the mechanism of yes and no, but not by a power of search. A typical form of this reactional nature of plants is the way they are polarized between sun and air and warmth, and the soil and water from which they draw in chemical substances. Such is the vegetative life.

The vegetable world seems, somehow or other, to have deviated from the main line of development of life, or maybe has remained stationary upon a certain plateau. It has proliferated upon that particular level to produce the marvelous things that the vegetable world is able to produce, but has not climbed above it to the next plateau where the animals have found a new quality and a new nature. This does not mean that we and the animals who have climbed above this have left our reactional nature behind. Whatever stage of existence we pass through contains something essential for our total being and that something is retained. It is as if we added a new storey to the house; but must necessarily keep the lower storeys if the house is to stand.

We therefore, and all animals, have a vegetable nature in us. There is much in our bodies that has to live like plants. Our bones, for example, cannot go in search of what they require; the food for the bones has to be brought to them, the bone-making material has to come, and if it does not come, the bone suffers. Even the flesh of our bodies has to live as a plant lives, depending upon what is brought to it or what is taken away from it by the blood. It is able to accept and it is able to reject. Only this total body, this total animal body, has qualities that go beyond the vegetable nature.

There can be, in man, very much that is artificial in the reactional self. Habitual reactions play a very great part in its formation, and they form a kind of screen or barrier, to prevent experience penetrating into the deeper parts of ourselves. The result is that we react instead of experiencing. It is physiologically like a reflex mechanism that crosses over in the spine without reaching the head-brain and therefore without reaching our awareness.

There are people who are not dominated by the material self, but are dominated by the content of this reactional self. This means that their will is seldom separated from their reactions. In one sense, they can be said to live by 'like and dislike'. They are unable to do what they dislike, they have to do what they like. Or they live by hope and fear. If the way their nervous system is constructed, is such that they are mentally active, then they will be narrow, logical people who will see everything as either true or false, either right or wrong. If they are people for whom sensation is powerful, then they will always be searching for pleasant sensations and the fear of unpleasant sensation will paralyse them.

There is another sensitivity connected with sex. In its simple, natural form it is the attraction between man and wife and aversion to any other sexual relationship. But as we know only too well, it can take innumerable other forms, some not apparently connected with sex at all. For example, there is a kind of self-aversion or self-loathing that will not accept that we are not the ideal man or woman we wish to be. This is usually no more than a strongly entrenched habit in the reactional self. You can see for yourselves what an immense field of study there is in the reactional self of man and its normal, abnormal and defective manifestations. Ordinary psychology knows many of the facts but it does not know how to account for them, or how to deal with them effectively.

In other words, this reactional self can be very different in its behaviour because people belong to very different functional types. One can be intellectual, another emotional, another instinctive and much concerned with the life of the senses. All of them have this in common, however, for them all is yes and no, attraction and repulsion. This can be so strong in people that everything else that belongs to the deeper finer regions of the 'me' in our human nature is virtually shut off and they just live from this part of themselves. This is a real barrier to understanding either oneself or other people, and it is very noticeable that people who are dominated by their reactional self have very little power of understanding others. All that they know is how they feel about them, not how they are.

Q. You have just referred to 'functional types', which is a technical term used by Jung in his book *Psychological Types*, and elsewhere. Could you say something about the connection between the scheme you are putting before us—which I find as a student of psychology most interesting and stimulating—and Jung's scheme? Would you also say something about the connection between the Reactional Self and the Unconscious which can be studied by association and dream analysis?

J.G.B. Jung's theory of types was developed as a result of his clinical observations. He constantly insisted that he was a psychotherapist first and a psychologist second. This accounts for the fact that his psychology seems to be overloaded with the negative aspects of human experience and also why it is not a truly *spiritual* psychology.

This said, let me add at once that, in my opinion, we have received from Jung the most valuable insights into human nature that have come from any Western thinker for centuries. It has been of the deepest interest to me personally to find that certain conclusions we have reached in the field of Systematics were stated by Jung in different language as a result of his psychiatric work. For a long time, I found it hard to reconcile Jung and Gurdjieff. For me, Gurdjieff has for more than forty years represented a *practical* system of psychology that really does work for normal people seeking to get beyond the limitations of normality; whereas I could not see how Jung's methods could do more than help me to discover what was wrong with me. Recently, I have come to an interesting conclusion and that is that Jung and Gurdjieff are interested in complementary, and therefore seemingly contradictory, aspects of human nature. In terms of Systematics, which most of you have not yet studied, Jung is interested in two- and four-term systems. Whereas Gurdjieff is interested in three- five- and seven-term systems. In a sense, one can say that the even-term systems are concerned with *Being* and the odd-term systems with *Becoming*. That will explain why I find Gurdjieff more important, for my own needs, than Jung.

Now, let us come to Jung's description of man and his nature. Everyone knows that he is one of the 'prophets of the unconscious', but differs from Freud in the way he describes the invisible part of man's psyche. His distinction of psychic attitudes—*extroversion and introversion*—has passed into our common language. I think it is most probable that this distinction applies to the reactional self; it is an *orientation of the sensitivity*. Picture two plants, one of which derives most of its strength from its roots and another which does so from its leaves. One looks within for nourishment and the other looks out. According to Jung the attitude is determined by the object. But the attitude is in the sensitivity, not in the sensation.

You asked about the *functional* types. Jung distinguishes two pairs; rational, consisting of thought and feeling and irrational consisting of sensation and intuition.[1] I personally prefer Gurdjieff's three functions: instinctive-motor, emotional and intellectual. The difference is possibly more one of classification

---

1   In one place (*Collected Works*, Vol. XI, p. 167, 'Psychology and Religion, East and West' (Routledge and Kegan Paul, London, 1958)) Jung connects the four functions with our basic needs: "In order to orient ourselves, we must have a function which ascertains that something is there (sensation); a second function which establishes what it is (thinking); a third function which states whether it suits me or not (feeling); and a fourth function which indicates where it came from and where it is going (intuition). When this has been done,

than a disagreement as to the facts. Knowledge of Jung's four functions are useful for diagnosing troubles of which the patient is not conscious. Observation of Gurdjieff's three functions can help us to work on ourselves to achieve balance.

In both cases, the functions are *forms of activity*; they are not divisions of the self. Both Jung and Gurdjieff insist that we should not look upon one function as 'higher' and another as 'lower' or inferior. The various functions are certainly part of 'me', but they are not 'selves'. My thoughts, feelings, sensations and intuitions are not *myself*. They are what happens to me, because I am constructed in a particular way and have been and am exposed to various impulses and disturbances. Ouspensky compared the functions to various instruments which work differently according to who uses them and to the amount of light that is present. When I spoke of functional types, I referred to the differences between people due to the strength or weakness of these different instruments. One person can think very well, another has a good memory for facts, another for faces or places. A third person has strong emotions and a fourth a very strong and competent body. One is active physically and another is by nature lazy. All these and dozens of other distinctions characterize my *functional instruments*. Certainly, the instruments are *my* instruments and a part of me. But the way I use them depends upon what *kind of person* I am. This is connected with my various selves. The material self uses the instruments in a totally different way from the reactional self. But they are the same instruments.

Q. Why does Pak Subuh say that the vegetable soul does not feel for the sufferings of others. If it is so sensitive, I should have thought that it would have natural compassion?

J.G.B. That is an important question, for it will help us to see just what it means that sensitivity is 'two-edged'. We should expect the 'stone cold' heart to belong to the material self, but there is another kind of unfeelingness. One can use the word 'ruthless' for

there is nothing more to say." So says Jung: but I would say that there is another function needed to answer the question: "What am I going to do about it?" I cannot feel that Jung's four functions are so exhaustive or so self-evident as he makes out. Gurdjieff's functions, perhaps just because he does not pin them down so rigidly, have proved, in my experience, to have been of greater practical help.

the material self, but not for the lack of feeling for others of the reactional self. This feels its own reactions, but it does not feel the reactions of others. The reactional self can be just as cruel as the material self, sometimes even more cruel, just because it has the force that comes from the sensitive energy. It has not the same aloofness that the material self has; therefore if something goes wrong in the reactional self, the result can be more disastrous than if something goes wrong on the level of the material self. That is because the force of life is incomparably greater than the force of matter. Sensitivity is a far more intense condition than the automatic quality that goes with material constructions.

One or two of you noticed, in the observations you made today, how this reactional self, when subordinated to a deeper part of the self, can become a very good servant. You saw how everything comes to life through this. If the reactional self is the master, then it is not pleasant, one does not live happily and comfortably; there is too much oscillation between pleasure and pain, between like and dislike. If it is subordinated to something higher in ourselves, then this very polarity gives us the sense of being alive. The attraction of this life feeling is what makes people expose themselves to danger. It is strange, but true, that in conditions of danger we feel most alive. It is also why people who have in them higher qualities will, in their intellectual activity, expose themselves to contradictions, and even absurdities, because they can see the life of the mind in this experiencing of contradictions. Whereas people who are contented to live on the level of the reactional self will tend to be dogmatic, always affirming one truth and rejecting another.

People dominated by their reactional selves cannot *understand* ideas, they will only believe or reject, and that is not understanding. What they have been trained or habituated to accept as true is, for them, absolute truth. Because of that they cannot confront contradictory ideas in order to understand a reality beyond. If they are in front of a contradiction, then either one side is true and the other is false, or the whole situation is absurd and intolerable. I am sure that you know such people! You know very well how there are people with one or another of these facets of the reactional self, so prominent all the time that it dominates their lives.

It is said that if man wishes to reach truth he must get beyond dualism, beyond the pairs of opposites, as Vedantists put it. This is sometimes put in a rather abstract philosophical way, as though there were some philosophical principle which rejects 'dualism' and accepts 'non-dualism'. It has always seemed to me that the dualists and the non-dualists are both talking in reactional terms. One can, with one's reactional self, affirm oneself to be a non-dualist, which is very strange and contradictory, since the reactional self is entirely built upon dualism. One can reject multiplicity and say all is one. People do so very often. I have seen this, how people, through their 'thinking instrument', have picked up the idea that All is One, and passionately oppose those who say that multiplicity—the wonderful diversity of the Creation—is real. They cannot see that their opposition is the very essence of dualism. It is quite true that we have to get beyond dualism, but that does not mean denying or annihilating this sensitive nature of ours, it means putting it in its right place. There is a place in our nature for this reactional self. If there were nothing in us that could know the difference between dangerous and safe conditions of life, between good food and poison, between pleasure and pain in the physical body, our bodies would be exposed to such dangers that we should probably soon let ourselves be destroyed. We need it in other ways too; there is something very important in this reactional self. Indeed, it is incomparably higher in the scale of being than anything that we can see and touch. The 'visible' world is the material world. The 'invisible' worlds begin with life. Our ordinary consciousness can take in the visible world and know it and act within it and on it. The world of life escapes from our ordinary consciousness. We are *inside life*; but we cannot see it. That is why Pak Subuh has said that the world that corresponds to the essential nature of plants is far greater than this earth and all that we can see and touch. As I shall explain later, the man or woman who is able to live freely in this world as ordinary people live in the world of material objects, has already made a great step towards Reality.

I think that you have begun to realize that this world of sensitivity is a domain within the whole scheme of existence. It is a very much finer and more extraordinary world than the world of material objects. If we let ourselves be obsessed with material objects and miss this quality of sensitivity, life becomes very, very dull, and it requires an artificial stimulation to keep moving at all. But very few people are able to enter into the world of life and see it as it is. Some of you may remember Pak Subuh's talk about this, and particularly the demonstrations he gave to show people the difference between the vegetable world, and the material world.

In all esoteric literature, there are references to a series of heavens. These are symbolical expressions for the different states of Being in which it is possible to live. The earth corresponds to the material world. The second world is that of sensitivity. We are all in this world too; but we cannot know it so long as we are not free. When we are free from earth influences, we can see that earth itself turns into heaven. The world of plants, the state of sensitivity of life energy, is a heavenly condition compared with ordinary sensation and thought. So it is said that the sensitive world is the Second Heaven. At present, you can only catch glimpses of the truth of this; but if you persevere, you will find that you can enter it and enjoy its beauty.

I do want to make sure that in speaking of the world of life as so much greater than the material world, I am not suggesting to you that the earth and material objects generally are 'low' or 'bad'. That is a false notion that has led many astray. Everything that exists is *equally* important for the total harmony of God's creation. A tremendous truth is expressed in the words of Genesis: "and God looked upon it and saw that it was good". The earth is good and it is a place for joy and fulfillment: but for us men it is a place of work and service also. The same is true of life and sensitivity. Every world can be a paradise—the earth was after all the first!— it only ceases to be when we fail to understand its purpose and our place in it.

It is necessary to say all this but still to repeat the truth that life is so much greater than mere materiality. The world of life is a very great world. We get some such feeling for life as it surges up and dies down in our own bodies. A great deal of our inability to live life, to experience the power of life, is due to the fact that our sensitivity has become fixed in habitual reactions. What should be the world of life has become for us a world of clichés; emotional, sensual, intellectual. We live by habits, yes and no, like and dislike, pleasure and pain. We react to this stimulus in this way because we are in the habit of doing so, and to that stimulus in the other way because we are in the habit of doing that. This is not how we should be. Our sensitivity should be very much freer than it is in most people. The transformation of the sensitive part of the self consists in setting it free from these habitual reactions. As I said before, this does not mean that the reactional self is to be destroyed in the process. It must become an organ of perception of almost infinite power and versatility, able to recognize distinctions that can never be recognized on the level of the material self. That is how this part of us should be; we should be able to participate in all life. You may have heard of Gurdjieff's tricky saying "If you could be conscious in your instinctive centre, then you could talk with worms, and what worms could tell you nobody else could". If we had this reactional self of ours working as it should, it is quite true, we would be able to talk with worms. We could talk with everything that lives, know its language and know what it is there for and why, how it works, what it feels and what it understands. We should perhaps be able to see for ourselves one reason why God has brought life into the Creation.

· · · · ·

At this point, the discussion was broken off for coffee and cakes. It was obviously hard to grasp the contradictory aspects of sensitivity. On the one hand, the reactional self was shown as a comparatively inferior part of 'me' and an obstacle to our spiritual progress, until it learns to surrender itself to the higher or deeper parts of 'me'. On the other hand, life was described as an immensely significant universal reality; sensitivity as the characteristic of the 'Second Heaven', and the world of plants as far greater than the earth and all the 'material' world. If the Reactional Self belongs to this great world, why should it be treated as a troublesome, inferior part of us? Most of those present could feel that the contradiction contained the secret of understanding, but they found it hard to express themselves.

This became obvious when the discussion was resumed.

· · · · ·

Q. What is the difference in the quality of rejection as it occurs in a person whom the reactional self controls, and in one who controls the reactional self?

J.G.B. When the reactional self controls, it reacts without reference to any factors that are not immediately present. It is 'heedless' of the consequences. When the reactional self is brought under control, then its reactions turn into perceptions, and the material for understanding. Properly speaking, the reactional self should be an instrument for perception.

It may be as well if I say something now about 'selves'. A self is not simple, it is composed of three different elements. Firstly, there are the instruments with which it works. These are more or less the same for all the four selves of man: the only difference being in the more complete or less complete use they can make of them. Secondly, there is the characteristic energy and the kind of experience that goes with it. So far, we have had only two of these: the automatic and the sensitive energies. These could be compared with the quality of fuel that we put into the engine. Thirdly, there is the 'I' or will. We have not said anything yet about who or what the 'I' means and why it is that I have always coupled the words 'I' and 'will' together.

As a very rough analogy, a self can be compared to a vehicle. With one kind of fuel it can crawl, with another it can go very fast, a third kind enables it to fly and a fourth gives it the power, let us say, of going through all the elements: earth, water, air and ether. The 'I' here is the passenger who sits in the vehicle and lets it carry him about. If the vehicle always uses the slowest fuel, the passenger is condemned to travel at a snail's pace.

There is also the question of what part the combination plays. The vehicle is always an instrument: or combination of instruments, feeling, thought and so on. It is also connected with the 'roads': that is, our external conditions of life. Then again, because there is a passenger, it is a passenger-vehicle and not just an ordinary cart. Put in different language, the selves sow seeds of which the entire man has to reap the harvest. That is because the 'will' is in it. When there is no will in a self, then it is only an instrument.

I am afraid this all sounds very complicated. A simpler way of looking at it is that a self is a part of a man that acts as if it were the whole man. If the reactional self has captured our will then we act as if nothing exists except like and dislike. If the will goes right out of the reactional self into a more inward place, then our likes and dislikes, pleasures and pains, have no power over us.

Q. Does this give you complete control over your feelings of pain? For instance, if you were being tortured, would it be possible not to react to physical pain?

J.G.B. Yes, I am sure it is possible if there is really a higher part of the self, able to dominate. I cannot say how far it can be done voluntarily because I have had so little experience of this myself, but I am absolutely sure about the possibility of it happening involuntarily. This came to me the first time from the experience I had when I was a schoolboy, when I broke my arm playing rugger. In the excitement that boys have when they are playing football, I wanted to continue, so I just tied the arm up and continued the game. I know for certain that I felt no pain at all, although it went on for say, another half an hour. Five minutes after the game ended the arm became excruciatingly painful. I remember how it struck me, that because I was so excited over the game, I did not feel the pain. So, excitement can be stronger than pain. Very soon after that, I went to France during the 1914-18 war. I saw and heard of a number of such cases, where the excitement of war, of battle, completely removed the sensations of pain, which only returned when the excitement went. All this showed me that there is undoubtedly in man a certain level of experience where the physical body has no power at all; that is, a man can 'kill' his body without its being able to refuse him, or the body can have the sharpest kinds of pain and he is not even aware of it. I am sure that people who have gained mastery over the conscious energy can produce the same result. This largely depends upon whether the person concerned is quite free from imagination, because I think the effect of torture is very much influenced by the imagination. This is very difficult to master, because it is of a higher order than sensitive energy.

Now, I want to start to explain the connection between sensitivity and consciousness. I shall complete the explanation tomorrow, because true consciousness belongs to the third stage.

The point is that people mistake sensitivity for consciousness.

When they say 'he has lost consciousness,' they really mean that the sensitive energy is cut off from his mind or his body. This is easy to see in the case of the body. It is what is known as *anaesthesia* or non-sensitiveness. When the same happens to our thinking, we call it 'loss of consciousness'; but it is nothing of the kind. I know from my own experience that in deep coma when all sensitivity ceases, we can still be conscious. I have spoken to many people about this and I am sure it is true. I have been beside people when they have died and have been able to observe how the sensitivity ceases, but the consciousness remains.

What is usually called consciousness is nothing else but sensitivity associated with the associative process of the thinking brain. When we go to sleep this withdraws: but as we can remember dreams, it is obvious that the associations and image building do not cease. The sensitivity of the thinking brain is no different from the sensitivity of the instinctive or emotional brains. Owing to our conditions of life, our will or our 'I' is more often trapped in our associations, and that is why we have the illusion that 'we are our thoughts'.

The example I gave you of my experience as a boy shows how a shock can drive away sensitivity. A severely wounded man—who has only a few minutes to live—usually feels no pain, is not even aware of his body, which moves by the automatic energy. Dr. Maurice Vernet has described crucial experiments which prove that the sensitivity is quite separate from the deeper consciousness. For example, it is possible to produce complete anacsthesia and then to inject lethal doses of poison, like curare, without any harmful effects. Electric shocks that in the presence of sensitivity would be instantly fatal do not injure a man who is completely without sensitivity. It is known that some murderers in America could not be executed in the electric chair. Probably, they fell into a state of hysterical general anaesthesia.

Anyhow, for us the all-important point is to realize that what we call ordinary consciousness is associated with the sensitive energy. Gurdjieff used to insist that what man calls consciousness is not really consciousness: but so far as I know, he never explained it in the way I have just done. As many of you know, Pak Subuh also refers to a 'finer consciousness behind the ordinary consciousness', but gives no explanation.

I owe my own understanding of this vitally important distinction partly, as I said, to Dr. Vernet and partly to my talks with the Shivapuri Baba—two sources about as far apart as they could be! When I verified the connection between sensitivity and the ordinary consciousness, I felt like Christopher Columbus!

Q. At one point, you said that by being fully alive in this body of sensitivity, we can participate in the life of everything, and another time you said that we cannot, that we are just sensitive for ourselves and not for what goes on in another person. How are we to understand this?

J.G.B. If this sensitive energy is really subordinated to a higher energy, then it can bring us into contact with anything we choose; but when it is not, then it stays in the state of separation. It is polar; positive and negative. When one masters polarity then one has all the force that is in it. When one has not mastered it then one is under the yoke of it, and that means that we can only feel one thing at a time. If I feel my own state, I cannot feel another's unless he is in 'sympathy' with me.

Using the terminology—which some of you know—of Gurdjieff's and Ouspensky's system, I would say that the Reactional Self belongs to what is called the 'emotional part' of centres. Some people used to find this confusing.[1] It was difficult in those early days to find proper translations of the Russian words, but if l were doing it now, I would speak of it as the sensitive part of our psychic functions. Physical pain, and other things too, will penetrate through the material self and touch the reactional self.

Q. Could it not be that if the sensitive part is too open to the pressures of life, one suffers unduly? I am thinking of the painter Van Gogh, who was really an extremely sensitive person. Was it that in some way he was too exposed?

J.G.B. If you discuss an unusual man like Van Gogh, you have to take into account further depths of his nature. I am sure that Van Gogh had something formed in him more than the sensitive self. I would have said that he was not dominated by the sensitive self;

---

1   You can find descriptions of the centres in my book *The Crisis in Human Affairs* (Hodder and Stoughton, 1948), and also in the books of Ouspensky, Nicoll, and Walker.

he was not dominated by likes and dislikes. It is evident from his letters and his life that there was something deeper acting in him. What is quite true, and I think very important to understand, is that this particular structure of the sensitive self can get into trouble, and then the reactions can get out of hand. The material self should act as a sort of flywheel that can slow things down, or at least regulate them. If everything is working rightly then there is a balance between the activity of the different selves. If one of the deeper—and more important—levels of the self-hood gains a degree of energy, or as Jung calls it, *libido*, in excess of what it is able to regulate, then the working of the whole person can be disturbed. Something of this kind happened to Van Gogh. You will see, as we go further, that there is a danger in over-stimulation of the deeper parts of the self before they have been transformed and spiritualized.

Q. In the Gurdjieff system, does self-remembering to a certain extent break up the reactional self?

J.G.B. Self-remembering is not a breaking-up process; self-remembering should be an integrating process. Its aim is to bring the deeper parts of the self into relation with the more superficial parts. But it is quite true that there are procedures in the Gurdjieff system—as there are in Zen and in various other techniques for the development of man—which are for what Gurdjieff calls decrystallization, or in your terms to 'break up' something which has got stuck. What does this mean in relation to the reactional self? It must be remembered that the reactional self in people largely consists of conditioned reactions, which can become very fixed, and the spontaneity behind this cannot then express itself. Those parts of the self where there are far greater and more significant powers, are held in check by the limited and fixed repertoire of reactions of the reactional self. Sometimes this has to be broken down in order to get things moving again. Also, one part of the reactional self can sometimes throw other parts of this same self out of balance. That is, the reactional self, instead of being a rounded whole, can be, as it were, overgrown or hypertrophied in relation to certain reactions, and underdeveloped, or even atrophied, in relation to others. For normality, all this has to be rectified, so that the reaction to one sort of stimulus and from one part of the person is not out of proportion to other reactions. Even for the attainment of a normal, balanced life, without the further aim of spiritual perfection, it is sometimes necessary for the fixed habits of reaction on the level of sensitivity to be broken down or dissolved.

Q. Some systems break them entirely; for instance, Scientology breaks down all these reactions so that there are no emotive masses connected with past experiences in the body. Might that not destroy a certain shield in nature which might be useful?

J.G.B. I agree that there are dangers in this. The sensitive part of man requires to be treated either with great knowledge, great understanding, or it must be left alone and allowed to change in a very natural way. I remember once watching Gurdjieff behaving absolutely outrageously towards a certain person—it was just such a breaking-down as you talk about—and he turned round to me and said in his queer English: "You not surprised what I am so impertinent?" I answered: "I am not surprised at anything you do." He asked me: "Why you think I can do this?" and I said: "Because you know what you are doing," and he answered: "Yes, because I have *science* so I can do this; who has not this science, must not do!".

It is a risky thing to operate on the reactional self of a person. There are more natural ways by which these conditions of the sensitive nature can be harmonized and developed. This is one of the marvels of Subud; there is something extraordinary in the working of the latihan in its effect on the reactional self, for it can produce a natural re-orientation of this part of man. I do not mean that there will never be trouble. I do not think that Subud can be guaranteed to be safe for anyone; any more than anything whatever can be guaranteed to be safe. We can make mistakes about everything. But when Subud is allowed to work properly, it is really marvelous to see how it can produce these rectifications without damage, without shocks to the whole structure.

Q. In testing, if an answer comes through the sensitive self, how would one experience it?

J.G.B. Not everyone here knows about 'testing', so I had better explain that first. In the practice of Subud, there is an opening and awakening of the deeper parts of the self. When these are working properly, they have access to sources of knowledge that are closed to the ordinary consciousness. Clairvoyance is an example of this kind of 'knowing without the help of the senses and the thinking mind'. Pak Subuh has shown those who practise the latihan that it is often possible to find the answers to questions that are troubling us, by formulating them in words and then putting ourselves into the state of the latihan. Sometimes, we can receive in this way answers or at least indications that can be a very great help in seeing the situation more clearly and in taking decisions. Pak Subuh has explained that the results of testing depend upon which part of the self is able to respond. It takes a long time before answers can be received which directly enlighten the understanding.

At first, the results of testing come from the material self; by movements of the physical body not necessarily always visible to others. Those of the reactional self begin to come later. You must remember that, however complicated its reactions may be, the reactional self always works on the basis of attraction and repulsion. There are many ways in which this can be experienced. The simplest and most direct is an inner 'yes' or an inner 'no' that has no words. It is sometimes conveyed through some feeling such as happiness or sadness, or through a sensation such as light or darkness. You can easily tell it from the 'receiving' of the material self in which there is no element of feeling. The material self can come under the influence of the latihan—in fact, it must do so if it is to be transformed into the right kind of instrument—but it can never be made to *feel*. So when it responds to the testing, it does so by some movement, such as a gesture of the arms or head.

By the way, I must be careful to distinguish here between *feeling* and *sensation*—in German *Gefühl* and *Empfinding*. The material self can have sensations. In the latihan, even in the earliest stages, there can be strong sensations that are mistaken for feeling. There can also be a physical relaxation with the corresponding sensation of peace and happiness without there being a corresponding relaxation of the sensitivity. People at this stage feel peaceful in themselves, but easily irritated by others. That is an indication that the reactional self has not been 'purified' as we say in Subud. The purified reactional self has pure *feelings* and does not like or dislike.

When the reactional self takes part in testing, it very often receives indications that are quite contrary to those that we should expect with our thinking mind. On hearing a question, one may feel happy or unhappy, one may feel a great sadness, or one may feel a great happiness and lifting up. That sort of thing belongs to the sensitive self. One may not understand or be able to interpret. One may easily make mistakes, because there may be finer influences at work that this reactional self is not able to take into account, but the difference between what it can receive and what the material self can receive is just this, that in the material self it is by *movements*, whereas with the sensitive self it is *reaction*.

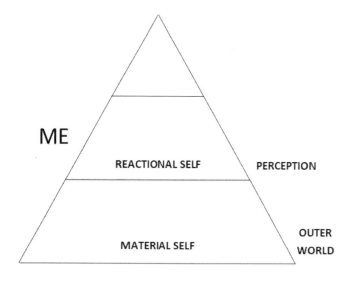

Fig. 1. The Symbol of Me

Now, we must end this discussion, but before doing so, I want to show you a symbol that I have found very useful in picturing the whole man, of which we have so far only studied two parts. By the word 'symbol' I mean a visible form that presents itself to our inner vision to help us see something that cannot be grasped in words alone. The symbol helps us to make a connection between the invisible or suprasensible and the visible or sensible or 'knowable' worlds.

The triangle narrows towards a point at the top. The narrowing represents 'inwardness'. The bottom line of the triangle stands for the entire world of our everyday experience; all that we can see and hear and touch is there. It is the world of material objects, of things. The corresponding level of 'me' is the material self. This is almost the same as the consciousness of the psychologies of Freud and Jung. It can also be called the knowable world. You will also remember that I referred to it as the Earth and as the first Heaven.

The second line stands for *Life*. It is the hidden domain where life has its home. We can never see life—only the outward forms of living things. It is also the place of the second part of 'me', the *Reactional Self*. It is a vast domain; not measured in millions of miles, but in depth. It is substantial in a way that material objects can never be. One could say that it has another dimension; the dimension of *Sensitivity*.

This is the Second Heaven. We live in it; but we do not know it, and because we do not know it, we misuse the powers that it gives us. We are alive, but we do not know how to live, nor what *Life* really signifies. As a result, our sensitivity becomes a burden to us and a cause of suffering, instead of being the means of freedom and a bridge from mere knowledge to the immense joy that comes when our understanding awakens. Tomorrow, we shall pass on to the study of that condition and that world where understanding is possible.

4. THE DIVIDED SELF

WE shall start today with the Symbol I put before you last night, the *Symbol of Me*.

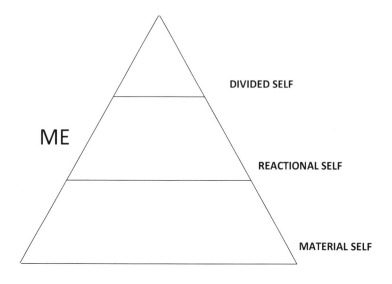

Fig. 2. The Three Lower Selves

As we shall make a great deal of use of this symbol in the remaining talks, l want to explain how you should look at it. The point at the top represents the 'True Self' of man. This suggests that we go 'upwards' from the material self to the true self. In reality, we go *inwards*. There is not a higher or lower in the way that the rungs of a ladder are higher or lower. You remember I have said that all parts of the self are necessary—*equally necessary*—for the completeness of men. Only we cannot start from what is within— we have to start from *where we are*.

The notion of *withinness* is important. Pierre Teilhard de Chardin makes this the one sure test of evolutionary progress as he discusses it in his *Phenomenon of Man* and other works. I do not believe that this is the whole story, because as you will see when we come to the problem of 'I' and 'I AM', the distinction of within and without is replaced by another equally important conception. Nevertheless, for the study of 'me', the notion of 'withinness' is very necessary. We have been moving inwards into the hidden nature of man. Sensitivity is more 'inward' than materiality. The difference between sensitive and non-sensitive existence is that something is formed, and has an independent existence within everything that lives, that is absent from non-living states. There is something within the simplest living thing that is not in the most complex machine. The idea of *within* is connected with experience; there is an inner experience in everything that lives and that inner experience is what we have called sensitiveness.

You will notice that I did not say that sensitivity is absent from non-living matter; but that it is not 'formed', that is, organized. If sensitivity is a universal energy, we must suppose that it is everywhere and enters into everything; but it cannot be aware of itself unless it has some kind of organization. It seems that this awareness is present in the very simplest possible forms of life. It is within the animal, within the cell, within the virus and possibly even within those wonderful nucleic acids that direct the formation of proteins.

Now, we must go still further in, from the sensitive energy to something that is behind it. We are more or less aware of something behind our sensitiveness, behind our likes and dislikes, our yesses and nos, but it is not easy to recognize what that 'something behind' is. It is still a part of 'me'; the whole of the symbol before us is 'me', it is not 'I'.

What is behind sensitivity? Each of these energies represents a great cosmic quality, as if the Creation were built up from certain basic qualities which combine in an infinite variety of ways to give the endless diversity of Existence. But the qualities remain quite distinct; as the quality of life is quite distinct from the quality of thinghood, so here is another quality quite distinct from that of life.

The first, and really the most important point is that we have now come to an energy that is behind and within sensitivity. I want you to verify this for yourself during the day. There is no difficulty in doing so, once you know what to look for. You can observe *with* your sensitivity or else you can *look at* your sensitivity. The first kind of observation tells *what is going on*: the second puts you *in contact with* what is going on. The first is what we ordinarily call 'conscious experience'. The second is the only genuinely conscious experience.

We have come straight to one of the chief character-istics of the third kind of energy; it gives us the power to come in contact with what is not ourselves. If you observe your own reactions, as you were doing yesterday, in order to see what it is that brings them into play, you will notice that it is a kind of meeting between something that enters from without—or from the past or future—and something that comes out from within yourself. There is something in 'me' that is seeking contact with what is 'not-me'. Those of you who have studied Systematics will recognize here the property of relatedness which belongs to the triad. In its simplest form, it is no more than the urge to express oneself, to affirm oneself, which we begin to find in the animal world; especially in what we call the chordata; that is, animals with some form of nervous system. This seems to have taken form in life on the earth perhaps two hundred million years ago, and it has developed an increasing complexity of structure throughout the animal kingdom. It does not seem to be present in individuals of any of the lower forms of life; it is not recognizably present in plants, worms or even insects. But it is not something exclusively human, for we share it with a very great range of animal forms. It is an urge to reach, to attain, to make one's presence felt. It is probable that this third power or energy is the same as Jung and other psychologists describe as *libido*. It is a mistake to try and make precise parallels between one scheme and another—especially in psychology where there is no way of making exact assessments— and therefore I do not propose to use the term libido, although it has by now become a familiar expression for most people. We could use the old, plain word *desire*, although I do see that this may be confusing at first as we usually take our desires to be urges of which we are conscious. They seem to belong to quite a superficial part of ourselves which we believe we know quite well. This is far from the truth, usually our true desires are disguised from us by the habitual attitudes of the Reactional Self. It might seem better to take some impersonal word like 'striving', or such terms as were invented by the evolutionary philosophers, like Bergson's *Élan Vital*, or the *Entelechy* of

Driesch, or perhaps, best of all, the *Idée Directrice* of that great biologist Claude Bernard. All these terms: Libido, the Life Force, Élan Vital, Entelechy, Idée Directrice and Desire refer to the same energy; the reality of which we can scarcely fail to admit as soon as we begin to study the surging of life from lower forms and those of the animal kingdom. In recent years, the word Mana has acquired great popularity among anthropologists and psychologists. In nearly all its meanings, Mana is probably the same as our third form of energy. It is that which endows images, places, people and words with power. I shall not use it, because it has special associations with animism which is too narrow a sense for our purpose.

You will see in a few minutes that the correct name for this third energy is consciousness. The word is not bad etymologically as it conveys the idea of 'bringing together'. Desires are the result of consciousness. We are drawn towards what enters our consciousness. Only you must remember what I said yesterday about not mistaking sensitivity for consciousness. We usually are identified with our sensitivity and 'lose our consciousness'. That is why our desires produce results without our knowing why or how.

All that desires seeks to make a connection with what it lacks, something that is not present at the moment. In the simplest animals, there is a striving for something not yet there; for example, an extant but very primitive kind of fish can be studied, whose appetites are almost entirely developed through the sense of smell. When they smell food, clearly some sort of experience happens in them that corresponds very much to what they will experience later when they have caught and eaten the food. In these primitive dogfish, there seems to be nothing that can be called consciousness or direction, or intention, but there is undoubtedly a striving, an urge to satisfy a need not immediately present; the fulfillment is not immediate, as is the case of reactions. It seems then that this energy has to do with an intelligence not present in some other forms of life.

So far, I have been talking about this urge in terms of its visible effect on us, the source of our actions. We must now try to penetrate to the very source of our desires and impulses. When this inner power, inner appetite or urge to impress oneself on one's environment, or to liberate oneself from one's environment, to search and to find, to have and to hold, has filtered through the mechanism of our reactional self and has expressed itself through the outer mechanism of our material, physical body, it of course takes the forms that we see. In the example of the dogfish, as soon as it smells a possible prey everything in it changes; there are changes in the chemical secretions in the bloodstream, it acquires a great influx of energy, moves at great speed in the direction of the prey, which it then follows by scent until it is able to catch it. I am quite sure that the dogfish experiences excitement, but all that we can see and study belongs to the outermost physical organism. Behind this there certainly is a pattern of sensitivity in the dogfish, but behind that again there is that something which drives it to satisfy its needs by reaching out instead of waiting for what will come to it like, say, a sponge or a jelly-fish or a plant. It seems obvious therefore that behind the body, behind the sensitiveness, deeper down, there is something in us which is urging us. It is this we have to look for now, but it must be borne in mind that it would not at all be desirable, even if it were possible, to uncover it, to expose this part; this can be a dangerous psychic operation. There is no doubt that what is called 'depth-psychology' is concerned with the organization of the energy that belongs to this third level.

When Gurdjieff wrote about this particular power or force in his book *All and Everything*, in the chapter called 'Purgatory', he referred to the danger associated with it, because on the one hand it is a creative power that drives us on, and on the other hand it can also be a destructive power.[1] It brings things together, but it can bring the wrong things together as well as the right ones. When desire becomes organized in us it becomes a self. It is the third part of 'me'. It is the third way in which we can know ourselves, and that knowledge is the knowledge of the pattern of our desires and impulses.

According to the analytical psychologists, Freud, Adler and Jung, man cannot know this pattern by interrogating himself in his

---

1   It is called in Gurdjieff's special terminology 'piandjoëhary' or the fifth energy. It is the fifth because Gurdjieff begins below the level of the material self with forms of energy that are not capable of being experienced in our ordinary consciousness. See *All and Everything*, pp. 761 and 790 (Routledge and Kegan Paul, London 1950).

ordinary consciousness. No doubt this is true because the ordinary consciousness is only sensitivity in the thinking brain, but it does not follow that man cannot become directly conscious of the third part of the Self. In fact, this is what Jung calls 'Individuation' and claims this can be found as the result of a rightly conducted analysis. As you well know, there are many different views as to what constitutes the principal content of the third self. Freud connects it with sex, Adler with the social impulse, and Jung with a more general urge towards completeness. You can study the problem usefully today if you will, from time to time, notice your activity and ask yourselves the question: "From where does this line of action come, this way in which I am behaving." If you can see this, then you are looking towards this third part of 'me'. If you cannot see it directly, you can probably infer that there must be 'something' behind your thinking, feeling, behaving, dreaming. Then you will begin to have some knowledge of this third part of 'me', which is certainly more subtle, more difficult to understand than the first two. We can best understand all this if we reflect a little on the great difference between reacting and seeking, or between a reaction and an urge, or between a reaction and a desire. Our reactions do not embrace, do not take things in, whereas our desires embrace and grasp things.

I would like you to reflect a little today on that distinction, and if possible to recognize what I mean by the force of desire behind our reactions. We can very often be aware of our reactions and see how they sometimes come from some hidden urges. Sometimes, they come simply from an outside stimulation; they may be a 'conditioned reflex' and have nothing that corresponds to our own inner urges at all. You can tell if there is something coming from 'underneath' if you feel some disturbance that you cannot understand.

. . . .

The school had little to say about the third level of the self. This may have been due to my having explained it in too abstract a way, without giving examples of the way it shows itself in our lives. In the evening discussion, there were some references to 'Movements'. This is the name popularly given by Gurdjieff's pupils to his gymnastic exercises and ritual dances, at which the able-bodied members of the school had been working every day.

. . . . .

Q. This urge that you are talking about, can it either be good or bad?

J.G.B. I cannot answer that unless you first will say: 'Good for what? Bad for what?' There are three ways of looking at desires. Firstly, they may be directed towards the outer parts of the selves; to like and dislike or towards sensation and activity. Secondly, they may be directed inwards towards the centre of the Selfhood. There is a third possibility that the desires may be in conflict with one another. Any of these three can be called 'good' or 'bad' according to the ideal picture that you have formed of what man ought to be. It is in man's nature that there should be a conflict of desires and that we should look upon our urges as good or bad. One would not put it that way when talking about an animal, because an animal cannot help being what it is. It does not choose its own urges, it has no power over them, because there is nothing higher in the animal, there is nothing behind its urges.

You probably found it difficult to make something of this. It is not surprising, because it is hard to get oneself sufficiently quiet to be able to see this situation. Usually our attention is so much occupied with the activity going on in the outer parts of the self, in the material and sensitive parts, that we cannot see what is behind.

Q. Is it this part that enables one to hold together the pattern of the Gurdjieff movements?

J.G.B. It can be so. If you have observed it, then it is so. If what you are saying now comes from something you noticed and observed in yourself, then it is valid and interesting.

Q. I have noticed that there is a difference between the way I am impressed by a movement when I watch you do it and when I hear you describe it. When I see, the interest enters some part, but then there is something else that makes me hang together.

J.G.B. That is why I am constantly saying to you that when you practise these movements you must have your mind empty, only then does your 'real' consciousness have a chance to help you. Only it can *connect*. You cannot do the movements by thinking as everyone discovers when they try. As soon as you begin to think about what you are doing, you are bound to lose touch. It is possible to do them by direct or indirect imitation; that is, to condition oneself to do them. That is the way anyone learns to do any complicated movements like using some piece of machinery, driving a motorcar, or ballet dancing, or executing precise and difficult coordinated movements—all of those can be built into the sensitive part. That is the ordinary way in which bodily skills of any kind are learned; but it is not profitable, from our point of view, to learn them that way, because that is not what we are after. It is not just for the sake of learning to do them—as one might do for one's profession—it is learning to understand ourselves better and to understand how we work. For that, we want to bring our attention nearer to our true consciousness, and in order to achieve this, we have to empty the sensitive pseudo-consciousness.

At this point, I think it will be useful if I say something about *attention* and its connection with these various parts of the self and also with our *will*. You should distinguish between *awareness* which may be quite passive and *attention* which is a manifestation of will. Our awareness is the result of our sensitivity. It is in the very nature of sensitivity to be sensitive—that is, to be aware. It seems as if the second line in the Me Symbol—which represents the reactional self—were made of sensitivity in much the same way as we use sensitized plates in photography. Only here the plate is sensitized in both directions so that it can receive images from outside and also from inside. This acts like a kind of cinematograph screen on to which images are constantly being projected. They can be projected from different levels, but the general way it works is that if there is a great deal of activity on the level of the material or mechanical part of the self, then this occupies the screen, and it is almost impossible to attend to anything else. If this mechanical part is doing its right work, then it leaves the screen undisturbed, but then you come up against conditions of the reactional part itself. If the screen itself is disturbed then you can focus nothing at all. This is the condition when we are havering and wavering between 'yes' and 'no', plunging from like to dislike, from joy to misery, from interest to boredom, from overactivity to sluggishness and back again. Under these conditions the sensitivity itself ceases to be a screen for receiving images and then we become mere 'reactors'. Only when the sensitivity grows quiet, is anything projected onto the screen; it is only then that coherent patterns begin to present themselves.

The practice of doing the movements in the way I have been showing you, of simply learning the scheme of it and then trying to be empty in your sensitive attention, so that a relatively simple pattern can be projected, is a most valuable exercise. If we want to learn anything quickly, there is no better way of doing it than this.

The energy of consciousness produces the urges that we recognize as desires, because it is always seeking to connect itself to something. If it is doing its proper work it connects us to ourselves—that is what Gurdjieff calls self-remembering. When it gets loose, as it were, it tries to get a foothold and that 'trying' is desire. Another power that arises from this same quality is that of *making connections in a pattern*. The sensitive awareness—our ordinary consciousness—can only accept or reject. If its attention is drawn to one object then it is withdrawn from another. It can work like a chain, from link to link. That is how our ordinary associative thinking goes. But with the true consciousness there can be the *holding* of a pattern. This gives it an extra dimension.

Another characteristic of the conscious energy is that it converts reaction into *relatedness*. You can always tell when there is a relationship and when there is only a reaction with another person. When you are only reacting, you may like very much, but that liking does not make a relationship. Sometimes you can dislike, and you can see that behind that dislike there is a true relationship. You can verify, if you watch how things are with you, that relationship is not a matter of like and dislike.

I want to remind you that in our symbol, life is represented by a single line—the second from the bottom. According to this picture, life is not the 'within-most' part of man. There is a deeper level which can be called 'beyond life'. The energy of consciousness requires life in order to act; but it is not just a kind of life.

Not only *can* there be life without organized consciousness, but almost certainly there was life without it on this earth for more than a thousand million years, from the time that life first appeared until the time that animals with a notochord began to appear. I am saying that so that you can see that organized consciousness is not necessary for life in the way that organized sensitivity is necessary for something more than just being alive.

It seems that Teilhard de Chardin was right when he said that here on the earth, there has been a movement towards greater withinness. This is the most valuable contribution Teilhard de Chardin makes in *Phenomenon of Man*, but he does not see, I think, the really important difference that comes with consciousness, and that is that it makes relatedness possible.

Now, we must try to understand what is meant by 'organized consciousness'. It can be called a *pattern of needs for connectedness* which issues in the form of urges, desires, impulses to action and traits of character. In each one of us, this pattern is more or less permanent. This is what I mean when I say it is organized. Of course, it is not a fixed pattern like an engineering drawing: but a set of tendencies that remains unchanged in most people throughout their lives. To a large extent, this pattern is innate; that is to say, it is formed in man before he is born. Because of this it can be called a 'self' or part of the total selfhood. What name are we to give to this 'self of desire'? In Sanskrit, it is called Kamarapa—the form of the desires. In theosophical terminology, it is called the Mental Body and the reason for this will be clear to you in a few minutes.

None of these names conveys to me what is most important about this third form of selfhood. The more I have come to know it in myself and in other people, the more I have been impressed with its ambiguity—almost I would say 'double-facedness'. Our desires are indispensable if anything is to be achieved. Even if all other desires could be eliminated, the desire for perfection, for completeness or rightness, for God or for the fulfillment of God's plan for us—at least that ultimate desire must remain. If we were to become totally indifferent to our fate, we should cease to be human beings and degenerate into witless morons. All achievement comes from desire; the force of conscious energy is probably the driving energy by which the entire Creation seeks its fulfillment. Even the Buddha, who preached the renunciation of desire, sat under his Bo Tree with the resolute determination to sit there until either death or enlightenment should come. What is that determination, except the concentration of all the force of desire into the one desire to be free from Dukkha—the burden of existence? In our own, very ordinary, lives, we need more desire, not less, because without it we cannot become truly 'conscious beings'. We are most of us very weak in this third level of the self, and we are only too well aware that the driving power is lacking. Gurdjieff said that the more desires a man has, the further is it possible for him to advance on the way to completion. Whatever way we look at it, desire is desirable.

Now, let us look at the other side. It is obvious that a man can be the 'slave of his desires'. In such a state, the man himself virtually ceases to exist—the desires rage freely and govern the entire life. Indeed, we can say that, as we enter this third region of the psyche, we are going into the jungle where the lion's only object is to eat as many lambs as he can, and the lamb's object is to produce as many more lambs as it can. There is very little 'lying down together' in our human jungle. Not only are our desires at war with one another, but, as I said earlier, the nature of consciousness is such that they can very easily be drawn outwards to the superficial region of the self. We can desire to 'have' instead of desiring to 'be'. Worse still, we can desire to 'appear to have' instead of desiring real possessions. In other words, our desires can be directed to imaginary goods, such as the esteem and admiration of others shown outwardly in the form of flattery and subservience. I need hardly say much more about this, for it will be obvious to us all that the man who is dominated by his desires is a weak man. He is not 'his own master'.

The two-faced nature of consciousness is connected with its power of making connections. In itself, it has no 'preferences'. Our consciousness will attach itself to something we loathe as easily as to something we love. If someone is horribly mutilated in a road accident, our consciousness is drawn to it, although our sensitivity shrinks away from it. Consciousness can also be drawn towards beauty and goodness even if we have to suffer in our sensitivity to attain them. Consciousness can draw us out into the world of things, and it can drive us inwards into our own hidden nature. It can connect us with people and create the 'social' urge. It can also make us desire domination and power. Finally, it can draw us towards what merely exists as so much organized matter, and it can make us search for the essential meaning that is behind existence.

I chose the name *Divided Self* for this part of 'me' for another reason, but I think that you will agree that it is true for the condition of the desires of the average man. The reason I adopted this name in *The Dramatic Universe* is that this self corresponds to that level in man where he is pulled equally in two directions: towards *Essence* and towards *Existence*.

The Divided Self really does stand between these two. It has an outer eye and also an inner eye. It is aware that there is another reality hidden from the outer eye; but it is equally drawn towards the tangible world of 'solid facts'. The real meaning of Divided Self is this particular division and all the others come from it.

Since the Divided Self is the seat of the powerful energy of consciousness, it holds in its hands the key to our destiny. It must be prepared to surrender this key to the next, and innermost, part of the self about which we shall speak tomorrow. If it holds on to the key, then we are bound to remain suspended in conflict of desires—a conflict that the Divided Self cannot resolve alone.

In order to understand more about the Divided Self, we shall start from a different point—that of *character*. By 'character', we mean a certain combination of trends, urges, desires, aims and ideals, appetites, all of which come through into our behaviour; but do so in an indirect way for they can be disguised by the conditioning of the outside layers of the selfhood. Character is situated in the Divided Self. It is our character that determines what relationships we are able to have. That is why it sometimes turns out that we cannot understand people who are close to us, like our own family; whereas we can understand other people who may be much less closcly connected with us.

One can say that the character is like a key which will open some locks and will not open others. In other words, according to our character, there are some kinds of life that we are able to live and other kinds of life that we are not able to live, because we are not able to produce all the necessary urges that will be required for that life. If somebody is put into a condition of life that does not correspond to character, he will not be able—except by a very great strain on himself, as a result of very harsh conditioning of his sensitive self—to exist in those conditions. It would be very desirable for him that he should learn that this is not the door his key can open and that he should change his conditions of life.

Another way of speaking about character is to talk of it as *type*. There are different types, and that pattern which gives a man this or that type belongs to this level of the self; but the word type here refers to what Jung calls archetypes and not to functions.

As we have entered a field that is regarded as the private preserve of the depth psychologists, I had better try to clarify the connection—as I see it—between the scheme I am putting before you and that of Dr. Carl Jung. I cannot say anything about Freud, Adler and others as I have read about analytical psychology almost solely in the works of Jung. Now, Jung makes a distinction between three levels or regions of the unconscious and the Self (with capital letter). It seems to me that these do correspond more or less to the reactional, the divided self and the 'True Self' about which we will speak tomorrow. The reactional habits of the sensitivity in each one of us could quite well be described as the 'personal unconscious'. The Divided Self, according to what I have just been saying, contains the pattern of our own character. Jung describes this as the *collective unconscious*. The reason becomes clear when we study Jung's papers on the subject. He would, I am sure, have agreed that the pattern of the deep unconscious in each person is uniquely characteristic of that person; but have insisted that the elements out of which it is put together are taken from the agelong experience of mankind in which we all share. I am inclined to agree with this view, but I find that Jung has been too much influenced by his clinical practice and tends to take too narrow a view of the content of what we are calling the Divided Self. As time went on, Jung got into the way of diagnosing his cases in terms of a few 'archetypes', that is, constructions or complexes in the unconscious.[1] Two of the most important are connected with the desire for sympathy and the desire for domination. He personifies the first as *anima* for men or *animus* for women and the second as the 'magician' for men and the 'great mother' for women. According to Jung's theory, these two archetypes are present in us all, but in some people they acquire an independent existence and begin to influence their behaviour in strange ways. When a man or a woman becomes aware of actions that are quite contrary to

---

1   You can read about these in *Two Essays in Analytical Psychology* (Routledge and Kegan Paul, London, 1953).

what he expects from himself, he or she is probably being actuated by one of the archetypal impulses. Jung sets about 'curing' this condition by encouraging the patient to recognize these hidden entities and to treat them as 'not-myself'. One way in which they are recognized is in dreams. The *anima* appears as a beautiful, sympathetic woman and the *magician* as one's own father or as a king, a prophet or a worker of strange miracles. Sometimes, they appear in the form of symbols which must be interpreted by an expert, as Daniel did for Nebuchadnezzar.

We are not concerned here with the therapeutic problem; but with the correspondence between Jung's archetypes and the characteristic forms or structures which go to make up the Divided Self. My own experience of dealing with hundreds of people, some of whom have been in serious mental disorder, and others of whom have been very normal people in search of God, has convinced me that the Divided Self is a reality and that it includes most of what depth psychology has discovered about the hidden parts of man's nature. I do believe, though, that too much insistence upon the archetypes can be misleading. We can now go on to see the way that Pak Subuh speaks of this region of the psyche. As you already know, he uses the Sufi terminology in which the third level of the psyche is called in Indonesian, the *Roh Haiwani* or Animal Soul. One reason for this is that animals are controlled by this part of the self: in fact, in an animal there is no organized energy higher than the conscious energy. In the animal there is not so much an individual character as the character of each genus of animals. We recognize, for instance, a certain dominating character common to all the cats, one common to all the herb-eating animals, another to the insect-eating animals and so on. So also within the genera, as between species, there is clearly a certain difference in character between, let us say, the sheep and the cow. These differences are recognizable to such an extent that often in the past and still today they have been used for describing people. It is often very apt to describe the character of people by referring to animals; because it is easier to say that somebody is like a fox than to try to describe in words just what that foxiness is. Or that someone is like a wolf, or a tiger, or a sheep, or a mouse. As I am saying these different words, each one of them evokes in you a certain feeling of the kind of urges present in the man who is said to correspond to one or other of the animals I have named.

It is quite possible that, in the course of the development of life on this earth, from the time that the mammals appeared and began to differentiate and become highly specialized dominant genera, that these different characters were being tested and fixed, and that the energy that carries these characters was being organized so that eventually, when man came on the earth, there should be the necessary differentiation of these character-bearing energies to enable man to receive his special nature which is so much more varied than the animals. The character of men is so varied that one can find among men characters corresponding to every single animal. And not only that, but combinations of characters, so that probably it would be possible to describe quite accurately the character of a man if one could say "The recipe of so and so is one spoonful of tiger, a cupful of lamb", and so on.

It is interesting to notice that it is hard to describe character by words taken from the material level: that is, from the things we can see and touch. When we use the names of animals in this way we are creating a much subtler kind of language, and what is conveyed is much richer. For instance, if we talk about a cow in the material sense, then it means an animal of a certain shape, colour and size. If we put our attention on the cow's vegetative life, we can see that we very seldom concern ourselves with this part of the cow's existence; that is, how it reacts. But when it comes to the animal level, and we speak of 'cow-like', then at once something is conveyed which applies to our human situation. It is very unlikely that this would be so if there were not a real affinity between something common to man and the different species of animals. I think there is no doubt about there being an affinity that is connected with the organization of conscious energy—that is, *character*. In so far as there are certain patterns that are not so much of animal character as connected with the common experience of mankind, it is no doubt legitimate to speak also of archetypes.

There is something I had not previously realized, which struck me very forcibly when I heard Pak Subuh talk of this, three or four years ago. He spoke of the animal soul in man, and said that every kind of animal seeks to dominate over all the rest, but each species does it in a different way. This is obviously connected with what Freud calls the 'Father complex' and Jung the 'Magician Archetype'. There is, however, it seems to me, a more fertile symbolism in the association with animal species. In Jungian language, we might speak of the 'Jungle Archetype'. Pak Subuh said that, for example, there are predatory animals, carnivorous animals: wolf and tiger, let us say. Obviously the wolf seeks to dominate in a different way from the tiger. You cannot mistake the difference, just as you cannot mistake in man when this desire is tiger-force and when it is wolf-force. But not only these; other animals seek to dominate, not by destroying, but by quite other powers. For example, the rabbit seeks to dominate and gain possession of the earth by its prodigious fecundity. It would be able to eat the rest of the world out of existence, if the world did not protect itself from rabbits. So would mice if they had the chance. Everything keeps everything else in check, and all need to be kept in check, from the apparently most harmless and weakest of animals to the most ferocious and also to the apparently indifferent, like the elephants or hippopotamus who seem to be concerned only with their own affairs. To pursue the Jungian method a little further, we might say that the myth of the earthly paradise where the lion lies down with the lamb, is the symbol of the harmony of the Divided Self for which man longs, but somehow projects into the past—perhaps into the womb!

If you reflect—as I did after hearing that talk—that every species of animal seeks to impose itself in its own particular way, and that every trait in the human character is an urge to impose oneself in a particular way, then you will understand much about consciousness and the Divided Self of man, but you must not run away with the impression that the Divided Self is entirely negative, only concerned to get the better of others. There is always something higher, but in most people this is dormant and ineffectual.

This is not the whole story, it is necessary to look at this Divided Self from another side. This desire to dominate is only one side of the picture. Every animal has another urge: to fit itself into the whole. There is a marvelous symbiosis of life on the earth, which manifests the mutual need of all living things for one another. The animal not only has the urge to dominate, to affirm itself, but has a need to occupy its rightful place. Similarly with man, there is in the Divided Self a two-fold urge: one is to assert oneself in relation to everything one is connected with, and the other is to fit into the situation. These two urges are character-istic of the contrary tendencies within the Divided Self. I would not go so far as to equate them with Jung's Magician and Anima archetypes. I think that they do not have to be 'dissolved' as he puts it. The aim is to bring them under the harmonizing and unifying influence of the True Self; that is, of the central part of the total 'me' that we are trying to understand. I will soon come to the really positive role that the energy of consciousness should play in our lives and the right place of the Divided Self.

The Divided Self can be said to have positive and negative parts. These can be called 'higher' and 'lower' because the first reaches towards the True Self and the second yearns after the material world. There are many descriptions of this opposition of impulses deep down in man out of reach of his ordinary consciousness. All that we see are the 'passions' as Aristotle called them. They are well described in Spinoza's *Ethic*; but I would refer you specially to the *Bhagavad Gita*, where you will see them in the form that the old Shivapuri Baba spoke of them to us a few months ago. They are given as pairs of opposites: such as fearlessness and cowardice, straightforwardness and crookedness and so on. These are all various urges, each one of which has its reverse and obverse, its upwards and downwards direction. It is probably necessary to consider the Divided Self as having this two-way spreading power. It spreads out towards the vegetable and material worlds; it is this that drives man to gain mastery over nature, to be the master of the things with which he deals, to be the master of the life that surrounds him. It is the source of that affirmation 'I must be master'. But there is, in this same self, the urge 'I must fit in, I want to find my place'.

Now, at last, we can turn to the true role of the Divided Self and the purpose for which conscious energy can be organized in us. I will start by giving the answer and then will explain it: *The Divided Self is our instrument for understanding* and the use of consciousness is to enable us to *understand*.

The difference between knowing and understanding lies

in relatedness. We can know something or someone: but if we only know, that something or someone remains separate from us. We know from the outside, by what the outside can tell us. We understand from the inside by conscious participation. Knowing is indirect and depends upon our instruments of perception and thinking. Understanding is direct and comes by contact. But contact requires two—one from each side. If I am to understand another, I must have something in me which my consciousness can bring into contact with that other. That is the secret of the Divided Self: it works by a kind of 'matching'. This will make it clear to you why Gurdjieff says that understanding is impossible without experience, and also why he speaks of *confrontation*. We can never understand a situation unless we have some experience of our own that we can match with it. We can never understand another person unless we have in our own pattern—our own character—something that can meet up with that person.

Now you will see why we have to have all those 'animals' in us. Every animal can be taken as holding the key to one particular way of understanding; a cow understands grass, a bear understands honey. Every species and genus of animal is necessary for the whole of life on the earth. Associated with every one of these there is a certain kind of experience. There is obviously a mouse-like experience, a cow or a sheep, a tiger or a wolf and so on. In so far as these are in us, they go to make up the richness of the inner nature of man. Through all those experiences, we are able to reach out; it is through them that man has a special and extraordinary power, not only of knowing the world in which he lives, but also of *understanding* it. We are able to participate because we have something in us which corresponds to each part of our world.

Now you can see why the Divided Self is the seat of understanding. In the psychology of Ouspensky and Gurdjieff, this corresponds to the highest part, which Gurdjieff calls the 'intellectual part of the centres', a terminology which was mystifying to us when we first studied it, but which has become much clearer to me since all these other ideas have been connected with it.

So that those of you who have not studied Gurdjieff's system can understand what I mean, I will say that Gurdjieff makes

the division of functions I have already mentioned: instinctive-motor, emotional and intellectual, and says that there is a
'centre' or brain that controls each of these powers. Now these
centres—according to Gurdjieff, and we can confirm it from our
own experience—each has three 'parts' that he calls *mechanical,
emotional* and *intellectual*. These correspond to the three selves
that use the centres. Thus the mechanical level of the emotional
centre is the emotional life of the Material Self. The emotional
part of the intellectual centre is the thought life of the Reactional
Self. The intellectual part of the instinctive-motor centre gives the
consciousness of the true nature of life in the Divided Self. The
intellectual part of the Intellectual Centre in Gurdjieff's scheme is
the seat of the first gradation of Objective Reason—which is what
we should call direct understanding. The intellectual part of the
Emotional Centre is the seat of *Conscience*. I am telling you these
things because I have found that this symbol I have been showing
you helps us to see how various systems of psychology fit together
in so far as they deal with the different parts of 'me'.

The interesting point is that Pak Subuh also tells us that only
when man has been purified to the third stage and the animal soul
has been freed from lower forces does he come to *understanding*.
It is only here, for example, that he understands what the latihan
is. Then he understands it because this part of him is able to get
beyond itself. Up to this point, he merely reacts or responds to
whatever the action may be.

Last night, I was asked about testing on the level of the
reactional self. All that can be received on that level is closing or
opening, accepting or rejecting. But when it comes to the Divided
Self there can be understanding, which means to see the situation
as it really is.

Each one of us is differently constructed. As I said before, there
is a recipe for the character out of the large number of different traits,
features, qualities and so on that can combine in the Divided Self. This
combination is like a set of chemical reagents by which all manner of
things can be tested and understood. You can see that the Divided Self
should be an extraordinary instrument; but few men ever learn to use
it. It is very difficult for us to reach this instrument, because nearly all
the time we are living outside of it instead of inside.

At this point we broke off to rest our attention. After some coffee we resumed. I had hoped that some observations would have been made on the distinction between sensitivity and consciousness: but evidently the idea was too novel to be taken in so quickly. Nevertheless, it could be seen from the questions that some progress had been made.

I am sure that there can be a deep education of the character. It is not so much a question of change as of transformation. The same trait can be positive or negative. For example, there is true pride and there is false pride. We should be proud that we are called to be sons of God, but it is false pride and wickedness to ascribe to ourselves qualities that we do not have. True pride is the same as humility. There is necessary fear and there is negative, destructive fear. There is fear of doing wrong and there is fear of suffering. The second must be transformed into the first. But we could not understand fear in others unless we could recognize it in ourselves. The same is true for all the elements of our character.

But people want to change in another way: they want to root out what they don't like in themselves and adorn themselves with beautiful qualities. There is very little chance of succeeding for that 'like and dislike' is in the Reactional Self which is too weak to change the Divided Self: for sensitive energy is far less potent than consciousness. Nevertheless, by persistence, or by rough treatment, changes can be made in the Divided Self and then there is danger. The last state may be worse than the first.

The real secret lies in consciousness. When our consciousness takes shape in us so that it can remain steady: then we can see all that we need to see and we can understand ourselves. Then we shall find that it is not what we have in the Divided Self that matters but the source from which it is controlled. As I said before, the more content there is, that is the more experience, the greater can be our power of understanding. When we can *see ourselves* we find that our character does not matter as much as we imagined. It is something deeper down than character that is important.

Q. If our power of understanding and our conscience are limited by the traits of our own personal character, can all this be changed?

J.G.B. Sometimes it is very hard for people to tolerate their own character when they begin to see it, and I know this very well because for a long time I hated my character for being what it was. One has to learn not to hate it; one has to learn to see that it can be made into an instrument, it can be made a means of understanding. We have to accept that it is what it is. Maybe if we tried to change it, we should be doing some harm and making it unusable; I mean unable to work as it should work.

Q. You said that the Divided Self could be damaged by trying to change it?

J.G.B. I am doubtful whether it is desirable for a person to make himself more of a tiger, for example, than he was born. I do think it is possible for something to be hurt in this region, because very intense external influences can penetrate the protective layers of the material and reactional selves and act upon the Divided Self, and produce changes that are often pathological. I think damage to the Divided Self could mean a loss to our own pattern. Instead of the different urges and tendencies fitting together, one part of this self can become isolated from the rest and develop independently. There would then be a very deep division within the self. This is one of the ways in which psychopathic conditions develop.

Q. Can you undo that damage?

J.G.B. Everything can be repaired if only we really wish it. Though the forces on this level are very great—out of all proportion to the forces that work on the lower levels—they are still nothing compared to the forces that work in the centre. If those can be brought to bear, they can repair almost any damage.

Q. When Mr. Gurdjieff spoke about playing roles, is this not like playing characters, or playing different people? Is it actually being those different people?

J.G.B. I think Gurdjieff remained the same to the last; that is, he himself had the same pattern always; but he certainly had a power that enabled him, as you say, to play different roles so perfectly that no one could know who or what he really was. It was a most extraordinary experience to see him in an instant change completely from one kind of person to another. To do this, he said, one must have one's own 'I', and we shall come to that later.

Q. People often try to open other doors which do not fit their own character, but I do not understand how aims and ambitions fit in here; you may be like a mouse and yet want to adopt other roles not mouse-like at all.

J.G.B. The character qualities are not, properly speaking, to be described as roles. Roles are outward ways of behaving. Even if people are not always aware of them, they can learn how to observe and know them. The traits of character are deeper than this and we are not able to be conscious of them directly until a very considerable change has taken place in our consciousness. You speak about a person being 'like a mouse', but if someone is really like that, he will probably have developed compensative roles in his reactional self which will disguise his 'mousiness' from himself and perhaps even from others. This is really the way in which we 'try to open the wrong door'.

I can see from your questions that it is necessary to emphasize that in the ordinary way *we are not conscious of our Divided Self.* There is no doubt of the truth of what Freud, Jung and the depth psychologists have taught us about the importance of the unconscious. Jung constantly repeats that the most important characteristic of the unconscious is that *it is unconscious* and that, therefore, we cannot know it by the kind of introspection that allows us to study our thoughts and our emotional states. Jung claims to be able to raise the *content* of the collective subconscious into consciousness—but he says that it is neither possible nor desirable to destroy them.

Gurdjieff says the same, in his own terminology and with his very different emphasis. We were always taught that the 'intellectual parts of the centres' were far beyond our reach 'in our present state'. Here I ought to say that I think there was too much of the 'far beyond our reach' in the way that Ouspensky and others presented Gurdjieff's ideas; but it remains perfectly true that we cannot be directly aware of this third level of the human psyche— that is, of me.

Pak Subuh says exactly the same from the standpoint of the latihan. The man in whom the *Roh Haiwani*, the Animal Soul which is the same as our Divided Self has been purified and awakened is already—according to Pak Subuh—far advanced upon the spiritual path. He is the man who receives the power to understand the Will of God. Pak Subuh describes three stages of spiritual development, represented by the figures of Adam, Abraham and Moses. Abraham has faith but not understanding. Moses receives the commands of God directly in the Burning Mountain. Whereas the children of Israel can see nothing but the burning fire, he enters into the fire itself and there 'dwells with God'. Of course this does not mean that the historical Moses had reached only the third stage of perfection; but that he is the symbol of it. Pak Subuh would, no doubt, agree with Jung about the content of the Divided Self. What in depth psychology is given by associations and dreams, Subud gives through the latihan. Those who practise the latihan find themselves making various strange noises and movements. Sometimes they will run about the floor barking and sniffing, sometimes they will howl like a wolf or roar like a lion. Pak Subuh explains that these manifestations indicate the presence of qualities corresponding to the different animals. Sometimes also people have visions and see symbols or make symbolic gestures. It is most probable that these are manifestations of the archetypes much as Jung finds in his patients' dreams. One of the remarkable features of Subud is the rapidity with which those who practise the latihan (technically called 'pelatih') come to such manifestations. It does not, however, by any means follow that they are able to understand them, even if Pak Subuh himself gives exact explanations of their significance.

I have not yet spoken about the social significance of the Divided Self and the part it plays in human relationships. Individual animals do not show such differences of character as do species and genera. It is also true for man that the pattern of his desires can only be understood by reference to human society. It is often said that man is a social animal. Probably this stems from the Divided Self. The Material Self is only social for its own purposes; it has no 'social sense'. The Reactional Self is quite unreliable as a social unit. Society cannot be constructed upon likes and dislikes. In fact the Reactional Self nearly always acts as a disruptive element in society. The Divided Self, on the other hand, is social by its very nature. This is probably why Jung was led to identify it with the 'collective unconscious'. The Divided Self is dependent upon the human collectivity; it lacks the capacity for independent, free action that belongs to the True Self of man. As I said earlier, it is 'suspended between essence and existence'. It cannot be what it desires to be, because its being is not 'for itself'. When it can find its right place, then the tension disappears and the force that it is able to transmit becomes the power of conscious understanding, not only for the benefit of that particular human being, but for the human society as a whole.

This does not mean that the Divided Self is a good citizen while it remains unconscious. Jung is quite right in saying that it wants to be recognized and caressed (the anima) and also to dominate (the magician). Pak Subuh tells us that the animals in us will not tolerate others. But all this is due to the malformation of the Divided Self, partly from hereditary taints, partly from bad conditions of conception and partly from harmful influences in childhood. These are accidents—very serious and terrible no doubt—but they do not characterize the Divided Self as it was intended to be.

There is an important lesson for us all here in our dealings with children. We must learn how to distinguish between discipline needed for the right development and functioning of the Reactional Self and illegitimate interference in the Divided Self. These antisocial defects could be much less troublesome if we could give our children conditions which would allow the Divided Self to settle into its true place in our lives.

Our time tonight is nearly up and I have not spoken about one of the most important questions connected with the conscious energy, so let me try to get this formulated as our last task today.

I am sure that you will recognize what I mean when I refer to the experience of 'looking on at what one is doing'. This is clearest in thinking. I can be thinking and not watching my thoughts; then something or someone comes and watches my thoughts as it were 'from within'. There are certainly two different kinds of awareness present. You will no doubt recognize that 'my thoughts' are the awareness due to sensitive energy, and 'watching my thoughts' is awareness due to conscious energy.

So far so good. But 'where are' the thoughts that I am watching? I could in the same way watch my 'seeing'. I look at an object and I see it: but I am also aware that I am looking at myself looking.

What is that 'myself' I am looking at?

Of course, these observations are well known to everyone even if they have never studied psychology: but I have not found a really satisfactory explanation of them except in terms of 'sensitivity and consciousness'. But we can add quite a bit more. The sensitivity behaves like a screen onto which an image is thrown: say like a zinc screen used with X-rays. Images are continually being thrown onto this sensitive screen from at least three different sources:

    A. Through the senses: sights, sound, sensations of touch, smell and so on.

    B. From the Reactional Self: memories, thoughts, images.

    C. From the Divided Self: images that represent some feature of the character.

It may help you to follow what I am saying, if I show it on our symbol:

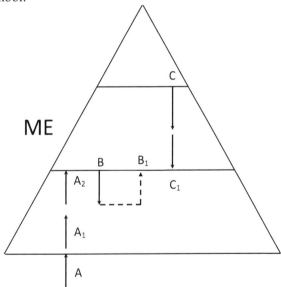

Fig. 3. Perception

A. is an object, e.g. a tree. A.1 is the sensation received through the eye, the optic nerve and the brain. A.2. is the image on the sensitive screen which makes us say 'I am seeing a tree'.

B. is the memory of a tree. B.1. is the image that makes us say 'I saw a tree'. Or else B. may be the whole class of tree images in which B.1. makes us say 'I have the idea of a tree'.

C. is a trait of character—let us call it 'love of nature'. C.1. can then be an image 'That beautiful tree'.

This is a much simplified scheme. One essential point must be added and that is the difference between 'I see a tree' and 'I see myself looking at a tree'. In order to have the double awareness, we must have conscious energy at the level of the divided self as well as sensitive energy at the 'screen' level.

The last point to notice is that many sense impressions stop at the first stage. We 'see without seeing'. Then there is only the automatic working of the machine. The 'screen' intercepts and catches the images; but it also intercepts our thoughts when they try to penetrate more deeply into ourselves. I expect that many of you have had the experience of trying to quieten your thoughts and reach a very deep self-awareness, and of finding yourself in front of a complete blank. And yet, at other times, without knowing why or how, we are carried deep down and find a wonderful world where there are not images but a beautiful clarity. Such experiences help us to understand that there really is an inner screen on which most of our so-called conscious experience is thrown. We call it our 'inner life', whereas it is very near the outside. Please believe me when I say that all, or nearly all, that I have told you up to now can be tested and verified in your own experience. I hope that you will remember this during the next few days and collect your own data. That is the only way to be convinced.

Tomorrow we must go deeper—quite out of reach of our ordinary consciousness to the very centre of the human self.

5. THE SELF AND THE SOUL

On Wednesday, we broke off to rest our minds. I gave a talk on my visit earlier in the year to the Shivapuri Baba and showed a film of the marvelous old man—then 136 years of age, but by then very, very weak. On the next day we returned to the theme of Spiritual Psychology, going straight to the centre where man should find himself as he is intended to be.

J.G.B. We must now pass beyond the 'veil of consciousness', as the Shivapuri Baba calls it, to find the True Self of man. We cannot with consciousness go beyond consciousness, or with thought go beyond thought. But both thought and consciousness can be led forward by reason—with the help of images and symbols—to some insight into that which they cannot reach.

The way that I have taken is through the study of energies. The depth psychologists have tried to unravel the secrets of the self by its indirect manifestations. Jung himself says that there is no evidence that such an entity as the 'Self' exists at all and he calls it a psychological concept. The Vedas and Upanishads have a simple solution: the self of man is the Self of All—Atman is Brahman. But that approach leaves the problem of the signifi-cance of the *individual* self unsolved and it has taken people away from the path of positive fulfillment. The Sufis say: fanā is baqā: extinction is resurrection which means that the self that dies to separateness is raised again in Unity with God. This is a mystical formula that may appeal to us very strongly: but I do not believe anyone can *understand* it until he has had the experience.

So I come back to my own more 'scientific' approach. There are different cosmic energies. They are the materials out of which God has brought this prodigious universe into existence. They form a series starting with the formless, indeterminate energy of heat, and rising through various material energies to the energy of life. The highest life energy is *sensitivity*, and we have seen how that forms the Reactional Self. Above the energy of life, comes the energy of consciousness, and that forms the Divided Self and with it brings man under the dominion of his passions or desires. Now we have to ask ourselves what can be 'within' consciousness. You see at once that this cannot be answered in that form. Let us put it in another way and ask what energy could be the master of desire? But in this form the question has a very simple answer: the master of desire is the power to use desire and bend it to one's own purpose. Such a power must itself be free from desire. It is impossible to imagine that a colourless energy, a kind of empty consciousness, could have power over the wild force of desires.

To master desires, one must be both free and strong. But this means that there must be a substantial, enduring centre from which mastery can be exercised. We have not come to that yet. For the moment, I am trying to convey to you some idea of the quality that we must look for in order to define the energy that controls all the other energies by which the selfhood of man is kept going. The machine is kept going by the energy of life. Life is kept going by the energy of consciousness from which comes our desires and our character. Something makes us conscious that is beyond consciousness. Something makes us desire and can also master desires; *that* is beyond desire.

Now we are all vaguely aware that there is a need to live which carries us along even if life is miserable. When this need to live goes, people die, and no one knows why this 'death-urge' comes over them. We can take the energy of the true self as connected somehow with this *need* to live which is stronger than life itself. We cannot understand it and we can never even be conscious of its place in us.

Gurdjieff has said, most profoundly, that a man cannot picture to himself the process of his own death. Being and ceasing-to-be are deeper realities than consciousness, sensitivity, and our automatic activity.

I think that we can say that the fourth energy must have some of that intense strength that attaches us to life. But this is obviously only a special way of looking at it. Alongside of the will-to-live is the self-will that makes us and our own affairs so much more important to us than anything else. In a negative sense then, we can speak of the *energy of egoism*. "I must live. I must have my own way. I am the one important thing in the world and everyone must recognize it. I! I! I!" That voice speaks in all of us—however much we may want to pretend it is otherwise. Is there anything stronger than that? Do not even violent desires give way before the power of egoism? Will a man not suffer anything, deprive himself of anything to satisfy his egoism?

But this cannot be the whole story. It is inconceivable that we should penetrate into the centre of our nature and find nothing there but vile egoism. Egoism can only be the misshapen image of what should be there: that is a free will, able to be both master and also servant. Man has been created with a special nature which allows him to be a free and responsible being. For that, he has been given access to this fourth energy to enable him to create his own destiny and make his own independent contribution to the furtherance of the Divine Purpose in the Great Creation.

In order to do this, man must, first and foremost, *become himself*, that is, become what he was destined to be. It seems then that this fourth energy is peculiarly bound up with the arising of selves. Until now, our study has been more or less impersonal. From now on, we can no longer separate the energy from the self through which it acts. The will-to-live and egoism, on the one hand, and the will-to-be-free and the creative power, on the other, cannot be pictured apart from a *self*, through whom and in whom, these powers are exercised.

We shall, therefore, start today with the idea of the True Self of man. Dealing with the first three levels of the self, I was able to introduce you to the energies and qualities, and afterwards to show how these are constructed into each kind of self. Today, we have to go the other way about it and begin with the notion that in the very centre of 'me' there is 'myself'. At this point me and myself merge. When we are studying the outer layers, we can speak of different degrees of withinness of me, but here there is no more within and without.

This is not all. Up to today, I have carefully avoided using the word 'I', but you may have noticed that it came out when I said "I! I! I!"—the cry of egoism in us. Here at the centre, I and me come together. This does not mean that 'I' is the *same* as the True Self, but that its place is *with* the True Self.

You will remember that it is the presence of 'I' that makes the instrument into a self. When the 'I' withdraws there is only a potential self. When the 'I' is there it is an actual self. The 'I' has no 'level' or 'height' or 'depth': it can go anywhere and wherever it goes there is a self that says 'I'. That is why the most trivial likes and dislikes can say '*I* like this', '*I* disapprove of that'. 'I' should not wander aimlessly from self to self, from automatism to sensitivity, from sensitivity to consciousness and back again into the machine.[1] The home of the 'I' is the true self. That is where it should be established as the ruler of the whole of 'Me'.

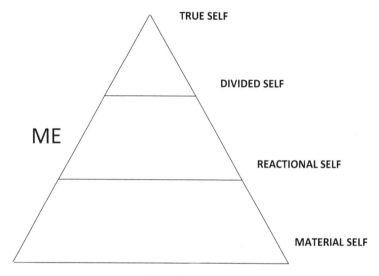

Fig. 4. The Four Selves

Before we go further, let me again draw the Symbol of Me which we can now complete up to the point where the True Self makes its appearance. The True Self is the part of man which is truly human and which contains the limitless possibilities of development and transformation which lie in man's destiny.

In the symbol, the True Self is shown as a point—the apex of the triangle. This draws our attention to the fact that here we are now at the centre. All the other selves spread out with their different subordinate qualities.

There is another way of looking at this that you may find

---

1   In *The Dramatic Universe*, Vol. II, Chs. 29-30, I describe the selves as composite, that is, combinations of essence and existence. Individuality, I say there, does not 'exist'. These difficult philosophical distinctions are not necessary for following the psychological exposition. For this reason, I did not speak about them at the Summer School.

useful, that is, in terms of materiality. We can say that the symbol shows the path that matter must tread in order to meet with spirit, or the path that leads from quantity towards quality. As we go from self to self, the energies grow finer and finer until at the top point, there is no longer any element of quantity. That is why we cannot speak of multiplicity in the True Self. We cannot say, either, that we have reached the realm of pure quality, that is, spirituality, because the True Self does exist in the way that matter does, for it is able to change and be transformed. The True Self stands at the meeting point of spirit and matter. If you will reflect on this, you will see that this is the condition of creativity. Only at this point can there be freedom to make real—that is substantial—changes either inwardly or outwardly.

You will understand that I cannot ask you to make observations about the True Self, for it is hidden away in the centre of our being but you can reflect upon the problem of egoism and non-egoism, and also what is closely connected with this: the significance of creation and destruction. Both of these are connected with the nature of the True Self in man.

· · · · ·

At this point, the School broke off to do the tasks of the day. In spite of the difficulty of the subject, the theme of the True Self aroused intense interest, and there were many questions and observations at the evening meeting.

· · · · ·

Q. Does this fourth self have anything to do with reason in the sense of an individual's purpose for existence, his reason for being here on the earth?

J.G.B. No. This is concerned more with *what* he is than *why* he is. The meaning and purpose of our existence are not in existence itself but in essence. Or, in the language we have been using: *matter* tells us what and *spirit* tells us why. We must try to understand what the true self of man must contain in order to fulfil its destiny.

Q. Is that freedom?

J.G.B. Yes, freedom is necessary. But perhaps we are putting the question the wrong way round. How can we understand freedom, if we do not understand to what it applies? What can be free in us? We talk about freedom, but what part of us can be free? If we knew that, we should know what freedom is. Do we really know what freedom is? We know various ways in which the word freedom is used; like freedom from something. If I am shut in a room and somebody opens the door, I am free from that particular imprisonment. I have been exposed to some danger, some infection, let us say, and then one day the doctor says "You are now free from this infection". When some restriction is placed upon us and that is removed, we say that we are free. But the freedom, in such a situation, has meaning only in relation to the restriction that is removed. What other meaning has the word freedom, apart from being relieved of a constraint of some kind? If one could find something about which one could say this is free, not free *from* anything; but simply *free*, then we would probably know what this central place really should contain.

Q. Could you say that this was a point where that self could see and really organize the other levels, and could yield them to a direction coming from above?

J.G.B. That is a very good question; but, in order to answer it, we must understand what we mean by 'from Above'. We need, at this stage, to begin to speak about spirit, although it properly belongs to tomorrow. To help you to follow what I am going to say, I shall extend our symbol so that we shall have a second triangle meeting the first in the point we are speaking about.

There are various ways of describing the distinction between spirit and matter. It has nearly always been regarded as an absolute distinction, in the sense that matter is totally non-spiritual and spirit totally non-material. This results in a problem that has worried philosophers since the time of Plato and Aristotle. If the two are totally separate, how can they act upon one another? How can one even know of the existence of the other? Closely connected with this is the question as to which of the two is 'real'. Some say that the only reality is spiritual and matter is an illusion. Others say that only matter is real and spirit is nonsense.

I am sure that you will recognize in such attitudes the limitations of the Reactional Self It is most improbable that such an 'either-or' can give a picture of the deeper reality. The mistake comes partly from misunderstanding the ideas of Aristotle. When he said that the soul is the form of the body, he certainly did not mean the shape of the body, but the power or energy that directs the formation of the body and keeps it going. Now, this sounds like the sensitive energy we spoke of in connection with the Reactional Self, and, indeed, in many ways Aristotle seems to have meant by 'soul' no more than we mean by the Reactional Self or Pak Subuh by the *Roh Nabati*.

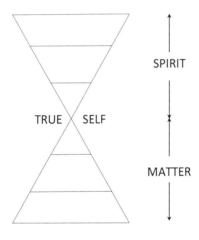

Fig. 5. Spirit and Matter

A more penetrating insight into the relationship between spirit and matter was achieved by St. Thomas Aquinas, who combined the theories of Aristotle. with the Pythagorean tradition, that reached him through the *Divine Names* of Dionysius the Areopagite. So far as I can pretend to understand the system of the Angelic Doctor, I would say that there is nothing in what I have put before you that is in conflict with his teaching. St. Thomas, like other scholastic philosophers, distinguishes between 'spiritual essences' and 'material forms'. There is not a question of one being real and the other an illusion. Neither is real by itself. Both remain possibilities, potentia, until they are realized by an act. We shall come to the idea of act in two days' time, but I think it will help you if I say something about St. Thomas' distinction between two different ways of apprehending the truth of things. One of these is Intellect and the other is Reason. Reason is the power that resides in the self-hood of man to draw the outer world into his experience and come to understand it. Reason works by stages; it starts from the outside with our perceptions of the material world. These perceptions lead us to form pictures (phantasms as Aquinas calls them) and these in turn can be the raw material for understanding. You will see that these stages correspond exactly to the first three selves of man. The Material Self is in direct contact with the material world. The Reactional Self knows it by images and phantasms. The Divided Self—when it is awakened and purified—can understand the real meaning of the presentations of the imagination.

Now we come to the Intellect. The word comes from the Latin *interlegere*, which conveys the same idea as our 'read between the lines'. The intellect recognizes directly the true meaning of everything; or, as St. Thomas puts it, the spiritual essences. When Reason is perfected, it comes to the same point as Intellect reaches by a single leap into the dark. That meeting point is our True Self. St. Thomas himself says that at the centre of man's being there is a place (*habitas*) where Reason and Intellect meet and where the direct insight into spiritual realities joins with the constructions of the purified reason.

For those of you who are practising the latihan and especially those who are gaining experience of 'testing', these ideas should be very illuminating. The true testing—which Pak Subuh says comes only with the complete purification of the four *Roh* or selves in man—should be the work of the Intellect; that is, a *spiritual* perception independent of material agencies. It should, however, be verified by agreement with the work of Reason. Let me hasten to add that our 'testing', at the stage we have reached, can have no *direct* connection with what St. Thomas calls the supreme power of man—that is Intellect.

I shall not go further into philosophical explanations, however tempting they may be. We have another and perhaps simpler way of distinguishing Spirit and Matter if we say that matter is quantity and spirit is quality. Or, perhaps, we ought to say that matter is reality experienced from the side of quantity, and spirit the same reality, from the side of quality. Again, in *The Dramatic Universe* I made the distinction between Fact as material and Value as spiritual, and said that the opposition between the two is reconciled in the Domain of Harmony.[1] The point is that although the two—Fact and Value—are always distinct, at the same time they are always together. It might seem that they could be compared to oil and vinegar that never mix, and yet can be blended to make a mayonnaise. But that is not a good analogy. As you will have noticed, we have found not one kind of matter only but a graded series of energies. These cannot all be spoken of in the same way. We can see only one kind of matter—that which is condensed as solid or liquid. We can *know* about matter in the sensitive state, and we can be aware also of matter in the finer and more intense condition that produces desires. There are different *kinds* of facts connected with the different levels of energy, just as there are different kinds of facts to be known about the self. So we must accept the notion of the *Relativity of Materiality*. Those of you who have studied Gurdjieff's ideas know how important this principle of the relativity of materiality is in his system. Our symbol represents the relativity of materiality by the fact that it is a triangle and not a line. If all matter were of one kind, then we should have only the bottom line of the triangle and there would be no unconscious, hidden depths of our human nature.

Now we must add the rather startling notion of the *Relativity of Spirituality*. This is not new. It is to be found in the works of St. Thomas Aquinas, who took it from the *Divine Names*. I shall say more about this tomorrow. For the moment, I am concerned only to show you that we can talk of the *ascent* of matter towards spirit, and the *descent* of spirit towards matter. They meet at the central point and that is why it is said that man has a two-fold nature compounded of spirit and matter.

Before we leave the subject of Spirit and Matter, I want to refer to yet another way of looking at it that belongs to the Hindu-Buddhist tradition. This distinguishes seven worlds, of which four are said to have form, *Rūpa*, and three are formless, *Arūpa*. The worlds of form or *Rūpa-loka* correspond to the four levels of the self. You will remember that Pak Subuh also refers to them as

---

1   *The Dramatic Universe*, Vol. II, Ch. 25, pp. 33-6. 139

'four heavens' or worlds. The *Arūpa-loka* are the formless worlds of the spirit into which we cannot penetrate with the discursive reason.

I could give you many other examples of the belief that there are seven different levels, that go from gross or visible matter to the pure spirit; but these will, I hope, help you to see that no one description is likely to be adequate. We must learn to read between the lines – *interlegere*—if we want to grasp these subtle and important ideas.

Now, let us come back to your question about the power of the self to organize the different levels and relate them to a direction 'coming from Above'. If we take spirit to be 'above' matter, then we can say that a spiritual power can enter the True Self and from there, be able to direct and organize all parts of the self. The working of Subud is based upon the belief that precisely this kind of action is possible and our experience confirms it.

Before we can say much more about this, we must return to the 'energy' that characterizes the fourth level. We are not wholly out of the sphere of materiality; there must, therefore, be some kind of energy that is at work here. It must be a wonderful energy that is finer than consciousness and stronger than desire. In *The Dramatic Universe* I have called it the *Creative Energy*, and I still think that this is the most appropriate name. It could be called the energy of the *act that makes real*, that would fit in with St. Thomas' description of this central place in man, but creative energy is shorter, and it has the advantage of bringing home to us that in this central part of his nature, man is made in the image of God.

When I said that we had to come to an energy that is finer than consciousness, you may have wondered how this could be possible. We are accustomed to think of as necessarily meaning the awareness concentrated at a point. We do not easily grasp the idea that we may be *within* the consciousness—like a fish is within the ocean. We think of water as something to put inside us: not as a medium in which to live. The creative energy makes it possible to live in consciousness like a fish lives in water. In all mystical literature, you will find references to the 'darkness in which God appears'. It is finely described by St. John of the Cross in his *Ascent of Mount Carmel*. In the Indian tradition, there is *Sushupti*, which is commonly rendered as dreamless sleep; but which is said to be beyond the highest consciousness. Pak Subuh has spoken of the same condition in terms of the *Black Light,* which is a favourite expression of the Sufis.

I could give you dozens of illustrations of the way that true mystics have tried to describe this fourth energy. The connection between mysticism and energy may seem strange. Mediaeval Christians would not have been taken aback to be told that their final 'leap into the darkness' was the operation of a special energy. The Greek word *energeia* is used in the New Testament to mean the *Power to Act*—both Divine and satanical. For example, in Ph. 3.21., St. Paul writes: "He will form this humbled body of ours anew, moulding it to the image of His glorious body, so effective is His *energeia* to make all things obey him!" One that is worth mentioning is to be found in the sacred book of the Taoist religion of China, the *Tao Teh King*. Here Tao is described as non-conscious and nonactive and yet as creating everything. The sage—who has reached Tao is said to do nothing, and yet through him a whole realm is in peace and happiness. Again, you are familiar with the term 'Voice of the Silence,' the contradiction in which is intended to convey that there is a state where there is no consciousness, and yet where all that is most significant comes to pass.

You will remember that, when we compared our symbol with the depth psychology of Jung, we connected the Reactional Self with his Personal Unconscious, and the Divided Self with his Collective Unconscious. Behind all this, as I said this morning, Jung postulates a *self*, which, he says, is no more than a psychological concept for we can never know anything about it.[1] According to Jung, the self is both the goal

---

1   Jung refers to this, for example, , *Cf.Collected Works*, Vol. VII, para. 399, 236, 'Two Essays on Analytical Psychology' (Routledge & Kegan Paul, London, 1953). He says "Intellectually the self is no more than a psychological concept, a construct that serves to express an unknowable essence which we cannot grasp as such, since by definition it transcends our powers of comprehension". Jung evidently assumes that comprehension can come by Reason only and does not allow for the Intellect which, according to St. Thomas, has precisely the power of grasping the essential nature of the self. *Cf.* Sum. Th. Ch. 87.

of Individuation, and also the source of the existence of the Ego. He also says that the self is pre-existent and stands apart from the changes that the person may undergo. All this can be accepted as applicable to the view that the True Self is the seat of the Creative Energy, with which man—as distinct from all other animals—has been endowed. Jung quotes with approval from that remarkable Chinese book of what could be called symbolical psychology, *The Secret of the Golden Flower*, which says, "when no idea arises, the right ideas come". In other words, the creative act does not come from our conscious striving, but rather from the cessation of striving. This is, of course, exactly what Pak Subuh says about the latihan and what Christian mystics tell us about the transition from active meditation to obscure contemplation.[1]

Now, I think we had better return to your own questions.

Q. Will you please relate the four energies you have been speaking about to Gurdjieff's Table of Hydrogens?

J.G.B. Gurdjieff taught that there are twelve cosmic energies or substances from the indivisible pure substance of the Sun Absolute down to the final materialization into dead matter. He called these universal energies by the name *Hydrogens*, to convey the idea that like the nucleus of the hydrogen atom—they are the building bricks of all that exists within the Creation. In *The Dramatic Universe*,[2] I constructed a similar scale by reference to the different kinds of energy that we find in Nature. There are four energies of the physical world, four vital energies and four higher or cosmic energies, the first two of which enter into the making of man.

I shall put these in the form of a diagram, giving the names that I adopted in *The Dramatic Universe* and also the corresponding selves. We only require four out of the twelve energies. Those below these four are outside of selves; that is to say, they enter our experience only by their action in living things and material objects. The two highest energies are beyond our reach, they are

1   *Cf.* my book *Christian Mysticism and Subud.*
2   See Vol. II, Ch. 32, Energies, where the twelve energies are derived by using the method of tetrads, which is more fully developed in the work on Systematics.

included for completeness. We might guess that they are used by Angels and Archangels!

Gurdjieff Table of Hydrogens	Dramatic Universe Energies	Name of Energy	Kind of Selfhood or Me
H12	E3	Creative	True Self
H24	E4	Conscious	Divided Self
H48	E5	Sensitive	Reactional Self
H96	E6	Automatic	Material Self

The Energies of the Self

Each of the four energies can be an instrument for knowing and an instrument for action. The fourth, the creative energy, has the special property that knowing and acting become one and the same thing. This is beyond understanding. Long ago, when I wrote *The Crisis in Human Affairs*, I referred to different kinds of language. The language of the true self is that of *gesture*. Everything that comes from the true self expresses what we really are. Unfortunately, this language is lost for those who have not transformed the reactional self. That 'screen' must become a crystal, so clear that it neither intercepts nor changes anything that passes through it. That is the 'still pool of water' in which all things are seen as they really are. That stillness is hard to attain.

Q. Is there not sometimes a quiet state behind one's activity?

J.G.B. Sometimes you are aware of a quiet state that is not interfered with by whatever else you may be doing. For example, you can talk and still have it; everything seems to be still inside, almost like a void. At least we can say this: that such experiences are evidence that there is 'something' behind all our activity, behind everything that is going on. It seems therefore as if there should be a place within us where all is quiet. But there still is consciousness or we should not know it. So that sense of inner quiet cannot belong to this fourth point. It is probably more accurate to connect this sense of inner stillness with the awareness of true consciousness that is behind our sensitivity. You remember I spoke yesterday about double awareness. The connection between the four parts of the human selfhood is illustrated by a simile that is extremely ancient. It is earlier than history, for it can be found in the oldest Egyptian and Sumerian texts and the earliest Vedic hymns. Man is likened to a chariot with horses and a driver. That makes three, and the fourth is the owner of the chariot. Gurdjieff describes it in a very vivid way in the last chapter of *All and Everything*. There is a still more vivid and beautiful description of it in the *Katha Upanishad*. The material self is likened to the chariot, the reactional self is represented by the horses, the divided self is the driver. The True Self is the owner of the chariot, the *Master*. If you consider that arrangement, the chariot is rolling along in contact with the earth; the noise and squeaks and so on, come from the cart. That refers to what we see and hear in the world of material objects. It is being pulled or pushed along by the horses; that is, the sensitive energy of life dragging us along. There is the coachman or driver urging it in a certain direction, and that is this third part of the self, the seat of our desires. Somewhere sitting quietly in the chariot, with his hands folded, is the master who owns the equipage. Perhaps if everything is well arranged, he can tell the driver where he wants to go. But, according to Gurdjieff, the driver is asleep and the owner is absent. Perhaps that feeling of 'stillness within' may be no more than awareness of the driver asleep behind the horses. Maybe he is dreaming pleasant dreams and we do not want to wake him. You see, the driver is the very one who should be awake. He is consciousness and he alone can understand what the master wants.

Q. When you are upset about something and one part is detached and seems to be looking on, is that nearer the fourth state?

J.G.B. If we could really be aware of the condition in which the True Self is sitting helpless while the chariot goes where the horses happen to notice something they like, we should experience terrible remorse. But the condition you describe is not like that. I would say that it is more like the driver, half awake, noticing that the horses have taken the bit between their teeth, while he is too lazy to do anything about it. Besides, *he* does not really care. After all, it is not *his* chariot.

Q. Is consciousness the method by which the owner imposes his wishes?

J.G.B. You have hit upon a most important point, but I doubt if you have understood it. Few things are harder for us to understand than the connection between the creative and the conscious energies. How can consciousness be 'used'? At the very most, we have had a few flashes of true consciousness in our lives. Do not forget that all-important point, that what we *call* consciousness is only sensitivity. What we *call* our inner life is only the moving images thrown upon the screen of our sensitivity. Behind that is consciousness. And behind consciousness again is the creative act. It is perfectly true that consciousness is the instrument of creativity, but you must try to picture to yourself how far beyond our ordinary experience this must be.

You are quite right to enquire about what goes on at this central point. With our reason, we can come to valuable conclusions about it. I asked you to put to yourself the question: "What could be the fault of the True Self; how could it go wrong?"

To understand this, you have to notice something rather queer and very interesting. There are two sorts of trouble likely to happen to the lower parts of the self: one is when there is disorder and confusion and the other is when the command is in the wrong place; that is to say, if the ruler is one of these outer parts of the self. This 'being in the wrong place' is a different thing from the place itself being in disorder. But when it comes to this fourth part of the self, there is not that difference, because this is the right place for the ruler to be; this ought to be the point of rule, of domination in man. Man ought to be there. Therefore the only thing that can go wrong here is that the content is wrong.

Q. This afternoon, while I was working at the telephone exchange, I felt an inward quiet and was in harmony with everyone else working in the same room. I also had a taste of how, in the past, I had sometimes allowed this to go into dreams, and also imagined things about it and I realized that this must not be so. I think it was that if this was to be the master, it must be the servant of something higher.

J.G.B. This is true and brings me to what I want to say here. This central point is where the *egoism* of man is seated. This is the trouble. Egoism means that one takes oneself to be the centre, one's own centre is the centre of everything. When it is like this at the centre, man does not acknowledge God or anything above himself whatever he may think or feel in his outer parts. This is a peculiar thing connected with the kind of energy here; this creative energy has the power of being linked with itself. It is an extraordinary power because it opens a freedom which could not be otherwise; but it is also an extraordinary hazard. The hazard is that one can stop at that point, one can be tempted to look upon this as the end. We can have some awareness of this centre in ourselves and recognize something which is different from the desire to dominate; it is the desire for me to be worshipped; it is a demand that myself will be accepted as God. You may think this is very strange and that nobody could do this, or only mad people could be so blasphemous; but this is what is hidden away behind the barrier of consciousness. Ask yourselves, what does egoism mean? Egoism can mean nothing else except to put oneself in the place of God [1]

It is possible to see this in another way. People can strive for perfection, for fulfillment, for betterment; they can struggle against the defects of their own nature; but they cannot struggle against egoism, because it is from this very egoism that the struggle comes. From egoism a man, without knowing it, may do all kinds of things that will not only appear to be, but really are objectively, noble, self-sacrificing, magnificent or useful, good and kind and so on, but they are all done from his own self-will. Another man may be much less visibly right than the first man; but there may be something much less fixed here in the centre and his motives may not come from self-will alone. Self-love or self-worship, and demands that are made upon others coming from egoism are very different from those animal impulses and archetypal urges of the Divided Self. The great hazard of human existence is here; that,

---

1   Self-worship is only one of the forms that egoism takes. In *The Dramatic Universe*, Vol. II, Ch. 31, we find six negative laws which together make the core of our egoism. They are delusion, self-worship, fear, waste, subjectivism and identification. This may seem inconsistent with the association of the True Self with World 24 and the negative triads with World 96. The point is that what would be permissible in a worm or a sponge is not permissible in a man.

having this special power of creativity, the self of man can be the seat of something which turns against the very purpose for which he is given this particular power.

I know that, during these last days, you have wanted to ask about 'I', but I deferred answering. I shall not say much about 'I' even now, but I can at least say this: there is not room for two in the centre; there is room for egoism or there is room for 'I'; which must mean that 'I' is the opposite of egoism. We have not yet reached the point where we are able to say just why it is so, and what it means that 'I' is the opposite of egoism, but it is possible to speak about egoism because this is a characteristic of this human 'me', this human self of ours.

There is this creative power turned upon itself, not reaching out towards the infinite, but drawing in everything towards itself. This difference between drawing in and opening out—possibly in an unlimited way—is the next thing I want to say about this centre. The nature of the centre of man, or of the true self of man, is that it is able to command or to obey. Egoism is a state of commanding. The more egoism there is, the more the self is determined to have its own way. The opposite is to be obedient and so to be connected with the realms of the spirit.

Why do we sometimes talk about the *place* of the centre? Why do the mystics, who have experience of these things, talk about the 'inner mansion', or the 'innermost place of the heart'? Why does St. Thomas Aquinas talk about the *habitas* or dwelling place of Reason and Intellect? Why does St. Teresa talk about the Interior Castle? And why is this self referred to as the spiritual or inner heart where God loves to dwell?

To answer these questions, we must go further into the nature of the creative energy. As with all else that exists it is part of God's creation and we may guess—though we have no means of knowing—that it is the instrument God employs in the creative activity that never ceases. We usually think of Creation—if we think of it at all—as the Act whereby at some moment long past God brought the world into existence; but we should also try to understand it as an Eternal Act beyond time and place. In creating, God fulfils Himself; thus it is an Act that is perfected in God, though performed outside Him. God creates the Universe as a dwelling place—not because He needs it, but because it is a means (there may be others completely inconceivable to us) that He has chosen for manifesting His own Nature.

You will see from this that we should look upon Existence (which is the Universe both visible and invisible) as both the place in which God works and also the *means* whereby He works. As we shall see in our last talk, the meaning of the words, "Let us create man in our own image" is to be found in the Act whereby God bestows upon man a particle of His own creative Power. Therefore, man has to reproduce upon the scale of his own very tiny—but not insignificant—existence, the creative Act of God. We must build our own dwelling place—a house not made with hands—and we must also create the dweller within, that is the Man we are predestined to become. This creation is both the fulfillment of our own nature and the accomplishment of the purpose of our existence.

With these explanations, I can come to the distinction between *self* and *soul*. The self exists with its own limitations and potentialities, but the soul is a new creation that has possibilities that are beyond the limitations of existence.

The soul is that part of man where his 'I' should have its permanent home. In that sense, it is a *dwelling place*. It is also that part of man that can expand and grow so that many things and even people can enter. In that sense, it is a *meeting place*. It is also that part of man which is destined to be the means of resurrection: in that sense it is the *working place* for the complete transformation of man's nature.

Let me say some more about what I mean when I say that the soul can expand. You should be able to recognize this in your own experience. Sometimes, you will have had the experience of an inward dilation, and the feeling that, in this state, you can take other people into you, not merely that you can enter into them and understand them—as can happen to the Divided Self—but to take them *into yourself*. You may have had that experience, which is more like a taste than the full reality. If you recognize what I mean, it will help you to have some idea of the way in which our souls are able to expand; I am sure you also know the contraction, the drying-up in the centre, when everyone outside is a stranger to you and nothing remains inside you except your lonely, unhappy self.

I shall use the word soul in a special sense to stand for the part of man that can grow greater, and can also diminish and dry up. When the soul of man grows as it should, then it absorbs all the parts of the self and uses them, as it were, for building its own dwelling. From these instruments, it is provided with all the furniture and instruments it needs. Self and soul are separate so long as egoism is in possession of the centre. They become one only when egoism is banished.

These ideas are so important that I will spend the rest of this evening in showing you two or three other ways of understanding them. Let us go back to the symbol and the four selves of man. All these have different degrees of materiality.

All that is material has limitations and characteristics that you can remember under three heads.

1. It can be known directly or indirectly through our senses. It is the work of Reason to know the states of matter that cannot be seen and touched. We know them through images and ideas, and we verify them by the effect they have upon what we can see and touch; that is, our own and other bodies.

2. It is always limited. Even those forms of matter that are not limited in size and shape—like gases, or radiation or thought—are limited in quantity. Even the finer states of matter can—in principle at least—be measured. We can say that there is so much sensitivity or so much and so intense a state of consciousness.

3. Matter has no values of its own. Nothing in the material worlds is important or valuable for its own sake; but only because of the use to which it can be put. Another way of putting it is that everything connected with matter is factual, and that all values come from the spiritual essences.

These properties of matter are not the same on all levels. As we move inwards, the limitations grow less and less, until, with the creative energy, we are at the meeting point of spirit and matter. Creative energy has power over all other forms of matter, it is at the limit of what the unaided Reason can comprehend directly. It cannot be measured or counted, and none of our usual categories of thought about the knowable world can safely be used in describing it.

The symbol shows it as a point. This indicates that it is pure intensity without extension. You can understand this better perhaps if you picture the creative energy as the King of the Kingdom of Matter. In a Kingdom there is only one King. He may have subjects numbered in millions and spread over the land; but the word of the king determines what all his subjects will do. All the power is concentrated in the king's word and so no question arises of how large he is or where he is. His word is able to reverberate throughout his kingdom. The creative energy has that sort of power, but it also has the power of 'taking into itself', which we can picture as creating a vessel or a dwelling. Yet another way of looking at the creative energy, is to put our attention on its *withinness*. It is the most inward of all energies and it can therefore penetrate everywhere. One consequence of this inwardness is that it can reach all the different levels; and, if it is saturated with egoism, it can impregnate with egoism all the other parts of the self. That is how it is possible for a man, who lives wholly in his material self, to be at the same time wholly egoistical.

I am digressing from the subject of the soul. The place of the soul is not only at the centre, but everywhere. But the soul is also a vessel which is able to contain more or less, according to its expansion or contraction. If you can see this, you will realize that few things can be more important for us than the 'enlargement' of our souls. A tight, narrow soul can be the home of nothing but a tight, narrow self. However well-developed all the other levels of the selfhood may be, everything depends in the long run upon the state of the soul.

Let us look again at the symbol and see how the upper triangle meets at the same point. I have marked that with the one word 'Spirit'. As I said earlier, there must be different degrees of spirituality. They will be our theme tomorrow. Meanwhile, we have to notice that the central point belongs to both triangles. The soul can be called the bridge between the two, and for this it must penetrate a nature that is both material and spiritual. In the True Self of man, there is such a twofold nature corresponding to the material and to the spiritual. In order to express this I shall add a small circle in the centre of the symbol.

I have represented the soul by a circle, to show that there is something spiritual above the point and something material below as well as the point in the centre. This means that the true human self has a three-fold nature. There is that which is in the lower part of the circle, that which is in the higher part, and there is also the point in the middle which does not belong to either. That point has great importance, because it can expand in another direction or another dimension, which we have come near to speaking about several times. It is very necessary for us to grasp that somewhere at the centre of our own being there is a place where we can pass over from the material to the spiritual, from the quantitative to the qualitative, from that which has form to that which has no form—*Rūpa* to *Arūpa*. This notion, of a change over from one kind of reality to another, is to be found in every tradition; because men, in all ages, have experienced the reality of this point of change.

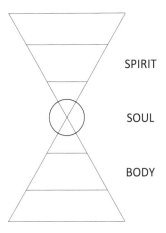

Fig. 6. Three Parts of Man

There is also that which is not committed to either; there is something that is neither material nor spiritual but of an altogether different nature: that is 'I'. This does not mean that the central point of the symbol is to be called 'I'. No. As I have said many times, 'I' has no place and so I can be everywhere. But I can be 'at home' or 'not at home'. The home of 'I' is not an ordinary home, because like the point in Euclid's geometry: "it hath neither extension nor magnitude". Nevertheless, 'I' am—or should be—one with my soul. That is why we can say that the soul has three parts: material, spiritual and the 'place of I'. You notice I am careful not to make 'I', as 'I', the third part of the soul. That would be a mistake, for it would suggest that 'I' is a kind of substance making a third with matter and spirit. Man has a triple nature. This gives him an extraordinary power of entering into relationships. He has an affinity with matter, he has an affinity with spirit, and he has an affinity with God the Creator of both. If he can only 'find himself' in his own soul, and he can find very much else beside this central place, he is able to enter into many different worlds, different conditions, and is able to become such that he can create and do.

Gurdjieff expresses this by saying that the perfected or completed man has in himself his own law of threefoldness (triamazikamno). Whereas the incomplete or imperfect man always requires something outside of him before anything can be completed, the complete man is complete in himself in the sense that he is not dependent upon anything outside him for his own actions, and that is possible because he has this threefold nature. This is, of course, true of the man in whom there is a real 'I'. It is not true of the man in whom there is only egoism, because egoism stands as a barrier between the material and the spiritual, whereas 'I' is a bridge between the two.

The explanation I have just given you will help you to understand one rather difficult thing said about the true self of man, because it sometimes appears as if it were an ordinary self—that is, something that actually exists—and sometimes as if it were a spiritual quality, or spirit nature. This is because of its having a foothold on both sides. It will be easier to speak about the soul because we can easily distinguish it in thought from the selves which are only instruments of the soul.

If you have followed the published talks of Pak Subuh, you will have noticed that, in talking of the true self of man, he uses two different terms; one is the *Roh Djasmani* and the other the *Roh Insani*. These words are not his own, he uses the Sufi terminology which is at least a thousand years old and is based on the extraordinary insight of the Sufi mystics over many centuries. The word *Djasman* in Arabic means body, but the word *Insan* means man;

not just a human being, but man in the highest sense of the word. When referring to man made perfect, the words lnsan-i-Kamil are used; whereas such words as *Adam* and so on are used for man in the sense of a person.

Why are two different words used for the same self? It is because there are two different conditions of the human self; it can be the summit of the whole of this material structure and then it is called the *Roh* Djasmani, that is, the master of the bodies. When the self has opened out to the spiritual world and realized its spiritual as well as its material nature, then it is truly human, the Insan. This clears up a certain difficulty, because the two words are both used to refer to this same fourth level.

So that you can see the connection between what I have been telling you and the way that Pak Subuh expresses himself I will take our symbol and put on it the names that he gives to the different selves of man, together with the English translations:

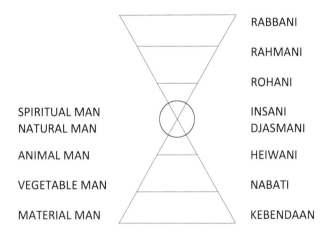

	RABBANI
	RAHMANI
	ROHANI
SPIRITUAL MAN	INSANI
NATURAL MAN	DJASMANI
ANIMAL MAN	HEIWANI
VEGETABLE MAN	NABATI
MATERIAL MAN	KEBENDAAN

Fig. 7. The Seven Souls in Sufism

I will not, for the moment, explain the three highest *Roh* as they belong to the spiritual realm we are to speak of tomorrow.

Q. Would you say how these correspond to Gurdjieff's seven levels of man?

J.G.B. This question was the first I ever received about Subud. It was in a letter I received from Keith Rogge in 1955.

At first, there seems to be a striking correspondence, but there is an important though subtle difference. I need hardly say that the idea of seven levels of man is not new; it is common to many traditions. Gurdjieff, as always, gives a special twist to the traditional teachings. According to his scheme, there are four men who are all on the same level of being, though different in their powers. These are Man No. 1, the Instinctive-Motor man; Man No. 2, the Emotional Man; Man No. 3, the Intellectual man and Man No. 4, who is already changed inasmuch as his powers are harmonized and he is free from inward strife.

I just said that these four are all on the 'same level'. There is probably some difference psychologically between the four selves and Gurdjieff's four men: but you must remember that I said at the beginning that the symbol does not really go 'up and down'; the four selves are all of the same nature: they exist and are states of matter or energy: whereas the higher parts of 'me' are not states of energy and they do not 'exist'. So if by 'on the same level' we understand 'of the same nature' the two schemes agree. Gurdjieff himself says that no one is born as Man No. 4 although this is what people should all rightly be. In this contradiction Gurdjieff expresses the doctrine of the Fall of Man.

Man No. 4 is 'normal man' able to acquire properties that are 'supernormal'. These take him into levels of being that are quite different from the first four. The first 'superman' is Man No. 5 who has acquired his own 'I'. Man No. 6 has powers that go beyond his own personal state. Man No. 7 is the complete man who has attained all that is possible for man to attain. Gurdjieff says that he is 'immortal within the limits of the Solar System'.

It is not safe to expect an exact parallelism between different ways of describing the hidden nature of man. For some time, I was perplexed by the fact that Gurdjieff's Man No. 7 certainly does not correspond to Pak Subuh's *Roh Rabbani*. The latter, according to Pak Subuh, is the same as the Divine Essence which is called, in Arabic, Zātullah, that is not God but the Spiritual Power of God, whereas Gurdjieff's Man No. 7, however rare and extraordinary he may be, is still a man, a created being, who, to put it crudely, has begun at the bottom, and worked his way up. The key to the mystery lies in the double nature of the True Self.

I will put on the blackboard the three schemes in parallel and you will see what I mean.

Sufi Scheme used by Pak Subuh	Gurdjieff's Scheme	The Selves of Man	Energies or Qualities
Roh Rabbani			
Roh Rahmani	Man No. 7	Spiritual	
Roh Rohani	Man No. 6	Essences	Spiritual Qualities
Insani	Man No. 5	Higher Nature	
Roh		True Self	Creative
Djasmani	Man No. 4	Lower Nature	
Roh Haiwani	Man No. 3	Divided Self	Conscious
Roh Nabati	Man No. 2	Reactional Self	Sensitive
Roh Kebendaan	Man No. 1	Material Self	Automatic

The Seven Levels of Man

Let us come back to our own symbol and to the circle I have drawn round the central point. In that circle there is the power to rule: the Zvareno of the ancient Zoroastrians. Whoever is anointed with Zvareno wields power over all within his reach. He is the King. If the King is 'I', then that soul can become the recipient of high favours from God. If it is Egoism, then even if it succeeds in penetrating into the spiritual world, it will bring the same taint into the spiritual qualities as it does to the material functions. There are limits beyond which Egoism cannot go; but within these limits it can exercise the power of Kingship.

Q. Is this egoism a misinterpretation of the 'I' or is it really a false 'I'?

J.G.B. I wish I could be sure of the answer to that. It seems to me that 'I' must always be 'I'; and, in that sense 'I' cannot be false. There can be a picture of 'I', which is projected on to the screen of the selfhood—the screen of the sensitivity. It is not the 'I' here that is false but the picture. Gurdjieff called it the Imaginary 'I'. But that is not the same as Egoism: it is simply the 'Turkey called itself a Peacock' as the Russian proverb says.

Egoism is not imagination. I am afraid we are bound to call it *'I' gone wrong*. It is not a representation or a misrepresentation of 'I': it usurps the place that 'I' should occupy. But I do not believe it could do so unless it had the essential property of 'I' that is free will. So it seems that we are forced to say that Egoism is the Fallen 'I'. But the question is a harder one than you perhaps realize.

Q. Where does Gurdjieff's 'essence' count in this scheme?

J.G.B. The word *essence* is used differently by Gurdjieff from the meaning understood by St. Thomas and the Scholastic Philosophers. I myself have been in great trouble about this. In different places, Gurdjieff uses the word essence in quite different ways. I shall not speak today about the scholastic use, as that will come tomorrow when we speak about Spirit. What I shall say now, refers only to the way Gurdjieff usually took the word—as *that which is man's own*, as distinct from what is borrowed: that is acquired by contact with other people, and life generally. Essence is mainly hereditary, but it has a pattern of its own. This pattern is bound to be defective on account of its source: that is human nature. A man's essence may have characteristics or weaknesses that obstruct his development, or prevent that transformation we are trying to understand. Gurdjieff insists that we cannot know our own essence without deep self-observation; so, probably, it is mainly connected with character and with the Divided Self. But then, Gurdjieff also says that the body is essence; and, in one very beautiful lecture he gave at Fontainebleau, he treated essence as if it meant no more than the pattern of our emotional life. These different presentations are not so inconsistent as they seem when stated in words.

Our task is to find and to know our own essential nature, to develop its powers, harmonize them, and bring them into their rightful use.

Q. Can the 'I' change our destiny?

J.G.B. It can, but not always. This does not mean that when the destiny appears to be undesirable it is to be changed. It may be that that particular destiny is necessary; but there have undoubtedly been people whose task on earth has included the changing of their own destiny.

Q. Is Egoism at the mercy of destiny or can it do what it likes?

J.G.B. It has a limited power to do what it likes. The Egoism certainly has freedom to do what it pleases: but I am sure that its potentialities are limited; whereas those of 'I' have no limit. Egoism can choose its own path, even if this is contrary to the true destiny of that particular being. It can use all the powers that are vested in all the different parts of the self.

The worst thing that can happen to Egoism is to gain power over others. Such unfortunate souls, which are at the mercy of their own Egoism, are called *Hasnamuss* by Gurdjieff. This word is a play upon two meanings of the Arabic words *Hass* which means 'special' and *namus*—which means 'honour'. The word *hass* is also used for the privy: so Hasnamuss means one who outwardly receives special honour, but inwardly is nothing but excrement. Outwardly he has power and sometimes even a magnificent position in men's eyes: but his end is to be excreted out of existence.

There are, according to Gurdjieff, three kinds of Hasnamuss, of which the third and most terrible, is the Eternal Hasnamuss who has misused great powers for the harm of all mankind. It seems to me that these three are distinguished not so much by the degree to which the True Self has been corrupted by Egoism, as by the extent to which Egoism has been able to draw high spiritual qualities to itself and pervert them to its own use. The eternal Hasnamuss is able to do such terrible harm because he is able to present his egoistic designs as the fulfillment of a high spiritual purpose.[1]

There are and always have been people corrupted by egoism in the core of their being, who have created from this egoism 'something' so strong and so enduring, that their only hope is for

---

[1]   This is vividly described by Gurdjieff in Lentrohamsanin, Chapter XXVIII of *All and Everything*. There is a still more penetrating and terrifying picture in Dante's *Divina Comedia* of the traitors whose bodies are still alive on the earth while their souls are frozen stiff in Hell (Inferno Ch. XXXIII). With the marvelous insight, so characteristic of all his work, Dante chooses Frato Alberigo, the monk who poisons his friends and family, to represent the type of Hasnamuss who behind the mask of spirituality poisons the souls of those who trust him.

the soul itself to be shattered and built again from nothing. There are many more, who are in serious danger of perishing in their Egoism, unless they are fortunate enough to suffer some painful shock that will awaken them to their peril. The trouble with such people is that they *cannot see themselves*. Even when they do great harm they do not see that they are acting in slavery to a blind egoism.

I am sure that some of you have, at some time, very sharply had this feeling that 'I alone matter', when there is a demand that everything should turn towards me. One is horrified when one sees it is so; but one finds that, in spite of this horror, it does not disappear. So one knows that somehow, out of sight, there is something or someone in us which has usurped the place of God. Then we must try our best to find ways of coming back to the true situation where we acknowledge our place.

There is a very important reality to be understood: this true self of man is in one sense the summit; and, in another sense, it is simply the turning point where one half of the journey is completed only in order to begin again, as we enter into the world of the spirit. The turning point for us all is the ending of egoism. Here lies the risk of disaster. If man has reached the stage where everything is brought into harmony for him, and this *Roh Djasmani*, or natural human self, has gained the mastery over all the rest—but has gained it, as it were in its own nature—then there is nothing further to be done in that sense, because it has made itself the master and does not acknowledge any other master. Then a soul has been formed which is fixed and which cannot be changed any longer, except by some other action from a different direction or a different source altogether. Such a soul must change its destiny or perish miserably.

Q. How does this shattering and remaking relate to the astral body, sometimes referred to as the fourth body?

J.G.B. The astral body is not the same as the fourth body. There are different ways of talking about bodies. They have different degrees of materiality; but there is no doubt that something is formed in man as the result of his life. The astral body is not on the level of the material body, but is formed of a finer energy, probably that of sensitivity. When sensitivity crystallizes, as it were, into something stable; then this is, probably, what is called the second or astral body. What Gurdjieff called the 'higher being body' is the same as the soul. In fact, he often uses the terms as equivalent—for example, in the chapter Purgatory of *All and Everything*. The doctrine of the 'Four Bodies' undoubtedly refers to the four selves of man. Each of these is potentially—but not necessarily—capable of independent existence. That is what we mean by a 'body'—a material construction that can hold together on its own without needing a vessel to contain it.

Q. What about the Christian idea of the resurrection of the body?

J.G.B. The resurrection of the body is one of the mysteries of religion. We cannot bring it into any natural scheme of explanation. According to the accepted doctrine, all souls will receive back their bodies at the Resurrection. Clearly, this is something outside of the power of Reason to understand.

Nevertheless, I do not think that the idea is so 'contrary to reason' as most people nowadays suppose. We can get some idea, if we remember the very special character of the creative energy, and add to that the idea that each one of us has a spiritual essence, or spiritual nature, that is not subject to natural laws. This spiritual essence acts like an organizing power that penetrates downwards. You can picture it with the help of our symbol. The form of our nature makes us what we are. Everything is formed according to some pattern. As far as the physical body, and, to some extent, the sensitivity are concerned, this pattern is mainly hereditary.

Q. What is the difference between a spiritual pattern and the pattern of our physical body? You say that this is hereditary, so I suppose it is connected with the Genes.

J.G.B. Yes: I think that there are several patterns. For example, in making an automobile, you will have a pattern for the body, another for the transmission, another for the engine and yet another for the driver—that is the Highway Code! Each of these enables one part of the ensemble to be constructed. We have a genetic pattern transmitted by the chromosomes. Within this there are patterns of sensitivity and character corresponding to the engine. Then there is the pattern of the driver, who either drives as he likes or obeys the Highway Code: in other words, he is an egoistic driver or an unselfish driver.

The soul is made in a different way. It creates and it is created. When it has become large and strong and has mastered—with its creative energy—all the energies of the selfhood: the automatic, sensitive and conscious energies, it can bring about the formation of whatever body it requires. At least, that is what may reasonably be deduced from all we have been saying: I cannot say that I have seen any convincing evidence that it is so. But let us suppose that such an act is possible: and let us go further and say that, in order to accomplish it, the soul lacks one power which will be given to it when the moment comes. That would make possible a literal resurrection of the body. The missing power would be the energy beyond Creativity which I said was out of man's reach.[1]

Having gone so far, I shall say some more about the soul as a vessel. It is not the kind of vessel that is inert, a vessel containing something different from itself. It is somehow the sort of vessel *that is what it contains*. That is the very nature of the creative energy.

We cannot be conscious of our own soul. There is one fully sufficient reason for this, namely, that it is formed from the creative energy which is not only beyond sensitivity, but beyond consciousness itself. We can, however, experience the *contact of souls* and so recognize the difference between outward contact through the senses, and the inward contact that comes when we *receive another into our own soul*. This is the true union between man and woman. Marriage rightly understood signifies that two people, two selves, have accepted one another in such a way that each has actually entered into the other, so that their relationship is not external, but internal. I do not mean by this 'internal' merely on the level of their sensitiveness, or of their animal nature; but right here in their very centre. That is why it is said that when there is true marriage it is indissoluble. Indeed, it is so, because there is an actual merging of souls at that point.

True friendship is a relationship like marriage except that there is not the same mutual completion of the male and female natures. True friendship is the mutual acceptance of two souls. Each freely admits the other into itself and for this egoism must give way. That is why friendship is a means of purification of souls. The soul that is free, or even nearly free, from egoism grows so great, that it can

---

1   *Cf.* Philippians, iii. 12.

open itself in friendship to all that need it. For such a soul it is a special satisfaction to obey the command: 'Love your enemies', because it knows that this drives out egoism.

A valuable light upon the transformation of the soul is given by the Sufi doctrine of the Three Mansions or dwelling places of which Pak Subuh has often spoken. The first of the three mansions is the place of union of man and woman. In it man and woman are able to enter into one another and really meet. There is the second, where all men can meet, where there is the true human being into whom all other human beings are welcome. The third mansion is the place where the soul meets with God.

Another way of putting it is that the soul is the place of *encounter*. This means the meeting with mutual acceptance. That can only happen in the soul, and it can only happen when the soul is free from egoism, which says 'I only, nothing else shall be here except me'. When it is like that, there is no encounter. The centre then draws its shell around it more and more tightly, so that nothing should get in. I shall be able to say more about the three mansions when we come to the spiritual half of our symbol. Some of you may remember Gurdjieff's analogy of the four rooms. The aim is to reach the fourth room where we can meet and know ourselves as we really are. In the fourth room we can have all that we want.

Q. Exactly where is the effect of the latihan in this scheme?

J.G.B. The effect of the latihan seems to come from the opening of the passage that goes through the central point and connects the spiritual and the material parts of our nature. This passage has been blocked because of our habit of turning always towards the material world. Of course, the effect of the latihan is extremely complex, because our situation is a very complicated one. It certainly does work as a purifying influence beginning with the material self. But it also stirs up the deeper parts of the selfhood. There is always a certain hazard in casting out devils. It seems fine to cast out devils, but supposing seven other devils come in, each one worse than the first? If one were to begin by trying to clear out this fourth room, that is the place of the Soul, then the results could easily be worse than if we left it alone. That is why Gurdjieff so constantly emphasized the need to go step by step, to prepare the first or outer room of the material self before something is done on the second, and only then go on to the third.

Pak Subuh, in talking about it, has said the action of the latihan starts from the outside, from the physical body. The physical body must be prepared before the latihan can move inwards to the vegetable soul. Otherwise, there can be a premature entering into the inner rooms and the wrong thing can be found there. So that, although the most important effect of the latihan is in the soul, this must come at its right time.

Q. What could cause a premature entry into the fourth room?

J.G.B. Pride, ambition, rashness, impatience and so on. These elements in our Divided Self are all connected with this danger. To be able to enter safely into the inner rooms, one must not enter with pride, one must enter with humility; one must not enter with rashness, one must enter with prudence; one must not enter with impatience, one must enter with patience. All that you will find described beautifully in the *Bhagavad Gita*.

We have gone as far as we could hope to do, without much reference to the spiritual part of our nature. Indeed, some of the things I have told you about today would be impossible without spiritual help. So we have an important task tomorrow: to study the whole range of spiritual qualities which can influence the life of man.

6. THE SPIRITUAL NATURES

It was with real trepidation that I approached the fifth day of the Summer School. In the years long past when we used to work with Ouspensky, the very word 'spirit' was taboo. We got into the way of looking upon it as standing for a vague and emotional belief in the 'unseen', and we prided ourselves on believing in nothing that we could not verify. This Cartesian attitude was so deeply ingrained in me, that it has taken a long time to see for myself that there is a non-material reality for which a name must be found: Plotinus, whom I once studied rather seriously, calls this the Intelligible—noeton—and presumably it is the same as the German Idealists call *Geist*. I did not doubt that there is a 'higher' reality: but I would not believe that it was different in its nature from 'ordinary' reality—only finer and more conscious. The notion of a reality beyond consciousness would have been totally incomprehensible.

The experience of Subud made me aware that there are non-material influences with which we can be related and the power of which we can verify for ourselves; gradually the immense reality of the spiritual natures began to become a direct conviction. I was particularly thankful to discover that I was not involved in the dualism of 'two substances'; because I could see that the relativity of materiality and the relativity of spirituality that is its counterpart lead to a continuous transition between the two domains.

As the summer school was concerned with psychology and not with philosophy, the students' main interest was in understanding what *transformation* means. I was able to approach the subject by way of psychological observations rather than a rational argument and this gave me more courage to go forward.

J.G.B. We have already spoken about the distinction between spirit and matter. But there are still one or two pitfalls to be avoided. The word 'spirit' is used in several ways which could confuse us. For example, if we speak about 'a spirit', it gives the impression that something exists in the same way as a body exists, though on a finer plane, and usually invisible. We have spoken about there being finer bodies in man, and I am sure there are, and that these finer bodies can exist separately from the physical body. Although they are very much finer, and their conditions of existence are totally different from those of the physical body, yet they are bodies, and therefore in some way material. I spoke earlier about the difference between having our kind of solid body and having a body made, say, of air or light. If we had a body made of light, it would be completely unlike this physical body; it could travel in ways that are inconceivable for us or even for a body made of air; but it would still be material, for light is a state of matter. If it were made of thought—one can picture a thought-body—it would be made of another kind of matter, the matter of thought. We can think of a body made of consciousness; that would be pure light; not the physical light of this world that our eyes can see, but pure light. We can even conceive a body made from the creative energy. That would be the soul of which we spoke yesterday. We cannot say that the soul is either material or that it is non-material, for its very nature is to be a bridge between spirit and matter. So if we are to talk about spirit today, we must understand that it is not the same as soul.

I have spoken about the words *Rūpa* and *Arūpa* used in the Hindu teachings; *Rūpa* means with form, and *Arūpa*, without form. That which is spiritual gives form, but does not take it. Matter takes form, but does not give it. Another good way of understanding spirit is to see it as the *world of quality*. Quality has no form, but it can produce form. A shade of blue can be connected with an object, but blue in itself has no form at all and cannot be thought about. If you try to think of blue and put away any idea of something which is blue, you can see how difficult it is. You imagine blue light or a blue sky, but it is the sky or the light that is blue. Blue as a quality is something that must be there, because all things blue share in this blueness. There are many qualities, and all these are spiritual in nature. There is a certain affinity between spirit and matter, as if they need one another in order to be real. Just as sweetness needs sugar in order to be sweet, and sugar needs sweetness in order to be sugar, so spirit and matter always need one another in order to be real.

Let me take one single example, and that is the sense of rightness, of appropriateness. You do a job of work. There is a quality that makes that work right, well done. This can be expressed only partly in material terms; we can know it is right in terms of the material world and those of the sensitive world and so on; but what is it that appeals to us when we become aware that there is *quality* present, and distresses us when we feel that it is absent? The difference between what it is and what it ought to be, can be expressed in material terms; but the *nature* of the difference, and the *reason* why we have a sense that one is right and the other faulty, is the spiritual element in the judgment and cannot be stated as a fact. I do not refer only to gross matter, but also to our habitual reactions and the desires that lie behind.

Take the example of the artistic taste, as when we say: "This work of art is beautiful." Very few people have direct taste; nearly everyone has only second-hand taste, in which their own sense of value is overlaid with habits, training, opinions that have been picked up, aesthetic principles that govern what one should admire and should not admire. All these are manifestations of the material and sensitive selves. But there is such a thing as pure taste which would enable you, without ever having seen anything of the kind before, to feel the rightness or the departure from rightness of some work of art, even if you have no idea of what is the school or the tradition to which this belongs, or have any training in the techniques used by the artist. It is no better when the divided self takes a hand. It may have convictions of its own; but they are not direct perceptions of value so much as a manifestation of the character of the critic. That is why there are such bitter quarrels between the different 'schools' of art. The true artistic taste cannot ever come from the True Self if it is overpowered by egoism. That is why it is said that art can have a purgative or purifying effect on people—if only they will allow it to do so. This applies, of course, equally to the artist as to the critic. The spiritual qualities are not facts, but they are realities; they do not exist and yet *they are*. There are qualities of rightness, justice, appropriateness and harmony in all kinds of constructions or forms; but the quality does not consist in the visible form, because the form is an attempt, always imperfect, to express a quality.

Every artist knows that in the most perfect moment of expression possible for him, there is always a sense of the gap that separates the actual work and the quality it seeks to express. That is what I understand as a spiritual element in our experience. You can see from this, that there are different kinds of spiritual elements, because there are different qualities.

Spirit is always calling to matter to join with it, and the material is reaching towards the spirit in order to express itself in spiritual qualities. This is going on in us all the time; there is in us something calling us towards these worlds about that central point, and there is also something they in their turn need. That central point, which I spoke about earlier as the place of meeting, is the place where spiritual qualities and material forms meet each other. They can meet there because forms reach their most complete freedom in pure consciousness, and spirituality at this point has become canalized, or focused into something that is individual; that is you, me, each one of us. This can be expressed as the difference between *what* you do and *how* you do it. We could also say that you can see how much you are concerned with the *quantity* of your experiences and with their *quality*.

Now, we must go more deeply into the meaning of spirit. I am going to put one idea before you that may help you to picture how spirit can be conceived without being involved in matter.

If you follow what I have been saying, you realize this means that the worlds of spirituality are not far away and inaccessible, beyond the sky or far down in the depths of our being. We live in the worlds of spirituality all the time, but we feel their influence indirectly; that is, so long as I am living here in my thoughts, then any spiritual influences have to come all the way through these different layers. By the time they reach the lower levels, they come in the form of some fixed conception like yellow, or goodness, or hope and so on, all of which are spiritual qualities, but have become names, and names for certain kinds of experiences that perhaps belong much more to these lower levels than to the real human self. So that, although the spiritual worlds are intimately close, right inside us, we only have an indirect contact with them until we are able to find ourselves. I do not wish to convey the impression that spiritual elements enter into the world of matter only through men-or man-like beings. There is a spiritual quality in the song of a bird and another in a flower; but these are the natural qualities inherent in the very nature of birds and flowers, spirit and matter are joined by a creative act in which man has had no part. In artistic creation, it is man himself who joins the two worlds. He does so in other ways—I have taken the work of art to illustrate my meaning, not exhaust it.

Does all this mean that there are no spiritual beings? I am sure that there are, but we want to be very careful not to picture them as if they were the sort of beings we know, with bodies or with thoughts, feelings and desires such as we have: we have these because our various selves are constructed so as to make them possible. A spiritual being will not have the limitations of any kind of self that we know. I am introducing you now to an idea that is very hard to grasp. It has troubled some of the greatest philosophers: but you can catch it if you will go by feeling more than by thought. It is that of *a reality that does not exist and yet has power to influence what does exist*. By 'does not exist', I mean that it is not made of any kind of matter. By 'reality', I mean that it is independent of any other support. Beauty is not, as the saying goes, 'in the eye of the beholder'. Beauty as beauty is not in need of being seen in order to sustain its own rich array of qualities. You know the story of Giotto, who when asked to send a sample of his work, took a brush and drew a perfect circle free-hand and sent it to the judges. By that he said to them: "You can judge my technique; but you cannot judge my art, for no one but I can see what I see." If he had sent an actual work of art, it would have been equivalent to admitting that spirit, to be real, is dependent upon matter.

You may have been able to follow me so far; but now, if I say that the spiritual realities are not just a collection of isolated qualities, but complex and highly integrated systems, and yet not *existing* in any material sense, you may not see what I mean. If I ask you: where was Giotto's circle before he drew it, you may reply that it was in his imagination, or nowhere at all. But I say that it did not need Giotto's imagination to be what it was. It was what it was and what it always will be; the spiritual quality of circular perfection. Now circularity seems to be a simple quality, but in reality it contains so much that when you begin to meditate on its meaning you find yourself in a world: the world of circles.

I am afraid that Plato has confused us all with his doctrine of *eidos* or idea. He tells us that these are the reality and that material forms are only copies. He would probably have said that Giotto saw the 'idea' of the circle and showed that he could copy it perfectly. But I am sure that this conveys the notion of a form or shape and not of a quality still less of a complex structure of qualities.

My own experience convinces me that qualities are organized into structures and that these are 'spiritual realities'. They have at least one recognizable power—that of organizing matter—which as you will remember includes sensation, thought, consciousness and all the stuff of which our four selves are made. These 'spiritual realities' can also be called spiritual beings.

In every tradition, there is the belief in spiritual beings that are non-material, and yet real. These are called angels, devas, malaikat, spiritual essences and various other names. We know them as angels, and, in the Christian tradition, we are taught that each one of us is accompanied through life by a Guardian Angel to protect us and guide our lives. I have no doubt that this teaching is true; only, of course, one tends to picture it in a too materialistic way. By 'materialistic' I mean one thinks of the Guardian Angel as some kind of beautiful being, who is close to us in a 'spirit body' that we cannot see. The Guardian Angel must be a spiritual nature associated with our own nature, but beyond our own self.

If we return once again to our symbol, I can show you the place of the Guardian Angels and of other spiritual essences of the same kind.

The Guardian Angel draws us towards spirituality and gives each of us the pattern of our spiritual life. If we can become aware of this, as it were *listen*, then we can receive both strength and guidance from it. In spite of all the mistakes man may make in his life, the Guardian Angel still preserves his destiny for him and guards it. It always keeps open for him the path he should be following, and makes it possible for him to return to that path even if he has lost his way. I believe that is the right way to speak of it, because its nature is eternal, not changing with time. It is what it is, and it is always there; what it holds for us, what it preserves for us, does not change.

Let me illustrate the idea by a picture. Let us suppose you watch people weaving carpets by hand, with the hand-knotting method used in Eastern countries. When people are sitting before a big tapestry and knotting, there is someone, maybe a child, who stands in front of them and holds the pattern for all to see. The carpet makers can always look up and see whether they are taking the right colour. If they have forgotten how the next knot ought to be, the pattern is always there for them to look at and see. The pattern of the tapestry they are weaving is presented by this child who holds it the place of angels in front of them. It does not mean he is protecting them from making mistakes, because if they do not look at it they will make mistakes. It is, to my mind, somewhat like that with the Guardian Angels.

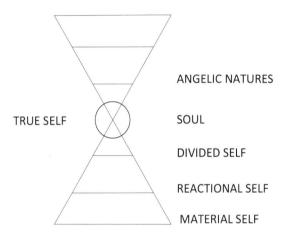

Fig. 8. The Place of Angels

I am sure you will realize, if you reflect on it, that although you have probably used the words spiritual and material quite freely, and perhaps even assumed you understood them, you have not really formed any notion of what is the difference between spirit and matter. I certainly had this difficulty until this began to be clear from my own experience. I tended to think of the spiritual simply as a finer kind of materiality. You might think that consciousness , for example, is spiritual, and if one could speak of such a thing as 'pure consciousness', then pure consciousness would be the same as pure spirituality. But it is not like that. Matter, however fine it may be, is still matter. Spirit, however much it may be individualized and focused, still remains spirit and is of a different nature. Quantity always remains quantity and never turns into quality; quality always remains quality and never turns into quantity. Facts always remain facts and never turn into values; values always remain values and never turn into facts.

All values belong to the spiritual world; all facts belong to the material world; and, therefore, everything that can be known from the senses is fact. The spirit cannot be known; it is something different, it is something that draws us and shapes our ends. If you say 'the spiritual nature of sugar is sweetness', you know sweetness is not something that can be measured. You do not get more sweetness from more sugar. Our nature being such as it is, we only know sweetness by tasting sweet things: but there may be other natures who can appreciate the quality of sweetness without any contact with matter. This is only an analogy, for sweetness is a very rudimentary spiritual quality. If you take a high spiritual quality, like Truth, we can know about Truth because we know things that are true statements that are true, people that are true, situations that are true—but we do not know Truth itself, in that way. This does not mean that Truth is not there, even if there is nothing there to be true; even in the midst of falsehood, Truth is still there. But in what way? Something in us says something like this: 'It must be there,' not 'I know it is there', but 'it must be'.

All obligations, all 'musts' come from the spirit. There are no obligations in the material worlds; things are what they are. They act from their various impulses and forces that work in them. But as soon as you enter the spiritual world, then you meet obligations, 'musts', 'this is how it has to be', 'there is truth because there must be truth', 'there is love because there must be love', 'Faith is real, not because we touch it or know it or understand it, but because it must be.'

That is why we speak of the Guardian Angel as the repository or our obligations. Our Guardian Angel holds before us the pattern of how life must be, and if we will turn to this, we can always be brought back to that pattern. This will give you some idea of what I mean when I speak of this spiritual world, the world of values, the world of qualities, the world of obligations, as distinct from the world of facts and forms and matter and energies, and also of selves and their powers.

I have spoken of the Guardian Angels this morning, in order to give you some idea of what is meant by spiritual beings. You should also remember what we have said about Reason and Intellect. Intellect is the instrument that is given to us so that we can have a direct insight into spiritual realities. Only you must not forget that all those who know what is meant by Intellect—or its equivalent in other systems—have warned us that the power to use this instrument is not given to many. For most of us, the utmost we can hope for is a few flashes of insight, and the laborious approach by way of Reason. I am referring to the pure spiritual realities, not to their manifestations in association with matter.

Now we must go to our day's work. I am going to suggest an exercise that may help you. Take some quality and sit still for a few minutes and empty out all material associations. For example, take the colour *yellow*. This will evoke the image of a yellow object or a yellow flower or just a yellow patch on the wall. Throw away any such image. Then your mind may turn to the idea of light as a vibration. You may know some physics or you may know theories of colour vision. Push them all out of your mind. Keep saying to every image or thought that comes "Go away. Leave me alone with my yellow". If you really try, you will have glimpses of a reality in the bare yellowness of yellow. Then go on to a more inward quality like *honesty*. Drive away all pictures of honest people, honest actions. Drive away thoughts of morality and the commandments. Send away everything that has any kind of materiality and remain with the honesty of honesty.

If you will try this exercise two or three times during the day, you will get some idea of what I want. Only, I warn you, it is useless to pretend to do it. There must be a real determination to get the Value without any support of Fact.

. . . . .

The transition from self to spirit did not prove so difficult for most of the students as I had expected, and there were lively discussions during intervals in the day's work. Some of the questions and observations in the evening showed that some at least had grasped the distinction in a concrete way.

Q. I saw that one of the difficulties I have relating to this spiritual world, is that in a sense the act of consciousness is different, it requires a passive consciousness to make this relationship. Instead of being actively conscious in relation to the lower worlds, I attempt to be actively conscious in relation to the higher world.

J.G.B. You have seen a truth which is very important, but almost impossible to put into words. We cannot penetrate into the spiritual world, by an act of consciousness. For many years I did not understand this, and I can remember how often I had the experience of coming to a blank, as it were seeing nothing beyond except blank darkness and wondering why it was not possible.

I was immensely helped by the talks I had, this year and last, with the Shivapuri Baba. He could speak of these things from direct experience—of that I was quite certain. He insisted upon the necessity, above all things, of coming to the 'Knowledge of God'. Obviously, he was not speaking of the knowledge that can be reached by Reason, but of the supreme gift of the Intellect. I did not really understand, until in one of his talks he said: "you are enveloped in consciousness; it is this consciousness which prevents you from seeing God. Put aside this consciousness for one moment and you will see God." This seems very bewildering if you have been accustomed to think of God as Supreme consciousness, or supposed that there must be an expansion of consciousness to reach God. Evidently, the word 'consciousness' has to change its meaning entirely when you pass from the material to the spiritual worlds. Another source of bewilderment are the references to the Dark Night, in the writings of mystics like St. John of the Cross. I have already spoken of the word *Sushupti* used by Yogis to describe the 'profound un consciousness' in which the Yogi enters it. These descriptions must refer to states that people have really known. It means, I am sure, that what you call 'active consciousness' can do no more than lead us to the central point. There has then to be some sort of reversal where consciousness ceases to be 'consciousness of' and becomes instead 'to be enveloped in consciousness'. then ceases to be 'our consciousness'.

Q. When we see something beautiful, then the passivity of our consciousness, the passive part of this act of seeing, transforms it into something beautiful. It seems to me there is a kind of analogy between this, which we ourselves can enter; and the reality of this, in which we ourselves are the whole passive part.

J.G.B. Yes. Here the experience of Subud can help us very much. We learn to recognize that non-doing can be positive, and that nonconsciousness can go deeper than consciousness.

What you say reminds me of an observation made in a group to which I belonged many years ago. It was so illuminating to me that I never forgot it. Henri Tracol spoke of having become aware of a reversal of the act of self-observation; that instead of having the awareness of observing oneself, one becomes transformed into a condition of being aware of being observed; and yet, this state of being observed was still a state of self-observation. Tracol was speaking in French, and he said: "*Au lieu de voir, ce fut l'état d'être vu*"—instead of seeing, it was a state of being seen.

This connects with what you are saying, and it can help us to grasp our relationship with the spiritual world. This is connected with that kind of reversal. Sometimes we pass by very significant remarks, because we do not know what they are about. They look like rhetoric, whereas they are, in fact, very serious attempts to express something. We are all familiar with the words of St. Paul about faith: "I shall know even as also I am known." You may have passed it over. In reality, it is an extraordinary expression and one of the many indications of how deeply he penetrated into a real knowledge of the spiritual world, where the state of knowing and being known cease to be separated. For us, they are very different, but we can sometimes come fairly close to where the knowing and being known get much nearer to one another. It can arise in our human relationships. There are sometimes moments when one is not able to say whether it is knowing or being known. How different this is from all our ordinary relationships where the subject and the object seem to be unconnected from within.

Q. In this part that touches 'I', people will have differences as people; in their characters, what they are in themselves, there is an equality which makes us all equal before God.

J.G.B. This is true. But it does not apply to the fifth level if you mean that. Where there is a distinction of above and below, there is not equality, for some will be higher and others lower. Where the distinction disappears, there can be equality. If we are to speak about levels of higher and lower beings, then we must say that the second is higher than the first, and the third is higher than the second, the fourth higher than the third. In the direction we are talking about and shown in the symbol, there is that distinction, which is more exactly one of within and without, than above and below. There are those who occupy a more responsible position in relation to the whole, who have a greater responsibility for the transmission of the purpose for which we all exist. It is harder to bear greater responsibility, therefore the higher positions in this sense are harder to occupy. Fewer people can occupy them or need to.

Yet what you say refers to a very great truth. I am mentioning this now so as to leave no doubt about its importance; although it really belongs to what I have to say tomorrow, when we shall speak about the connection between 'I' and 'Will'.

Q. Does it mean that below the fifth level, there are not responsible beings?

J.G.B. I did not say that. I said there were different *degrees* of responsibility. In order to be responsible, one must at least be sensitive. Therefore, responsibility in man begins when his sensitivity acquires a degree of organization that is not wholly at the mercy of every external stimulus. At every stage of transformation, responsibility deepens and intensifies. *Responsibility* means to answer for that which cannot answer for itself. We are responsible for inert matter; that is, for material objects, for plants, for animals, for our own bodies, for other human beings in so far as we can be sensitive to their real needs and not merely imagine them.

The material self is responsible for everything in the material world, because it is the highest kind of existence in the material world; but it is not responsible for what happens in the higher worlds, because it has no power there. The second self, the reactional self, when it is truly free from the material forces, is responsible for everything in its own world and, of course, also for the world that is below. This is the general principle of responsibility, that on any given level a self is responsible for what is outside it; but it is not responsible for what is within, because it can neither understand, nor do what is needed to help what is finer than itself.

Q. Will you say what it is in us that understands these things? How do the ideas you have given us, of Reason and Intellect, fit in with Gurdjieff's higher and lower centres?

J.G.B. Yes. I must try to answer this question for myself as well as for you. The word 'centre' here means the brain or mind that directs a particular function or power of man. As there are seven fundamental functions, there are seven centres. We think, so there must be a centre that directs our thinking. We use our bodies to act upon the material world through our movements, so there must be a moving centre. The seven centres were named by Gurdjieff:

VII	Higher Intellectual Centre.
VI	Higher Emotional Centre.
V	Sex Centre.
IV	Thinking Centre.
III	Emotional Centre.
II	Moving Centre.
I	Instinctive Centre.

The first four, from the Instinctive to the Thinking centre, are the instruments of knowledge and action that we use in our everyday lives. They may work well or badly; and, as we saw in talking about the 'selves', their work is quite different, according to which of the four selves uses them. The Sex Centre occupies a special position, as sex is a function of the True Self of man. For its expression, the sexual power must use the ordinary functions; but its real nature is seen only in the union of the souls of husband and wife. So, in a way, the sex centre can be said to stand between spirit and matter—or perhaps we should say that it *ought* to occupy that position. When we allow the sexual function to be captured by the lower parts of the self, all kinds of distortions inevitably follow. I think that you can easily understand that there is sex of the material self—merely physical; sex of the reactional self— love and hate; sex of the divided self—desire for domination or submission; and sex of the True Self, which can be the most wicked and destructive egoism, or it can be the true union of male and female souls.

Then we come to the so-called 'Higher Centres'. Every description that Gurdjieff gives of them and of their work, shows that he regards them as what we should now call spiritual powers. The Higher Emotional Centre belongs to the spiritual part of the True Self—the upper half of the central circle in our symbol. It can be taken to represent the highest that human Reason can reach. The Higher Intellectual Centre is certainly the same as the Intellect of St. Thomas Aquinas. It seems that only the Higher Intellectual Centre can have *direct* perception of the spiritual realities. This agrees entirely with all that Gurdjieff says about it. It is also worth remembering that Gurdjieff says that the full and conscious working of the Higher Intellectual Centre belongs only to his Man No. 6 or 7. I shall come back to this shortly.

Q. Is there a deeper kind of conviction that God exists, for people on the higher levels?

J.G.B. That is a good remark. I think we can say something like this: all the first four selves can only have different degrees of knowledge and understanding. The material self can only know about God as a theory, it has no feeling for the reality of God. With the second self, there is more than theoretical knowledge; there is something which feels the distinction between what is towards God, and what is away from God. There can be a genuine feeling for right and wrong in the reactional self, and with that feeling of right and wrong, there is also some feeling for the reality of God. The third can come nearer, much nearer. The purified Divided Self has understanding of Truth. He sees that God *must* exist.

Q. Is it then from the fifth level that a change of direction comes, an experience, or something which changes the life slightly and tends it towards God? It seems there are these two parts; one coming from something high above which we cannot understand, and the other part which is our lives, and that some guidance filters into our lives and tends towards God.

J.G.B. Yes, I am sure that is right. The teaching in religion about the Guardian Angel that I referred to this morning, can help us very much in trying to understand the fifth level. The doctrine that we have guardian angels means that there is a spiritual being who is somehow connected very closely with each one of us, who is able to be a link between our 'selves' and what is still entirely out of our reach. This Guardian Angel is like a source to each one of us individually from which spiritual influences can flow. They flow through the channels of the different selves, and reach our ordinary consciousness, so that after various experiences of this sort, it acquires a tendency to seek for something, which at first, may not seem at all like drawing towards God. It is perhaps even just felt as a need, a need to have something more in one's life than what can come from the external material world, or from one's own bodily and sense experiences. Owing to the condition of the intermediate selves, this message from the Guardian Angel may be unrecognizable, it may be disregarded and play no part at all; and man is as if he were cut off from it. But everyone has this and probably everyone has some moment when this reaches them. Some are fortunate enough to have it strongly and clearly, so that they cannot be satisfied unless they find the spiritual reality.

Q. This Guardian Angel is not our higher self, is it? I have always been confused about that.

J.G.B. No, it is not the same. An angel—though not material—is a being, and one being is always distinct from another being. There is a most intimate connection nevertheless, for the Guardian Angel exemplifies the ideal character to which our nature should conform. We can be very differently related to this ideal: it may be 'outside' or it may be 'inside'. So long as we still live in the lower parts of the self, our Guardian Angel remains outside of us, a spiritual being alongside of our material being. This is how it is experienced when there is a moment of awakening which makes us aware of the presence of the Guardian Angel, as if it were really a voice speaking to us, other than our own. That is because there is so great a gap between the three lower selves and the spiritual natures.

We have seen that within the true self of man, there is also a spiritual nature. I think that when man approaches this centre of himself, the Guardian Angel, as it were, begins to be able to enter within him, instead of standing beside him. It can then unite with him and become his intimate eternal companion. The transition from the otherness of the Guardian Angel to its sameness, to its oneness with us, is connected with the whole process of transformation of man.

Q. Can we relate the Guardian Angel to the Great Life Force as it works in the latihan? When we test and get an answer, would you say that this is the Guardian Angel giving us help?

J.G.B. It seems to me that when we receive guidance that is right and necessary for our own lives, this most probably reaches us through the personal help of our Guardian Angel. He is our link with the spiritual world. Now, let us see how these notions are presented by Pak Subuh in reference to the Subud experience. I have noticed that sometimes he says something of extraordinary significance quite spontaneously and apparently out of context. This is one reason why it is important to record what he says. Very often he will repeat, over and over again, things that come from the known traditions; but sometimes he expresses something which is different, and seems to come directly from a source of spiritual understanding outside of tradition.

In one particular talk, I was taken aback to hear him say that the opening in man is made by an angel, and this angel is *Roh Rohani*. Now the *Roh Rohani* is the word he uses for the fifth nature. You will notice that it is the one nature of all the six where the adjective is the same as the noun; *Roh Rohani* can be translated: the 'spiritual spirit.' He said that, in the opening, you receive the contact from the *Roh Rohani*; and then it is this *Roh Rohani* that guides the latihan, and gives to your latihan its particular individual shape, and the form of its gradual transformation.

When I heard him say that, I saw a number of connections; I saw that we have to be rather careful not to use words indiscriminately, like the unfortunate statement that it is the Holy Spirit that opens us—that I made in *Concerning Subud*, chiefly because I had heard the words *Roh-el-Kudus* used in Indonesian. When translated literally this means 'Holy Spirit'. Later Pak Subuh explained that by this word he meant simply the angelic spirit or power. This is a good example of the need to be very cautious in taking words from one tradition, and translating them literally into another.

From the standpoint of theology—especially Catholic theology—
it makes all the difference that the opening is not claimed as the
direct action of the Holy Spirit—which would be supernatural—
but from that of the *Roh Rohani* which, though spiritual, is still
natural; that is, a created power. It also helped me very much to
understand why the action of Subud is so highly individualized for
each one of us, and how each has his own pattern. Although it is
directed by a spiritual power, that corresponds precisely to what
each one of us needs; yet, all the wrong conditions existing in the
four parts of the self, may so disturb or distort this working that
further results may be disastrous. This risk has to be faced.

I think that we are entitled to believe that in every human
being there is a spiritual nature corresponding to the fifth nature.
It can simply be called the *spirit of a man*. We are accustomed to
say that man is a three-natured being: body, soul and spirit, but we
very seldom distinguish between soul and spirit. The two words
are sometimes used as if they meant the same. For a very long
time, I could not make out what was meant by *spirit*. Two ideas
helped me: one was to find that St. Thomas Aquinas says that
Spirit and Intellect are the same. The Intellect is the spirit of man
and is to be distinguished from his *anima*, or soul. The second
was just this point of Pak Subuh, that the opening comes to us
through the *Roh Rohani* and that this is something individual for
each one of us. It now seems clear to me that the *spiritual essence*
of man is a very definite part of his totality; it is that which bears
the pattern of his possibilities—*potentia*, as St. Thomas would call
it. It is not material and *it is not a self*. This last point is important.
It means that the spirit does not exist in the way matter exists.
This connects with what I wrote in *The Dramatic Universe* about
Selfhood and Individuality.[1] We can therefore say that every man
has a spiritual as well as a material nature, and we can speak in a
very precise way about the *spirit* of a man as distinct from his *soul*
and his *selves*, which latter can be regarded as the powers of his
body. I cannot leave this without pointing out very emphatically
that none of these three is the man. We speak of *his* body, *his* soul,
and *his* spirit. Who is *he* that owns the three parts? Do not forget
that question, because we must answer it tomorrow.

---

1   *The Dramatic Universe*, Vol. II, Ch. 29, 29.1.

We must go back to the spirit and distinguish between the spirit as the pattern of *potentialities*, and the spirit as *realized*, and united with the soul. Only the latter can rightly be called a man of the fifth level. Gurdjieff's man No. 6, or Pak Subuh's fifth man—the *Roh Rohani*.

Pak Subuh has repeatedly emphasized that this level is something very high and very rarely attained, and that very few people belong to the fifth nature or level. If we all have a spirit nature, this seems to be a contradiction. I have been trying to emphasize that there are two very different situations; one is where this spiritual power is *acting* on the self; and the other, where the spiritual power has become *united with the self*. The condition of that union with the spiritual power is that we should truly be prepared for it. It cannot come in the right way until the True Self, the human self, is really empty, above all of its egoism. I think there are times when it has entered for several of us—even if only for a moment. Then everything is different. But the place is not truly ready and the spirit cannot remain.

The mystical life of man has been described as having three stages: the stage of *purgation*, the stage of *illumination* and the stage of union. The first stage is that in which the self is in course of preparation; it is being cleansed and expanded, it is being made ready. Various conditions of bewilderment, and various ups and downs, will occur as the action goes through the lower parts of the self. But the time comes when the soul begins to open. Then comes the stage of illumination when spiritual insights are received. These are quite different from the consolations that may come in the first stage, and are more connected with what we spoke about earlier as the reversal of consciousness. When the soul begins to be really empty, then the fifth or spiritual power can enter and transform it from the state of separation to the state where there is direct participation in the spiritual realities. If the soul is not finally delivered from egoism this can only last for a time.

There may even be a bleak reversal, when everything seems to have gone, and there is no sense of any spiritual reality whatever. The alteration of bright and dark states characterizes this middle stage. The final stage is when this centre is completely empty and there is no longer any egoism present. Then the spirit can enter and make its permanent home in the soul. I need hardly emphasize for those of you who have had experience of Subud, that the utmost caution is needed in the interpretation of experiences that may seem to belong to one or more of the stages of perfection. This is where a Spiritual Psychology is most needed. So long as there is no deep action in the sub-conscious parts of the selfhood, the condition of the soul can be judged by the overt behaviour. This ceases to be true when purgation deepens. You must remember that the risk of being deceived in spiritual matters is present in every path; and, in the long run, there is no protection against it except humility. Knowledge, however accurate, can fail us, the desire for perfection may still have egoism at its root, even the love of God may be contaminated with self-love. If you wish to understand how these same problems can arise for people with a true religious vocation. I advise you to study the spiritual exercises of St. Ignatius Loyola.[1]

Q. What about people who deny God with their minds or profess not to have any belief in spiritual powers; but yet show by their lives that they are truly human and full of compassion and have great feelings of responsibility?

J.G.B. There can be really spiritual people who deny God simply because they are denying a word; because the word 'God' does not mean God for them. But they may have a knowledge of God beyond words. They may have been misled by faulty teachings and they may not know how to interpret their own spiritual promptings. But so long as they do follow them, they can come to the union of soul and spirit, and even become saints.

Q. What is a saint?

J.G.B. A saint is a man or woman who is completely and permanently liberated from egoism. When such a being is ready, the spiritual power of the fifth level can enter into the soul and unite with it. Then the creative energy of the True Self is wholly guided and directed by the spiritual power. Such a soul can be the instrument for the working of miracles and for the spiritual

1   I have found Fr. Joseph Rickaby's edition (London, 1915) very useful. On pages 65 and 143, you will read St. Ignatius's 'rules for the discernment of spirits' that fit in very well here.

awakening of others. In short: a saint is the representative of the fifth level of being.

Q. Is this fifth level where our own striving ends and we can only knock at the door?

J.G.B. Yes. Everything that man can accomplish for himself, even under the best conditions, is to open the way for the spiritual qualities to enter. Even the most holy man cannot by himself get beyond his own soul. The central point of our symbol stands for the furthest limit that man can reach by the exercise of his own powers. He can only reach it, he cannot purify it of its egoism, without the Grace of God. Man cannot enter the spiritual world unless he can leave all matter behind. This is possible only for a purified soul. We all can receive from the spirit: but, as St. Paul so tellingly describes in his account of the *Charismata* or spiritual gifts, these are not distributed equally to all. And since that is so, some people complain of 'injustice' and ask the question: "Why should some receive this and not others?" We can understand about that only if we realize that this is not the whole story.

Pak Subuh has said that purification ends with the purification of the human self. The end of purification is the casting out of egoism. When egoism is cast out of the centre of the self; then it has become a *holy soul*. There is nothing further to be accomplished. But, in another sense, there is still much to come: because, when that purified vessel is ready, whatever is required can be put into it. Into such a purified vessel, there can enter a spiritual nature which is beyond the human. This is sanctification, given to a being into whose purified self has entered a spiritual nature.

We must hold on to this, that the end of the path so far as our own nature is concerned, is the purification of the inmost self. This brings about the state of inner purity or emptiness. The soul has no power to decide what shall fill that emptiness. Let us suppose that a soul has been chosen, predestined, to be the vehicle of a spiritual nature of the sixth order. The soul is free. It may accept or not accept all that is involved. Though it is not in the soul's power to seek it, it may be in its power to refuse it.

Q. When Moses said he would not speak, do you think that was a case where Aaron had to become involved?

J.G.B. I think it is always true that these higher places are for the fulfillment of definite tasks. The task Moses was to fulfil was different from the task of Aaron, but he could not fulfil his task without Aaron.

This reminds me to speak about a most important character-istic of the spiritual order, and that is that there is no *spiritual duplication*. Everything spiritual is unique. You can see this in a very simple way if you reflect upon the nature of *qualities*. Every quality is what it is. There cannot be two identical qualities even among the qualities that are attached to material objects, such as colours and shapes. There is only one square shape, there is only one blue colour. Of course, there are squares of different sizes and materials, there are different shades of blue; but 'square' and 'blue' cannot be thought of as either one or many.

Let me say at once that this is only an analogy to help you to follow what I am going to say. 'Square' and 'yellow' are not true spiritual qualities, unless we can divest them of any connection with material objects or mental images; and, if you tried the exercise I recommended this morning, you will have seen that this is beyond your power.

There are genuine spiritual qualities that we do represent to ourselves; such as faith, obedience, patience and hope. In *Concerning Subud* I called these *Sacred Impulses*, and it is not a bad name for them.[1] They are sacred because they are spiritual, and they are impulses because they organize and direct the soul that responds to them. If these spiritual qualities or sacred impulses are combined into a pattern, they will form a spiritual potential. Each human being is endowed with such a pattern. *That is his Spirit*. Now such a pattern must be unique. One does not make several identical patterns, except in the material world where they are limited in time and place and can wear out. But the pattern of a work of art—say a sonnet—is unique. However many sonnets may be written, they all have fourteen lines and they are all written in iambic pentameters. Even this is too 'material' an analogy. We might take the example of character, as we found it in the Divided Self. The character is a pattern, but it is still a material pattern, even if the 'materiality' of desires is very subtle and beyond the

---

1   *Concerning Subud*, 2nd ed. Chapter VII. I owe the term Sacred Impulses to Gurdieff who used it in much the same sense in *All and Everything*.

reach of our sensitivity. The spiritual pattern is of a different kind. It is not what we *are* as existing, but what we *can be* potentially. It is the combination of qualities that we *could* express in our lives.

The point is that this spiritual pattern is unique, even upon the fifth level, where it is connected with individual beings. There is no doubt that this is why it is said that the spirit of man is unique, and that it is quite different from his bodily characteristics.

This is also why it is said that every angel is unique. As the scholastic philosophers put it: the angelic essences are genera each with one member only. This means, in simple language, that every angel is a pattern of spiritual qualities that is unique and never repeats itself. Such a pattern is eternal and indestructible, because it is not involved in the conditions of existence to which all material forms are subject. The spiritual essence of a man is also unique; but it serves a different purpose from that of an angel, for it has to become involved in existence. Bodies and their functions are all made on the same basic pattern; therefore, in one sense, all men are alike. They are 'made on the same pattern'. But as regards their spiritual qualities, they are all different, because every man and woman has one unique destiny, shared by no other being in the universe. How that destiny is fulfilled depends upon several other factors besides the spiritual pattern which alone can be said to be 'pre-destined'.

Now, when it comes to the very exceptional spiritual patterns predestined to produce men and women with a special role in history, it seems that special conditions of existence also are provided for the development of the self. Evidently a very strong soul is needed to endure the stresses of a great historical role. It can happen that the self at some level—usually that of the Divided Self—comes under the domination of forces that, instead of preparing the way for the conquest of egoism, on the contrary strengthen it almost beyond redemption. When a soul develops under these conditions it can have great power, but it loses touch with its spiritual pattern. This is how tyrants and dictators are made, and you will recognize the Hasnamuss we spoke of yesterday.

You most not suppose, therefore, that to have an exceptional pattern of spiritual qualities, is a guarantee of attaining sanctity. There are pitfalls in the path of every destiny, great or small, but perhaps they are most deadly when the spiritual essence is rich in qualities. You will find in our symbol help in understanding all the strange and wonderful, and also all the ordinary and seemingly uninteresting lives that men and women have lived and do live on this earth.

Before we leave the subject of the purely spiritual essences, I should add something about the nature of the angels. I may have given the impression of isolation: each angel a pattern of spiritual qualities, unique and alone, not entering into existence nor having any possibility of changing his situation. Of course, angels are a mystery. Even if we do see them sometimes—and I am convinced that I have seen them—all that we can see is the temporary material form that they take in order to make themselves visible to man. Sometimes they are not seen, but their presence is felt. All these angelic 'manifestations' tell us nothing about what angels really are. It is only because *with our reason* we can be certain that there are spiritual qualities that we can, with our reason, conclude that there must be angels. The Intellect, when it enters into the purified soul, can take it to visit the angelic worlds and find out for itself what they are like. But even without that, we can be sure that angels do cooperate with one another, and that they produce the combinations of qualities by which the destiny of the universe is regulated.[1] When we hear of 'choirs of angels', we should not take this as mere rhetoric but as expressing a very real and very important element in the spiritual world.

Q. Are all the beings of this fifth level good?

J.G.B. No spiritual essence can be perfect except the seventh level, which is the perfectly pure essence of which I may be able to say something before we finish. All other spiritual essences must be incomplete and therefore imperfect. That which is imperfect cannot be perfectly good. If we are to believe—and this is something we cannot know—that there is freedom in the spiritual world, then the combination of imperfection and freedom makes it inevitable that there should be sin also. We are taught in

---

1   In *The Dramatic Universe*, Vol. II, Ch. 35, pp. 312-14, I refer to these powers as Demiurges, and say that they are preeminently concerned in the maintaining of the universal order. I am not sure that this interpretation is not too narrow.

religion that there are fallen angels, and that consequently sin did not begin in the material world, but in the spiritual.

If there can be spiritual beings that are evil, so also can there be men with spiritual powers corresponding to these levels who are partly or even wholly evil. You must remember that what I am telling you now refers to levels that we cannot know with our ordinary perceptions and thoughts. Even the purified Reason can only understand the *principles* that must be true for spiritual essences; it cannot have a direct insight into their nature. That is reserved for the Intellect, or what Gurdjieff calls the Higher Intellectual Centre.

Q. Would the collective or one great human soul come in here?

J.G.B. Yes, I think that is the next thing we must speak about. I think it means the same as we should understand by a great prophet or messenger of God, like Abraham, Moses, John the Baptist. I think most people would agree that the Buddha and Muhammed, the founders of two of the great religions of the world, belong to this same category of spiritual essences. Only, I must say here that it is most dangerous to draw conclusions from traditions that have reached us at tenth hand or more, and that can tell us, at best, what other people have believed. The only evidence upon which we can rely, is not what the traditions tell us about such and such a man, but what has been his influence in the world. To transmit such tremendous spiritual forces as have worked and are still working in Buddhism and Islam could be possible only for a soul whose spiritual nature was upon the sixth level.

Now just what do we understand by this sixth level? The difference is between an individual spiritual pattern and one that is universal. I mean by this that there are two main possibilities: one is the pattern that makes an individual soul of a single being, and the pattern that is common to a great number of souls. When you spoke just now about the Soul of Man, you must understand that this is a prodigious idea. We are bound to admit that mankind has not reached such a state of unity that we can feel that we all share in a single soul. Nevertheless, the idea must certainly be true in potentia, that is, as the spiritual pattern which mankind is destined to realize. It is the idea of the Universal Church—the Corpus

Christi or Body of Christ on earth. This is a mystery that cannot be understood with our Reason, although we can certainly believe that there must be such a spiritual pattern. It would seem that this pattern belongs to the seventh level; I can say no more about this because it belongs to the domain of theology, not psychology—not even spiritual psychology!

But we can think of the sixth level as that from which come those beings whose love for God and mankind is so great that their souls can expand and take in thousands or even millions of people.

Q. You said that on the seventh degree there is this unity, which I suppose Christ referred to when He said "I and the Father are One". And yet He could also say "Why hast Thou forsaken me?" So there seems to be this unity and absolute division. Also, a couple of years ago I asked what Muhammed brought which was beyond Christianity, and you said it was this knowledge of the complete 'otherness' of God. Could you bring these two together?

J.G.B. Your two questions concern theological mysteries, but each of them can be understood better by reference to the other; so I will answer them together.

Islam is the Qur'an and the Qur'an is Islam. It is essentially the religion of the Book. As presented in the Qur'an, Islam is a religion without theology for the simple reason that it proclaims God the totally unknowable, because totally different from anything that we can possibly know. But this 'otherness' of God is not remoteness; nor is God an unattainable Absolute such as we were offered by the Idealist philosopher. Every true Muslim believes that God, though unknowable, is immediately present—nearer to him than his own most intimate self. God is the most within and the most without: but in both senses He is totally other than all His Creation or any part of it including man. As Christians we can accept this: but there is a very great difference of emphasis in our belief.

Anthropomorphism—that is the attempt to depict God in human terms—is denounced as blasphemy in many passages of the Qur'an and some of these passages are levelled against our Christian belief that in Christ we know God. The passage you quote: "I and the Father are One" is expanded in the long reply to Philip which starts: "he that hath seen me hath seen the Father" (*John xiv, 8-31*).

This seems to mean that by knowing Jesus the man, the disciples could know His Father, God. Indeed we Christians do tend towards anthropomorphism, even though we would deny any intention to do so. Christian art does picture God the Father as a man: no Muslim painter would dare to do any such thing. Christians do speak of God as being pleased or angry, as showing Himself to saints and visionaries sitting upon His throne in Heaven. All this seems to Muslims to be sheer blasphemy. Our belief that Christ is God, is called the error of *shirk*, that is the attribution of partnership of God, the One, the Indivisible.

It is very comprehensible that Christians and Muslims have in the past completely rejected one another's beliefs. And yet no one who has lived with a devout Muslim would venture to deny that they are truly religious people, many of whom live their religion far more completely and sincerely than most Christians. Here we have one of the most striking illustrations of the principle of complementarity, or the nature of the Dyad. No compromise is possible and yet we must say that our Christian belief is true with all its theological details of God, Christ and the Trinity. We must also—I am sure—say that the Muslim belief is equally true with all its insistence upon the Uniqueness and the Otherness of God.

This is not the only way complementarity enters into the answer of your question. There is the mystery of the two-fold nature of Christ. Christ is Man and God, always, eternally and completely. Not man on Mondays and Wednesdays and God on Tuesdays and Thursdays, but always and completely both. God is infinite, uncreated and unknowable. Man is finite, created and knowable. How can the infinite and the finite be present in one and the same person? Only by the virtue of complementarity which not only allows, but requires, that the perfect dyad should be the union of two incompatible natures.

We are required to believe that Christ is all God and all man, not man in his body and God in his soul or spirit. The earthly body of Jesus was God's body. The soul of Jesus was God's soul. But both body and soul were also human. About this there can be no compromise, or the tremendous significance of the Christ dyad is lost. The cry of despair on the Cross "Why hast Thou forsaken me?" is not that of Jesus the man forsaken by God; but Jesus who fulfils the decree of God—which is also his own decree—that mankind should be redeemed by the sacrifice of the crucifixion. All the suffering of the world's sin enters into that cry, and it is truly the cry of all humanity, past, present and future. But it is also God's cry uttered by His own decree, in fulfillment of his own act of Love whereby the sin of man was to be redeemed.

If you ask how it was possible that God should utter the cry of despair I can only point back to the Muslim creed that God is utterly and completely different from all that we can imagine. This belief, though unspoken, is as deeply rooted in our Christian faith as it is in that of Islam. The preface of John's Gospel reminds us that we cannot comprehend the Word of God even though it came and dwelt among us. God can put aside His otherness and manifest even on this earth as in the Incarnation; but this does not mean that God in His infinity and His otherness can be wholly known or wholly comprehended. Only love which does not seek either to know or to comprehend, but only to give itself and hold back nothing, can pass naked and empty into the fullness of God's presence. But love will not return and give us lessons in theology.

Q. Will you say how the spiritual essence, that each one of us has, can influence our lives? I have always been puzzled about the distinction of soul and spirit. You have helped a lot, but I want to know how I am to come to terms with my spirit?

J.G.B. I will tell you the conclusion I have come to after many years of pondering over this question. First of all, I am sure that it is right to speak of man as having three independent parts: body, soul and spirit. These come from different sources and their nature is different. The body comes almost entirely by heredity, and to a less extent by the influences that act on the parents before and during conception and while the body is in its mother's womb. The soul is made out of the material of the selfhood. The part with which we are born is mainly, I believe, in the Divided Self; that is, our character. This can be called the *material essence*[1] because it is a pattern of energies. The sources of the material essence certainly include some part of

---

1   This by the way is the term used in the *Maitri Upanishad* to describe just this part of man. See the translation I made with the help of Swami Purohit in *Values*.

heredity; but it is obvious, in looking at children, that there are nearly always traits of character that are quite unlike anything in their parents. I am inclined to accept the theory that the energy of consciousness is indestructible; and, that when a person dies without having accomplished the completion of the soul, then the unused material enters into a general reservoir of 'human essence material'. I believe that Henrik Ibsen, in the episode of the button moulder in *Peer Gynt* gives a picture not far from the truth. In quite a different way, with his concept of the 'collective unconscious', Jung expresses the same idea. Within that 'reservoir of human essence material' there are the archetypes to which Jung attaches so much importance; but there are also far more personal elements of character, and some of these may even be associated with memories of past events. That is how I explain to myself the 'I have been here before' memories that so many people have reported. I would, therefore, not exclude as impossible what is commonly called 'reincarnation', that is, the return of a more or less fully organized selfhood with the character and also the consequences of a previous life.

There is, however, one very important point to be remembered here, and that is that we are speaking of the material essence and not of the spirit. Let us speak about that next. The spirit, as you will have understood from our talk today, means for me the same as *spiritual essence*. It is a pattern of qualities that is not in any way material, and therefore it is not subject to the conditions of time and place. You will also understand that, in this view, every spirit must be unique and can only be the pattern of one particular human life. There cannot therefore be any question of the reincarnation of the spirit of man. We must go further and deny that the spiritual essence can come 'from anywhere'. Only a material form can be in one 'place' and go to another 'place'. The same is true about past and future. We cannot say that the spiritual essence 'was' or that it 'will be'.

We must, therefore, conclude that our reasoning about the spiritual essence leads us to a conclusion that agrees with what is taught in religion; that the spirit of man comes from 'Above'. If we look back at our symbol, we could imagine that the top line represents the limitless ocean of spirit. The second line is like great clouds from which the rain falls drop by drop. Each drop is a spiritual essence.

Now, let us come back to your question. What part does this spiritual essence play in our lives and how can we know it? Let us take as a start, one of Gurdjieff's aphorisms "Conscience is the Representative of God within us".[1] Our search for our spiritual essence is the same as our search for conscience. It seems very probable that our conscience is the material form of our Guardian Angel; that is, the form which is impressed upon our energies by the presence of a spiritual power that is part of ourselves. The Guardian Angel, being spiritual, has powers beyond conscience. They are not identical, because there is a more actively formative power in the spiritual essence which is not represented by the Guardian Angel. It is quite impossible to 'prove' it to the satisfaction of our reason; but I am convinced all the same that my Guardian Angel does help me, and has more than once got me out of very awkward situations.

Perhaps the most important help to us in knowing about the spiritual essence, comes from the realization that our destiny is not determined by our *character* (Material Essence), but by our *spiritual qualities* (Spiritual Essence). We are liable to be too much concerned over our character. Our Reactional Self gets to know about it from our manifestations and begins to like and dislike. There is a false kind of hatred of oneself that comes from disliking the traits of character that do not 'look well'. In reality, the only thing in ourselves that we should hate is *egoism*. We should take our character as a fact to be dealt with like other facts. We have some power to change it and considerable power to control it, but this must come from the True Self. By our efforts to make our character conform to the needs of our destiny, we strengthen our souls. I cannot go much further than this. The spiritual essence cannot be known as facts are known. We unite with it by our *assent*.[2] This is, I am sure, the same as the act of *submission* that is the foundation of the Subud latihan. Our Dharma is our spiritual pattern. *Susila Budhi Dharma* means the connection made between

---

1   *All and Everything*, p. 372.

2   *Cf. The Dramatic Universe*, Vol. II, p. 18, for an explanation of the difference between knowing facts and assenting to values.

the spiritual pattern (Dharma) and the activity of the self (Susila) through the power that resides in the soul (Budhi).

Q. Did I understand you to say that our character can be changed? How is this to be done?

J.G.B. There are two ways in which one can speak of changing the character. You remember I compared it to a jungle. The animals are wild and some of them are dangerous. They are dangerous to man because they are afraid of him. Man can set himself to exterminate the animals that he is afraid of or that interfere with his plans. But he can also make friends with them. If he ceases to be afraid, they will lose their fear. Then they can all serve him—as the leopard and the wild bear really did serve the Shivapuri Baba. It is the same with the character. So long as we are dominated by egoism, we have fear at the very centre of our being. Egoism must be full of fear, because it can never wholly disguise from itself that its end will be miserable. To get its own way it will destroy anything. Men can, out of egoism, change their own character. That does them no real good, because it will separate them still further from their spiritual essence. Men can also, out of desire for good, struggle with the defects of their character.

If this is done without egoism, they will be helped by their own essential qualities. But they will probably end by discovering that it is best to accept one's own character, and tame one's own wild animals—not exterminate them. Jung calls this 'accepting the unconscious'. We must learn to look upon this character not as 'ourselves', but as what we have to live with.[1]

In a sense, the taming of our animals can be called a change of character. For example, I see that I want other people to respect me. When this desire is 'wild', it will demand respect, right or wrong. But, when it is tamed, it will make me act in a way that is worthy of respect, whether other people think well of me or not.

The problem of character cannot be solved by itself. It is useless to have a 'good' character, if within it there is a core of

---

1   See C. G. Jung *Two Essays on Psychoanalysis*, p. n2 'the man who knows how to separate himself from the unconscious… not by suppressing it… but by putting it clearly before him as that which he "is not". Again, in *The Secret of the Golden Flower*, p. 123. 'If it can be lived with in such a way that conscious and unconscious demands are given recognition as far as possible, the centre of gravity of the total personality shifts its position.'

egoism. Therefore, the question does end up in the True Self of man, with its threefold nature. It is here that is waged the conflict of which St. Paul speaks: "Inwardly, I applaud God's disposition, but I observe another disposition in my lower self, which raises war against the disposition of my conscience, and so I am handed over as a captive to that disposition towards sin which my lower self contains. Pitiable creature that I am, who is to set me free from a nature thus doomed to death?" (*Romans VII, 23-4. Knox translation.*) This warfare is within the True Self of man and its outcome is decisive for his destiny. As man becomes aware that he is acted upon by the opposing forces of his material essence and his spiritual essence; and, as he sees that he cannot resolve the conflict by his own strength, he has, sooner or later, to come to the moment of decision, about which I shall have more to say tomorrow.

If the outcome of the struggle is the discomfiture of egoism, then the self is transformed into a 'spiritualized soul'. This means that the fifth spiritual nature can enter and takes its place within the self. Then this becomes the truly spiritual man, the man made perfect. When that is achieved, that soul is on a different rung of the ladder, his world is not like this world. This is a different condition and those who reach this condition are not like other men. This can be seen from the outside, from their lives, from the powers they are given powers incomprehensible to other people. There have been, and there are, beings of this order. Their lives are lived differently, and they have powers which do not cease with their death, so that people can turn to them after they are dead and receive spiritual help from them.

These characteristics of the fifth man are so clear that we cannot fail to recognize them. For example, it is possible to say that such and such a man is a saint. A saint is quite different from ordinary men; he is no longer tied to a particular place, no longer even tied to his present heavenly state, but to be met with, to be encountered. There have always been saints in the history of mankind; not only Christian saints, but Muslim saints, Jewish saints, Hindu saints, Buddhist saints, and saints of no religion at all. To be a saint, the spiritual nature must enter into the self. *There is no egoism.* This is the first condition of sanctity. Because there is no egoism, all sorts of powers can be exercised, that cannot be exercised in the presence of egoism or only with great danger to the soul and to others.

Q. Are there beings who acquire spiritual powers and misuse them?

J.G.B. It must be so. It is the nature of the Creation that everything within it is imperfect and that together with imperfection there is freedom. As I said before, we believe that there is only one creature who is free from all imperfection. That is the one we know as the Virgin Mary. But Her Cosmic Nature is beyond our comprehension.

Q. Is there direct experience of the Love of God on the fifth level?

J.G.B. Yes, the Love of God is experienced directly by our spiritual essence; but this is not the same as the direct transmission of the Will of God. Revelations of the divine purposes come only to the beings of the next order. That is why they are called prophets. They are of a different kind again. It must be so, they are not formed, they are sent. This is why they are called prophets and apostles; that is, 'messengers'.

The beings of the sixth order—whom Gurdjieff calls Man No. 7—are not necessarily historical figures. According to several traditions, especially those of the Middle East, since adopted by Islam, there must always be one being of the sixth degree in human form on earth. He is called the *Kutb* or *Axir* and it is believed that his presence alone saves mankind from complete apostasy—that is loss of contact with God. You can see this tradition was alive among the Israelites at the time of Our Lord, for they kept asking Him "Art thou that Prophet?" They would not conceive a man higher than Moses or Elias. In my travels in the Middle East, I have observed that the belief that there must be one supreme prophet on earth is still very strong. I remember how struck I was once in Asia Minor, when a dervish referred to the presence on earth of the *Mutessarif-ul Zaman*, which means almost the same as the words 'Vicar of Christ', by which Catholics refer to the Pope.

I do not know whether the tradition that there can be only one man alive who has been filled with the Universal Spirit is right.

But it does seem to me that this can help us to understand what is meant by the Universal Church. All mankind is sustained by the Spiritual Powers of the sixth order, but not all willingly associate themselves with it—that is recognize that their salvation cannot be a private matter, but must be integrated into the total spiritualizing action that is working as leaven throughout the world. You will understand that what I am saying is only a 'reasonable interpretation': the Universal Church is a mystery that our reason can never fully comprehend. That is all that I can say about the sixth spiritual order.

Q. When something that feels like love enters in the latihan, is that the fifth level entering?

J.G.B. Yes. We do have sometimes an overwhelming awareness of love that is not love of anything or of anyone. It may be love of God, but there is no *thought* of God at that moment. This is a spiritual experience—a direct contact with the quality of love as it is in the spiritual world. It can be the same with faith. There is a belief *in* someone and there is belief *that* some statement is true. But there is also a kind of faith that is neither in anything nor about anything. We are filled with a joyful certainty so well expressed in the words of Julian of Norwich: "All shall be well, and all shall be well, and all manner of things shall be well." That again is a true contact with the spiritual *quality* of faith, not with the material fact of belief; though of course both are necessary for us. The pure spiritual qualities are faith without facts; love without object; hope without reason. The same applies to the sense of what is right and other spiritual powers which Gurdjieff called 'Sacred Impulses'. They are spiritual, but cease to be purely spiritual when they become attached to something, although they are not debased. Love is not complete when it is only this pure spiritual love; love has a fuller purpose than that. It has to manifest as compassion, as tenderness, as the readiness to bear burdens for others. All this happens when love has entered into the world of forms, the lower triangle in our symbol. It does not in that process become less, it becomes something more because love grows by giving itself. But those who have never experienced the pure spiritual love are unlikely to understand all visible kinds of love. That is why it is a very great gift, and something to be very thankful for, if one has had a pure taste of any of these spiritual realities without any form at all.

For example, *wonder* is a spiritual quality. Nature does certainly evoke wonder in us; but pure wonder is not attached to nature. When this sense of wonder comes over you, as you walk in the mountains for example, you realize that this is not because of the mountains or because of yourself or any other material cause; but because you have become aware of the spiritual quality which makes the Creation wonderful.

I am saying all this to encourage you to feel that the spiritual world is not far away, very high up above our heads. It is intimately close to us. We experience it in nature, in beauty, in the truth of ideas, in all qualities that are not quantities masquerading as qualities. But, as I have said several times, there are also levels of spirituality. The natural qualities can be called 'nature spirits'. They are about the 'thinnest' kind of spirit there can be. Then there are the spiritual essences of the fifth level: angels and the spiritual essences of man. Then there are the higher spiritual essences: archangels, prophets and messengers of God. Above that, is beyond our reach and I will not try to guess.

Q. Will you tell us more about the meaning of the soul as a vessel or mansion? What is the soul before it is a vessel?

J.G.B. The undeveloped soul is formless. It is not exactly the possibility of a soul—as I used formerly to think. It is rather that the soul-stuff is there, but it has not acquired a stable form. It has to go through a process that will purify and strengthen it and make it permanent. Then it can be the eternal vessel of our spiritual nature and it can also take in our entire selfhood. Gurdjieff spoke of this transformation of the soul as crystallization. It is also called the formation of the fourth body. Whatever it may be, it is something which has to be formed by a process. He says it is formed at the expense of the lower parts of the self; that is, they have to give up something in order that this should be formed. The sacrifice which has to be made by the lower selves is the condition of the formation of the soul. After this, it is a question of being endowed with new qualities.

Gurdjieff gave an analogy for this when he compared the

ordinary state of man to a crucible full of various metallic powders that can be agitated and brought into all sorts of different combinations. This is the condition of the man who is entirely under the influence of his Reactional and Divided selves. By the process of submitting these lower parts of the self to the creative energy of the centre, a fire is lit under the crucible which eventually will melt these powders and fuse them together into an alloy. This is no longer separable, but has now become one mass in which all the qualities of the different metals have become set. That is, instead of the fluid condition of the qualities, they have become something permanent in man. Then, having obtained this solid permanent alloy, it is possible to give it certain new qualities and the bringing of new qualities represents the descent of the spiritual nature into the self.

I think this analogy of the different powders, of the crystallization and the formation of an alloy, is useful for illustrating certain features; but, in some ways, it gives a wrong impression, because people tend to overlook the special significance of the analogy. There is one kind of process which is the process of formation, an active process of conversion of what is unstable into something stable. Then there is an entirely passive process where new qualities are brought into the stable alloy.

This analogy can illustrate the three processes involved in the transformation of man. One is purification. The faulty condition and content of the selves must be rectified. The climax of this process, and infinitely the most important step, is the elimination of egoism. The second change is fixation or crystallization. This comes, as Gurdjieff says, from the 'struggle of yes and no'. The soul cannot grow strong without this. The third factor is the entry of spiritual influences—the soul ceases to be controlled by the pressures of the external world that dominate the lower selves and comes under the direction of the spiritual power. The three factors can act differently in different people; but, I am sure each one of the three is indispensable if we are to achieve the destiny prepared for Man.

We have now reached the point where we must ask ourselves: what does all this signify for us? Who and what is Man? This we can answer only when we shall have spoken about 'I'. That is not yet represented in our symbol and has to be spoken about separately. Up to this point, all our conversations have been about 'me'. The selves are a part of me. My spiritual essence is a part of me. And my soul is the completion and fulfillment of 'me'. Now we have to answer the question: "*Who am I* and where am I among these three parts of me: body, spirit and soul?"

7. I, THE WILL, AND THE MAN

The last day of the Summer School began with a longer talk than usual as the problem before us was the hardest of the week. It has taken me more than forty years to come to my present realization of what *I am* means and there is no way of sharing that realization with another, unless he or she has had the same experience. It was, therefore, necessary to talk round the subject of 'I' and 'Will' in order to have some point of contact.

J.G.B. We can at last speak about 'I', the presence of which is one indispensable condition that entitles me to call myself a *man*. During the week we have spoken about the various parts of a man. We have taken 'me' to pieces and studied each piece separately: the machine, the reactional and divided selves and so on. We have separated self and soul so as to see how the one is transformed into the other. We have separated Matter and Spirit in the hope that the reality of spirit should become clearer for us. We distinguished between the material essence and the spiritual essence, and, in terms of knowing it all—we made the distinction between Reason and Intellect that certainly deserved more attention than we have given it.

Before we go any further, I want to insist as strongly as I can that man is not just a collection of all these separate parts held together by their need to be connected in order to be complete. Man is man—an indivisible whole. Body, soul and spirit are not three members of a partnership that could split up and each set up in business without the others. The unity of man is far more important than his divisions. In Systematics, the unity of the system is the first condition for its being a system at all; the distinctions of terms, however important they are, come second.

The unity of man does not come from the way the different parts are put together, but from his own essential nature. You may be expecting me to say that it is 'I' that makes man one; but this is a mistake. Nor would it be at all right to say that man is one because his will is one. On the contrary, the will is unified only in the man who has been transformed and who has a complete soul. We should know, only too well, that our psyche is a battleground of warring wills. Man is one in the sense that our body is one: it cannot live unless all the vital organs are intact. There is, however, one tremendously important difference, between man and his body. The body comes into existence by a natural process; but the man must become real by a process that goes beyond the limits of nature. We are all men and women in the sense that all our essential parts—body, soul and spirit—are there in an undeveloped state. This can be compared to the fertilized ovum, which has all that is required for its subsequent development, but is not yet what it is destined to become. The fertilized ovum in the womb of its mother is already fully and exclusively human—it cannot become anything else but a human being. So with us, all that is needed for the attainment of full manhood is there; but the growth and the development have still to be accomplished.

There is, however, one point at which the comparison completely breaks down. This is the *unnatural* condition of the *natural* man. He cannot develop naturally and normally because he is under influences that will not permit it. These are the influences of the Original Sin. Man is drawn outwards towards the material world and this prevents him from responding to the guiding and directive influences of his own *spiritual essence* of which we spoke yesterday.

Consequently, if he is to develop, there must be a reversal of the flow of influences. We Christians believe that this has been made *possible* for all men through the Redemption: but we do not imagine that it is guaranteed to any of us unless we accept the implications of this reversal. I do not suggest for a moment that in order to come under the influence of one's own spiritual essence, it is indispensable to have been baptized as a Christian: we believe that *all* humanity, of all ages, has been redeemed by the one act: and that all who have accepted the implications of the reversal can be transformed even if they have never heard of Christ.

The point, therefore, is to understand what these implications are—that is all that a 'spiritual psychology' can do for us. The rest belongs to the theologians.

You will remember the distinction I made between the material essence (which is pretty well the same thing as the character of the Divided Self) and the spiritual essence (which is the destiny that is possible for us to realize during our life on earth). The first consequence of the reversal is that a man should be more concerned with the needs of his spiritual essence than with the desires of his material essence. This is where we must be very careful. It may seem from what I have said that there are two separate 'realities', matter and spirit, and that we must choose between them. It is not one bit like that. There is only one reality—for matter and spirit are not *really* separate.

One of the most important and illuminating features of our symbol is that it shows the *relativity* of both matter and spirit. It goes further and shows that matter and spirit actually do meet and blend in the centre of our self. The soul is neither material nor spiritual, but spirit-matter.

I said that all Fact is material and all Value is spiritual; but this does not mean that Fact and Value can be separated except in our thought about them. In every experience there are always these two elements. Even the most material of situations must attract our attention if it is to be known as a fact, and it can only do so because it represents some value, however trivial. A completely valueless fact would be so uninteresting that we could not notice it and it would find no place in our experience. We pass by innumerable 'valueless' facts every day of our lives, without having any contact with them. I do not mean that they are absolutely without value—nothing can be—but their value to us is so slight that they cannot attract our interest. It must also be fairly obvious from the exercise I set you the other day that we cannot experience pure 'factless' value. There must always be some material element in every experience, if only in the form of a mental image. What I am saying now probably does not apply to the Intellect or Higher Intellectual Centre which certainly has the power to apprehend purely spiritual values.

The reason I am telling you all this is to get you to see that though matter and spirit are always distinct, they are always together. In order to unite them there must be some third element which is neither matter nor spirit and yet can catch hold of both and work them into something new and different. Without beating about the bush, I shall say that this third element is Will, and the new and different element is Reality. I shall say that will acts upon matter and spirit so as to realize them. In doing so it 'spiritualizes matter' and 'actualizes spirit'.

As this is such an important principle for understanding all that we have been working at during this week, I shall put it in a different way. In *The Dramatic Universe* I have used the word 'Harmony' to designate the meeting place of Fact and Value. A factual situation, in order to acquire value, must be harmonized with the appropriate qualities. A value must be 'clothed in fact' in order to be realized.

Let me illustrate what I mean. An artist is to paint a portrait. He wants to make a picture, not a photograph; he is not satisfied to show *what* is there, but wishes to show *who* is there. But the 'person who is there' is hidden away. Maybe he can depict traits of character; the mouth can show cruelty, cunning, generosity, sensuality, determination and a dozen other 'beasts of the jungle'. But suppose that he is not satisfied with this, and wants to bring out the *person* behind the character. In other words, he is looking for the spiritual essence. But this cannot be seen or even pictured in thought. He has somehow to drag it out of the spiritual world and marry it with the material the outward form of the body, the sensitivity, the desires and perhaps the state of the self within. If he is more or less successful, he has created a real work of art. He may be a Rembrandt or a Franz Hals, he may be a Renoir or a Picasso; his style and his school are not the point. If he is a true artist he will have performed a *creative act*. When the act has been performed, fact and value are no longer separable. The portrait is a work of art, a creation; the result of an act. As such, it is neither a fact nor a value. When we look at so much paint on a canvas, we see a pattern of facts. When we pass judgment on its qualities, we assent to a pattern of values. But in doing either the one or the other, we have gone away from the *act*. The 'blood and toil and tears and sweat', that went into the act, are inseparable from its reality. We say that we stand in front of a *work*; and this work expresses the property whereby the act has been accomplished. The power of the work is in the *act*, not in the fact nor yet in what the work seeks to express. The merging of matter and spirit is not like mixing oil and vinegar; it is more like a chemical action where acid and alkali combine to make a salt. The salt is the result, but the savour of the salt is in the act that brought about the chemical change.

This intimate interpenetration of the different elements goes through and through human nature. The soul is the result of a combination of selfhood and spirit and it is something quite new and different from the elements from which it was made. What is made in this way can only be the outcome of an act.

Now we can pass on to our second question 'Who am I?' This can be answered in various philosophical ways; that is, ways that may satisfy our Reason, but do not, of themselves, give us the complete conviction that comes when we say 'I see. Yes, that is so because I see that it is.' Let us hope that we may come nearer to that conviction before we finish today.

Firstly, we can say: *I am act*. I am in my act. In my act, I lay hold of the Reality which is both the source and the proof of 'I'.

Another way of putting it: *I am the seer*, I am the doer, I am the one who experiences my experiences. I am not the seeing, nor am I what is seen, but I am what joins seeing to what is seen.

Still another way: *I am the innermost*. There is nothing inside 'I'. I am inside everything.

Fourthly: *I am Will*. What I am I will. What I will I am.

And just one more: this is Gurdjieff's formula: *I can—I wish—I am. I can wish, I am can.*

I am sure that you can see that all these formulae point in the same direction; but they do not get us to the point where we can say that we have seen and understood what 'I' signifies in relation to 'me'.

Let us go back to our symbol, and start by assuming that the right place for 'I' is at the central point. But the very last thing we should say about 'I' is that it is the 'still point of the turning world'. 'I' am never still; at one moment I am in my thoughts, at another in my eyes or hands, at another in my likes and dislikes. Then again, I am wholly caught up in some animal passion of desire or fear or self-assertion. And whenever my centre is threatened, there 'I' am in defence of my egoism. If I am sometimes lifted into the spiritual world and am occupied with the contemplation of timeless realities, I cannot tell how I came there or what will drag me away again.

Again, I am forced to admit that there are no thoughts so mean or so disgusting that 'I' am not able to be dragged after them; so that I begin to wonder whether 'I', instead of being the crowning glory of my manhood, is not the most miserable and worthless part of it all.

When I find myself in this state of agonizing self-searching, I remember that 'I am will', that 'I can, and therefore I am' and I realize that there must be a different condition of 'I' from that of helpless participation in all the kaleidoscopic changes that are evidently proceeding in 'me'. Then I see that 'I' need not be carried along by the stream of happenings. I remember a verse of George Meredith that made a deep impression on me when I was a boy:

"... and this the woodland saith
I know not hope nor fear; I take whate'er may come.
I raise my head to prospects fair,
From foul I turn away.
Sweet as Eden is the air
And Eden—sweet the ray."

If nature can turn towards beauty and away from ugliness— as so wonderfully and so constantly she does—can I not do the same? Can I not turn towards fair spiritual images and away from foul ones? And, of course, this is just what I can do; and, in doing it, I recover my conviction that I am will.

For years and years, I went on that path; determined to use the power that is in me to turn towards the spiritual realities— in Gurdjieff's language—to remember myself. Again and again, I was overcome by despair. 'I' seemed as weak and helpless as ever; and then some new stimulus would come and I would be encouraged to try again and keep on trying. In the end, I became convinced that it is true that I am will and that there should be a way by which 'I' can become the master of my own house. Later I came to understand, and, really and truly, to see for myself that this could not be done by my own unaided powers, and that the transformation I was longing for could only come about in a very different way from what I had supposed.

Our symbol will help you to follow what I am going to say. This time, I am going to add something quite new to it.

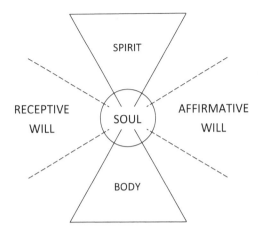

Fig. 9 The Whole Man

The symbol has now been transformed from two triangles into a special kind of cross. There are now five distinct elements:

1. *Body.* This includes my three lower selves; material, reactional and divided, all of which are 'organized energies', associated with my physical body, though they can exist without it.

2. *Spirit.* This means primarily my own spiritual essence. I think, but cannot be sure, that it includes also my Guardian Angel.

3. *Soul.* This is my True Self. So long as my egoism remains it is divided between the spiritual and material influences. It is the battleground of conflicting influences. It is also the vessel that contains my potentialities as a complete man; both material and spiritual. And it is the bridge that is to be built within me between the two worlds.

4. *Affirmative Will.* This is the aspect of 'I' of which we have been speaking. It is the I can and therefore I am. It can also be called the 'male' will.

5. *Receptive Will.* This is the aspect I hinted at just now. It is the will that submits and accepts. It is the will to be helped rather than the will to act. It is *I am wish.* This is the 'female' will that is in all of us.

Many questions will occur to you as you study this symbol. First of all, where is 'I'? The best answer I can give is that 'I' enters by the two channels to the right and left. It can go anywhere and wherever it is, will be at that moment the *centre of gravity*. Where 'I' am is the momentary centre of my being. The aim that I must set before myself is that 'I' should be permanently established in the centre of my soul so that I can fulfil the first purpose of my existence: to be a link between spirit and matter.

How can I perform this task? If I am to bear the strain I must be strong. Strength of 'I' is expressed by the words 'I can'. How does 'I' gain strength? It is by *act*. When I fail to act, my soul weakens and shrivels, when I act, my soul grows stronger. If my soul is strong, it will attract my 'I' to itself. I must wish. How do I wish? I wish because I see. Consciousness makes it possible for me to wish. I see what is matter; I see what is spirit. I see the significance of quantity in the material world; I see that of quality in the spiritual world. I wish for harmony and union between them. This wish attracts 'I'. I can see only if I have the right perspective; as one can only see all round if one is at the top of a mountain. The true place of seeing is in the centre and this is where the 'I' must find itself.

When 'I' am attracted to the material self, I will have no sense of quality. What passes for quality here amounts to 'how much is it worth?' Value is seen in material terms. On the sensitive level, value is interpreted in terms of like and dislike. What I like is worth something; what I dislike is to be thrown away. Reaction takes the place of seeing. There is no value but like or dislike—I am 'like' or I am 'dislike'. In the Divided Self are my desires, my ambitions, my fears, my needs. Value is now only 'I want'. There is no 'I wish'. Then, in the centre comes the great hazard, that I may deny any will but my own and fall into egoism. Then it is 'I demand', 'It is my right', 'Everything is for me', which is the condition of the 'I' when it is shut up in the centre. When the centre of the self begins to open, then the 'I' is able to have an open wish. It is no longer the self-centred wish but the wish that receives and accepts. When 'wish' and 'can' are harmonized, then only I AM. This is the union of the male and female principles within our own nature and seen in this light, we can find another formula for 'I', namely: *I am the union of I can and I wish*. Evidently, this union is possible for every human being in whom the power to wish and 'to can' has been planted.

The symbol is all in one plane in Fig. 9: but properly you should see it in three dimensions. The dotted lines should go vertically up and down in a different plane from that which contains matter and spirit. We could arrange the four main elements as a tetrad in this way.

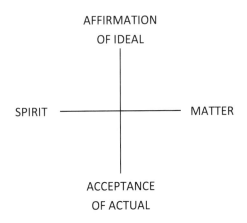

AFFIRMATION
OF IDEAL

SPIRIT ———————————— MATTER

ACCEPTANCE
OF ACTUAL

Fig. 10. Tetrad of Will

This shows matter and spirit as the 'field of action' of the Will—balanced, as it were—between the male or affirming principle and the female or receptive principle.

This suggests that in the completed symbol, the state of 'I' is not a matter of place or level. It is very important to understand this. As I have said, it is very rare for man to become truly spiritualized; that is, one in whom the fifth level has become united with the self. The spiritualized man or the saint are rare. Rarer still are the prophets and messengers whose spiritual essences come from beyond this earth altogether. At first, this makes it seem as if our destiny were somehow cut short. If you and I have no hope of becoming saints, then it seems as if our prospects are limited to becoming useful human beings. That is true if we look at human destiny only in terms of the material and the spiritual field of action. When we begin to look at it in terms of 'I' and the will, the whole position is transformed. Then great and small cease to count; everyone is capable of the act that makes real. In the

Harmony of Creation, the small act is as significant as the big act. Out of many small acts, Reality, the purpose of the whole creation, is being forged. Every deed, every act that is in truth the unification of the spiritual and the material is real. Or, putting it in ordinary language, *everything done with quality is a real act.* Everyone is capable of the act. However small they may be, they are of infinite importance compared with the mere activity where the union of spirit and matter fails to be realized.

I am not using the word 'infinite' in a figurative way. Just as a solid is infinitely more massive than a surface; so is a real act infinitely more weighty than mere actualization.

This is vividly represented by the story of the widow's mite. Her act is reverberating through all history so that mankind can never forget it. And yet, it was a small act whether in material or in spiritual terms. She was not a very spiritual woman or her role would have been different. She obviously had no material strength, because she only had one farthing to give, but she had the act. She could give without reservation all that she had. That is real act. To give with reservation just what is convenient to give, is not an act that draws 'I' to the centre, but rather strengthens the hold of the lower parts of the self.

How many ways there are of giving! Every level of selfhood has its own kind of giving. But there is one kind of giving which is act, which is real; that is, the giving without reserve, the giving free of the demand for any return. This applies not only to what we call charitable acts. Everything done by human beings can have the property of a free act. This is what we should be looking for in our lives; that *what we do should be free and therefore real.* In the act, there should be the full quality compatible with the amount of quantity present.

This brings us to a question of as much concern to us ordinary people, as it is to philosophers and theologians. We must all, at some time, have asked ourselves the question as to whether our will is free or not. We *seem* to be free. We *must* be free, if we are to be responsible. There would be no sense in asking questions and seeking answers or in troubling about anything whatever, unless we were able by our own free will to influence the results of our actions. And yet we see that the greater part of our actions are done without choice and cannot be called free. Even when we are aware of a choice, we see that we come down on the side that has the strongest pull on us. When such thoughts take possession of us, we are bewildered. What is the use of saying that I can, if what I do is so obviously the result of some influence that I did not myself create?

I need not say more about this; because we are studying psychology, not philosophy. We can say without hesitation, that *psychologically* we are convinced that responsibility and therefore freedom are real. We are also convinced that, if we look carefully enough, we shall find that our actions can always be explained in terms of causes and influences outside ourselves. This manifest psychological contradiction does not distress us, unless we allow it to obsess us. Why not? Because we feel that it, somehow, misses the point. The solution of the problem can be seen quite easily with the help of our symbol in its present extended form. I should perhaps say at this point that the solution I shall give you follows fairly closely that given by St. Thomas Aquinas, but I have made one additional point that I believe is essential to the completeness of the argument,[1] as I understand the matter. It turns upon three distinctions that we can, with a little trouble, verify in our own experience:

1. Spirit and Matter.
2. Will and Being.
3. Affirmation and Receptivity.

We already have the distinction of Spirit and Matter in our symbol. We should by now recognize the distinction in various ways, such as Value-Fact, Quality-Quantity, Spiritual Essence-Material Essence, Spirit-Body. The two constantly exert opposing influences upon our selfhood. Both of them are diverse and their influences are infinitely varied in kind and in intensity. Taken together, as I said just now, they are our field of action.

I have not previously mentioned the second distinction. It

---

1   St. Thomas' solution is given in detail in the treatise *De Malo*, Of Evil, mainly under Question No. 6. A more general and elementary presentation is in the *Summa Contra Gentiles*, ch. 48. I have also made use of *The Philosophy of St. Thomas Aquinas* by A. D. Sertillanges (Editions Montaigne, Paris 1940).

concerns the two pairs of triangles. Matter and Spirit are both manifestations of Being. Being has gradations, from the purest spirituality to the grossest materiality, all is Being. Being is: whatever is. Will is totally different in its nature from this. Will cannot be put upon different 'levels'. There are differences in Will, but they can best be looked upon as the *intensity of connectedness*. We speak of a strong magnet and a weak magnet, or a strong chain and a weak chain. Will is strong or weak in a manner that bears some resemblance to this, though the illustrations being taken from material objects cannot be anything but suggestions. Another way of describing will is as the *power of taking things as they are*. Two people may look at the same situation: one will see it hazily and make mistakes, the other will see clearly and judge correctly.[1] Lastly, we can say that *Will is the Power to Act*. If you can combine these three formulae and see what is behind the words, you will be on the way to grasping what I mean, when I say that Will is totally different from Being.

Now, we come again to the third distinction. In front of any situation, it is possible to be active or to be passive. This is a rather inaccurate way of distinguishing between *Affirmation* and *Receptivity*.[2] We can assert ourselves—'take arms against a sea of troubles'—or we can accept—'suffer the slings and arrows'. Hamlet's dilemma, as we all well know, is the dilemma of us all: but Hamlet did not see the solution, or there would have been no tragedy. It must be obvious from the way I have put it, that there are some situations that call for affirmation and others that call for acceptance.

Now the point of the three distinctions is this: all three combine to give us freedom and responsibility. Because we are between different influences—spiritual and material—the *choice* is before us. Because we are able to *see and judge*, we can make the choice. Because our will has the double quality of affirmation and acceptance, we can translate the choice into act.

The power to see, to judge and to act resides in the 'I'. This power is the third element that completes the soul. The other two

---

1   The connection between Will and Attention and Decision is discussed in *The Dramatic Universe* Vol. II, pp. 73-5.

2   These arc discussed in detail in the chapter 'Will and the Triad', *The Dramatic Universe*, Vol. II, pp. 69--97, especially in sections 11.27.6 and 11.27.7.

are the material and spiritual natures, or the lower and higher natures of the self. When *I am*, then the lower and higher natures are blended into the soul. The soul is the home of the 'I'. It is there that we must be if we are to have and to exercise our freedom. Let me remind you here that we said that the energy of the True Self of man is the *creative energy*. It is this energy that creates the soul. It is this same energy that is the direct instrument of the 'I'. Through the creative energy, the 'I' can exercise its power to act. The creative energy, you will remember, is beyond consciousness. That is why it can be intimately linked to the will. If we were conscious of it, there would be two separate experiences of 'will' and 'act', but we can easily verify that will and act are one. They are one because the creative energy can translate judgment into act without any intermediate step. One consequence of this is that we find that we can act, without being *conscious* that we are acting. For example, if I decide really decide with my will—that I shall perform a particular act at a particular time, I shall find myself doing it before I am aware of it. Many of you have had this experience when we worked at the exercise of 'putting something into tomorrow'.

This is only one way in which these ideas can help us. I want to show you more about the way to use them in order to live our lives better; but first I must say some more about the soul.

When I spoke of the point in the centre, I said that this could expand and become a sphere. This means that our *soul can grow*. In order to grow it must receive food and this comes from our acts. It is 'I' that feed the soul and also 'I' that build the house and put it in order. As the soul grows it can take more and more into itself. This could be represented on the symbol by a series of circles, each with a greater and greater embrace.

I have drawn four circles to symbolize four conditions or states which the human soul can attain. The innermost circle represents the state where man has found himself. He is able to say *I am* and it will be true of his own real self. This state does not imply freedom from egoism; in other words, it is not necessarily a *good soul*; but it is a strong one that is not dominated by the lower parts of the self. The second state is that of the union of male and female principles. This soul is free from inner conflict; but it is still subject to the limitations of its own material and spiritual pattern. It has no universal quality yet. The third is the compassionate soul that has grown so great and so strong that it can take all into itself It loves all—friends and enemies, known and unknown—alike. But it is also aware of the gulf that separates it from the perfectly pure spirit that is represented by the top line. The last circle is the soul in the state of union—when it is able to meet God and finds God at home within itself. This touches the line of perfect purity which I suggested yesterday we could perhaps connect with the Virgin Mary. The symbol here suggests a very important point—that is the combination of perfect matter and perfect spirit in the Virgin Mary. She was a woman with a body exactly like that of any other woman and she was—and is—also universal in her spirituality overshadowing the whole creation as its representative before God.

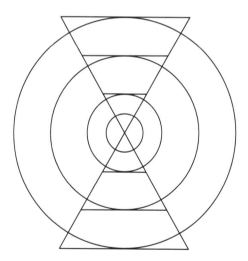

Fig. 11. The Four States of the Soul

You will remember the three 'mansions' I spoke of the other day. The second circle is the mansion *Beit-ul-Muharrem*, the secret mansion of the union of man and wife. The third is the *Beit-ul Mukaddes*, the blessed mansion where soul meets soul. The fourth is the *Beit-ul-Ma'mour*, the mansion of the Divine Decree, where the soul meets God and receives His commandments. Under other names, these four states of the soul have been described by mystics and visionaries who have experienced their reality.

For us, the importance lies in the meeting or, as it is sometimes called, the *encounter*. Encounter means a meeting that is a *real contact*. This is not possible for the self, but only for the soul in which there is 'I'. The lower parts of the self can have various kinds of exchanges; primarily through the senses. We see and touch one another. We can also be sensitive and react to one another. We can be moved by the deeper passions of the Divided Self. But in all this, there is no encounter, no true recognition of one being by another. Because of this the lower selves are lonely. They long for a contact of which they are incapable. The place of contact is the True Self; but if Egoism sits upon the throne, it will only admit others who will crawl on their hands and knees. That is not contact. Indeed, egoism is the loneliest thing in the whole creation; it rejects God and man alike.[1] But when 'I' enters, then there can be a completely different contact. It is a contact of wills—not merely of instruments.[2]

This contact of wills that needs neither matter nor spirit is what we all long for—but the price of it is that egoism must have gone out from the centre. We are so far from this that it might seem to belong to another world—and yet, we can know it for a moment. Sometimes, we are taken unawares and we look into another person's eyes without egoism. We see another soul and recognize it; and know, in the same instant, that we too have been recognized and accepted. We cannot keep this for more than a moment, because our egoism returns and spoils all. But there will come a time when we can hold such moments longer—especially as between man and wife; or as between true friends. With these encounters, we come to the realization that life is an empty shell without that 'I' that is able to meet another and recognize and

---

1   In Dante's *Inferno*, the lowest level is one of frozen immobility, where the souls can see nothing because their tears freeze over their eyes. Lucifer, representing Egoism, has three mouths but three-quarters of his body is encased in ice and snow. No one can approach him and he can see no one but himself. He cannot even taste the egoistic souls whom he crunches in his three mouths.

2   This again is beautifully portrayed in the *Divina Comedia* (Rav. Canto XXI 70--93) when Dante makes his prayer before Beatrice who only smiles and says: '*Roi si torno all'eterna fontana*' to show that their union was one of Will in God.

accept.

Now, I am sure that I need hardly add that this has little to do with high spiritual qualities. The humblest soul can encounter the greatest without fear or shame. We do not often meet it in a degree that approaches that of the great soul that can love all the world— but meet it we do, and it can teach us that the 'I' of man has no level, neither great nor small. The power of the 'I' is to embrace and hold fast to the unity of spirit and matter, and to embrace and hold fast the unity of souls.

The final and decisive encounter is with God. Only then do we learn who we are and all secrets are revealed. Then the soul is judged by an absolute judgment and there is no more freedom of the separate wills. The will must either accept God wholly or be condemned to remain separate and helpless.

I have not said enough about the two-fold nature of man's will. Perhaps we shall come to it again, when you have made your own observations.

. . . . .

This was the last day of the summer school. The practical tasks were finished and there was ample time for discussion. So much was said that I have had to cut down the report. Sometimes the conversation strayed far away from the theme of Spiritual Psychology.

Nevertheless, it was evident that a real step forward had been made in understanding the three-fold nature of man. The evening session began with a question about the attitude we should have towards the 'material world'.

. . . . .

Q. Your symbol goes from the outside to the inside. Until you spoke this morning, I took it to be 'up and down' with visible matter at the bottom. I thought this meant that matter is lower and further away from God? I want to know what you say about this; because most religious teachings seem to tell us that matter is something low and despicable. I believe that Pak Subuh says that matter is satanical and that the material soul can also be called the satanical soul. Do you agree with this debasement of matter?

J.G.B. It is certainly un-Christian to look upon matter as satanical. All who accept the Bible must remember the first Chapter of Genesis: "God looked upon it and saw that it was good."

As I said this morning, the whole symbol of matter and spirit should be taken as the total field within which God and man—as God's representative—do their creative work. It is true that there is a direction 'inwards and outwards'. Matter, visible matter, is the 'external' world. But that does not mean that it is bad or even inferior. It is indispensable for the whole balance of creation and therefore it could not possibly be considered evil in itself.

Again, if we look at it in terms of our human situation: we see the body. It is an indispensable instrument and the very condition of our completion. It is through the body, that our acts are accomplished. Intentions that do not lead to actions are self-destructive; we are told that hell is paved with them. Moreover, man is not complete without his body, any more than the creation would be complete if there were no material forms. Man is one entire whole, body, soul and spirit. The soul cannot act at all without the body and it cannot act rightly without the spirit. The soul cannot fulfil its purpose of linking matter and spirit together unless it has a body to give it a hold upon matter. That is why the resurrection of the body is an essential part of our religious belief. This may seem paradoxical; but if you will reflect on it you will see that a belief in 'survival' without a belief in bodily resurrection, entails a dualism of substances which is quite different from the triadism of body-soul-spirit. As philosophers have painfully realized over the centuries the separation of substances can never be reconciled unless we go beyond dualism. A dyad of spirit and body, such as is implied in most spiritualistic beliefs, will not really work, because there is no way of establishing communication between spirit and matter—even in life, let alone after the body dies—unless there is a third 'something' to hold them together. The 'third' is the soul. But the soul in its turn is helpless, without matter and spirit.

We can look at it in another way. The visible world is wonderful and awe-inspiring. The more science discloses its marvels, the more are we overwhelmed by its immensity, its limitless diversity, the beauty of its working and the marvelous harmony of its laws. We cannot despise such a world, without doing violence to our most direct and most intimate perceptions. How many times we must have felt in our hearts the echo of the hymn that says: 'and only man is vile'. It is not matter, but man that gives us evidence of satanical forces.

How is this to be explained? The main point is that spirit and matter are neither good nor evil. *Good and evil reside solely in the will*. There are good acts and bad acts and there are indifferent actions or mere actualizations. We have seen that the rightful place for our will—our 'I'—is in the centre of the soul. When it goes out of that place it sins. It is drawn out towards matter, because of egoism. We have power over matter, so it can nourish our egoism. When our 'I' chooses to live in the outer world of matter and puts its trust in material things, then and then only we can say that it is satanical.

Pak Subuh never said that *matter* is satanical, but that the material soul is satanical. I do not think that this is hard to understand. Man should be master of the material world, not its slave. When he seeks to dominate through matter, he becomes the slave of matter. That is called 'selling one's soul to Satan'.

But you must see clearly that the trouble is not in matter, nor even in the enjoyment of the material world. If God saw that it is good, we should also see that it is good. And what is good is to be enjoyed. It is possible to enjoy in act. When we look at the beauty of nature this can be an act. We say 'an act of worship'. Everything that we do can be an act of worship. You remember that I said that, for the will, there is no higher or lower. There is only right and wrong. To take good care of a spade or a suit of clothes is right act. To enjoy nature, or wife and children without being enslaved by them is right act. Every right act is an act of worship.

Q. Should the act be done in quietness?

J.G.B. Inner quiet is a necessary condition of judgment. We cannot act without judgment. We cannot judge without seeing. We cannot see without inner peace. That is what we mean by dispassionate judgment.

Q. What does the taste of reality mean?

J.G.B. The taste of reality is in the *encounter*. We have got to learn what it means to encounter. I think the true taste is there. The quality of my wish depends upon my taste being consciously informed so that I am able to recognize the spiritual quality present in this particular moment. In only a limited number of situations can recognition come by thinking; and they mainly concern material questions. For example, one can see whether a sequence of arithmetical calculations is correct or not. This is a material process, a machine could do it just as well, if not better. But there is also the first seeing of the step that permits the calculations to be made; that a machine cannot do, it requires something different. Sometimes, the seeing of that step has such a creative quality that, when you become aware of it, you realize something has come through the seeing that could not have been there without it. How do you recognize the marvelous quality of that particular act of seeing? It is by a kind of inner taste; something in you that is able to encounter the truth. If you have not got that, you cannot recognize it.

'I' is not to be looked upon as a kind of stop-go affair that says 'yes' to this and 'no' to that, and has no other power. 'I' means much more than that. 'I' can make use of the elaborate mechanism of the different parts of the self, from the material to the true human self. 'I' is the lawful ruler of all this. This does not come just by saying: 'I want this and I do not want that' and leaving it to the mechanism to get on with it. That is not realization. There must be something creative, something which could not happen, if 'I' were not there. I create the act. It seems to me that it is just because of this creative power given to man, that it is said that 'God created man in His own image'.

Q. Do you think that there has to be brought into every level a choice, an encounter which goes on all the time?

J.G.B. No, this could be out of proportion. When the right relationship between the spiritual and the material natures has been established, the 'I' will be there and all will go harmoniously. It is not a matter of an intervention, even of the 'I' being aware of everything all the time. Certainly not. If there is a good and just ruler in a country, everything will go rightly, he does not need to know everything that is going on. I should warn you that this analogy is only useful up to a point and after that it becomes misleading. It is not the task of the 'I' to rule by doing everything itself but rather more like the Chinese Tao: if there is a sage in the country—that is, a possessor of Tao—then, although he does nothing, that country will be well ruled. But he is not the emperor.

The small acts of people who have come to a balance between their material and spiritual natures, whose 'I' has found its place in the soul, are sometimes wonderful. This does not mean that their acts are all performed intentionally; but when we notice the act, we meet them in that act. I have seen that a small act like handing a piece of bread across the table can be important and unforgettable. Why? Because it was a moment of encounter. We may meet a stranger in our lives, just for a moment, and something real happens. You recognize in that moment that there is a human being, and you know that he has recognized it in you. This is a momentary thing; but still it is the encounter of 'I' with 'I'.

Q. Returning to the animal impulses of domination and desire for assertion and all that, moments happen when we are witnesses of that going on in us. For instance, desire for admiration or recognition, or being important or something like that, and yet we feel completely helpless to do anything about it. Where is the significant act in that moment?

J.G.B. What you ask is part of the general question of 'I' in the wrong place. In the situation you describe, 'I' has got into the reactional self. The reaction is from our character, to some real or more often fancied injury, or to the possibility of asserting our power. There is *sensitivity* to the stimulus, and *consciousness* of the reaction. When 'I' am caught in that way, I am helpless. The affirming will has been caught into the selfhood. We are like an animal caught in a snare. The only chance is to put ourselves in the receptive will. This is the way of *prayer*. Only you must understand that prayer must not be just another reaction. It must be an act of will. It is a 'letting go' as we used to say in one of Gurdjieff's exercises. This 'letting go' deep down within oneself is, of course, what is required of us in the latihan. That is a significant *act*. I need hardly remind those of you who practise the latihan, that letting go is a positive act of the will. But it is a receptive as distinct from an affirmative act.

Q. When you spoke about the handing of bread, the unforgettable act, I was reminded of the disciples of Emmaus who recognized Christ in the act of breaking and handling the bread, and I wondered if there was a connection here?

J.G.B. Yes, indeed. In what does the supreme power of the earthly life of Jesus consist? It is that it is all act and never mere activity.

Q. Even His speech?

J.G.B. Why not? Certainly His speech.

Q. I was often puzzled why they did not recognize Him before?

(another) Q. They recognized Him in the sense that they asked Him to stay...

J.G.B. The difference is really between knowing and seeing. First they knew, then they saw. First, He approached them through knowledge, by expounding the scriptures to them. They were touched in their hearts, but they did not yet see. The episode reminds us that reality is not encountered through knowledge, but in act. As long as He enlightened them by expounding the scriptures, this could only produce a response in their reason. It was bound to produce this response, they could not let Him go, but they did not yet see. They saw in the moment of act. Then their Intellect was awakened and they saw the Risen Christ.

Q. This is beginning to illuminate something for me about unreality. I think all my life everything has seemed unreal. Why is that so frightening? Is it because one never has one's 'I' in its right place?

J.G.B. A person who has never had his 'I' in the right place is unaware of danger, he does not know what it is. You would not have this fear if you had not a hidden memory of the Reality you have temporarily lost touch with. That fear will awaken you. But those who have seen but do not fear and so fail to make the act, go into that region called 'outer darkness'. If one is able to have that fear, that is the beginning of the act. 'The Fear of the Lord is the beginning of Wisdom'.

Fear of the ego is quite a different thing, it is the sense of emptiness. It is not the fear of something, it is the fear of nothing. Is that what you are talking about?

Q. Yes, it always seemed illogical, because one did not know the reason...

J.G.B. True fear is a precious thing, because so long as it is present in us, we will not lose contact with our soul. When man becomes heedless and unaware of his danger, then terrible things can happen to him. True fear is not paralysing, nor is it an animal fear, it is something different in its nature.

Q. Is 'I' always present when 'me' is absent?

J.G.B. That is not quite the right way to put it. I have spoken about egoism as a sort of central condition; but there are all sorts of false 'I's that impose on our imagination. For example, I may be convinced that I cannot drink milk. What has that to do with 'I'? There is a kind of stupid little impostor that has got into my reactional self and this dances about and says "No milk, no milk". It is not egoism, it is too small for that.

Q. But that is 'me', as far as I am concerned...

J.G.B. Yes it is 'me', but you would not be aware of it, if 'I' were not attached to it. This is what makes the understanding of 'I' so bewildering. Wherever there is a *will*, there is 'I'. You may say 'this is *want*, not *will*' but it is not really right to say 'this body wants' in such a case, because it may not even be true; why should you malign it? It is *I want*. The point is that this is not the right place for 'I'.

'I' can be shattered into fragments, or it can be built up into one. When I spoke about the strength of the 'I', the *I can*, this is the strength of the binding together of the fragments. But in the state of man when his 'I' is broken up into fragments and dispersed all over his selfhood, it is difficult to distinguish between 'I' and 'me'. What you speak about is the state when, from one of these tiny fragments, you become aware of something more whole, more stable. The isolated part is the enemy of the whole, from which it has run away. It is in this sense, that the fragments of 'I' prevent us from being aware of the reality of 'I'.

No impartial self-observation can leave us in doubt that 'I' is not one but many in us so long as we have warring desires, uncontrolled reactions, and are in slavery to every passing influence. The man who has one 'I', always the same and always in the centre, is the transformed man of whom it can truly be said that he is the child of God. Among millions of human beings, there are few who have such an 'I'. But those who have it and have understood its meaning for them also understand that their own 'I' is born in them from God—not made from the self or from the spirit.[1] So that we can say that in the true and complete sense of the word only God can say "I am that I am". When that is experienced as reality a very great step has been made.

Meanwhile, we have to continue to live in the condition of fragmentation where there is no stable will, no permanent 'I'. We hope that we are in a process of being reassembled and 'made whole'. There is much to be said about fragmentation and reintegration of 'I's. But in using words like fragments and integration, I may have evoked in you the picture of a *thinglike* nature that is broken into bits, or a bundle that has been untied and fallen apart. These pictures are dangerous for it would be quite wrong to speak of 'part of an I'. It is rather that the I attaches itself to a part when its true place is to be master of the whole. The fragmentation is in the material form: but the 'I' can be 'tempted' to give itself to a fragment.

Each time it does so it manifests according to the make of the fragment. That is why we have warring 'I's' and the conflict of wills that seem to contradict the belief that man is one. It is only when the 'I' is linked with the creative energy that it has power to act. Then and then alone can it be said that a man has a free will. So long as the 'I' is linked to the weaker energies, it can only exercise the power to choose—'yes' to this and 'no' to that. Step-by-step, the 'I' that has lost itself in the fragments must work its way back to the centre.

Q. I think I understand what you mean by what you call the world of reality; but why is it absolutely different from a big expansion of consciousness in the spiritual world?

J.G.B. I think failure to recognize this difference is the cause of much confusion. There are two words used in the Sufi language about the condition of man. One is called *hal*, which means state, and the other *makam*, which means station. A man may, by the action of some spiritual power beyond himself, be lifted into a higher state than corresponds with his own stage of development. This may be a transition from sensitiveness to consciousness, in which case he will have 'illuminations' that he can understand. Or it may go beyond consciousness into the darkness of the creative energy. He will not experience this directly: but he will feel a

---

1   St. John's Gospel, i. 5.

power working within him and this may give him the assurance that there is a 'Reality beyond consciousness'. These states can never last very long—because the soul is not strong enough to bear them. Nor is it desirable that they should, for they are not necessary for his progress. When they pass, he is no longer on the level to which he had been lifted, but if something has been left in him from it, then he is different, because he has been there. But this is not the same as *makam*. *Makam* means the station which he has actually reached; this corresponds to what I called the growth of the soul. There is such a thing as being raised for a time to a high level of spirituality; and there is such a thing as coming to a certain inner stature, to a certain inner power. They are different. One is simply a state to which one is brought. If it is genuine, it is a grace from God. The other is something that has been reached through the process of transformation, through gradual acquisition of a stronger soul, a more completely integrated will. The first is temporary, the second permanent. I said 'if it is genuine' because there are also false states reached through an unlawful use of the energies of the psyche. These may be self-induced or brought on by some evil spirit that deceives people, by imitating some of the features of a true 'state'.

When I understood all this, I could see that someone who had reached a high station would not necessarily always be in a high state of consciousness. This was a puzzle to me until I realized that what the Sufis speak about are two quite different conditions.

Q. I have for a long time been labouring under a fundamental misconception about this whole scheme of things, and it has to do with my idea of transmutation. The way I have always seen transmutation is the possibility of actually transmitting substances from the bottom of this symbol to the central point. I have begun to see that this is not a right idea; it does not bring in the right for these areas to be themselves. It does not grant them an independent existence. Self-development in that way, is perhaps what Mr. Gurdjieff was talking about when he referred to 'the crystallization of the consequences of the maleficent organ Kundabuffer'. In that sense our hope is this 'I', in enlarging this 'I' so that it expands into one circle on the diagram, and in this way brings all subordinate areas into harmony with each other?

J.G.B. Yes, that is nearly right. It is the whole point, except for just one thing you said about 'enlarging'. The 'I' is not the circles of expansion. It is the soul that grows greater. The circles represent the soul just as the lines represent the selves. It is difficult, until you see this, to distinguish between selves and soul. *The selves keep their places.* They have not to be either promoted or dismissed. They have to be where they should be, but they have to be brought within the soul so that it can take care of them. There is a difference between having a small soul and a great soul. The small soul person can perhaps keep his servants in order by force. The magnanimous person takes them all in and they are all taken care of within. This is magnanimity.

Q. Can we help others in this way? Is any kind of real help possible? I mean spiritual help as distinct from material help, which obviously we can give.

J.G.B. In order to give one must have. If one has material wealth one can give it. If one has spiritual wealth, one can give that also. This is the doctrine of what is called 'the transfer of merits'. It is a very important doctrine that sometimes seems to be very strange, and perhaps for some people a stumbling-block. It is that the merits of a positive act of the 'I' in one person can actually be transferred to another who is in need of them. For example, there is the story of the death of the great Indian saint Ramakrishna. There was a very worldly man, wholly caught in the material forces, who found it quite impossible to love the Great Mother, which was Ramakrishna's form of devotion. He came to Ramakrishna and asked if he would help him. The saint, according to his own account, undertook to do this and took all that man's sins into himself. He developed cancer and died not long afterwards. I believe there is an important historical truth in this story, but in any case it illustrates this notion of the transfer of merits. This other man, with no merit of his own, was saved from hell by asking Ramakrishna for that help. Ramakrishna transferred his own surplus merits to him, but he had to pay the price in his physical body.

Belief in the transfer of merits is part of the doctrine of Christianity. There are religious people who devote their lives entirely to prayer in order to be allowed to bear the consequences of the sins of others. This doctrine, which seems strange, is based upon a reality; and that is, when a soul has become strong enough and great enough it is able to take others into itself. The Christian doctrine is that mankind as a whole has been redeemed through Christ. Christ descended into hell, and without this, His mission would not have been completed. But in spite of the redemption of mankind, men continue to fall into sin. Those people who have, so to say, a surplus of merits can, with their merits, open up new possibilities to others. If you can grasp this idea you will also accept the notion that the real true 'I' of the man with a magnanimous soul is able to enter into the negative regions and do something there.

I do not know if you have read the story of Francisco and Jacinta Abobora, of Fatima in Portugal. These two children, with their cousin Lucia, had visions of the Blessed Virgin Mary. To them, and through them to all Portugal, the Virgin predicted the best authenticated miracle of modern time when, on 13th October 1917, 70,000 people saw the unbelievable 'dance of the sun'. Now, the point is that these children were told by an angel and by the Virgin that they could bring about the conversion of sinners by their prayers and voluntary sufferings. They were only children eight and nine years old, but they cheerfully accepted a most agonizing life and died within two or three years with full confidence that they would be taken straight to heaven. They were assured that, if only enough people could be prepared to pray and suffer in this way, Russia would be converted and the world would be saved. Although they were so young and in a worldly sense insignificant, their act has had tremendous consequences which we do not yet fully appreciate.

All of us are free to accept some part of the world's burden. Mankind cannot ignore all this and just go along the line of self-affirmation alone.

It is very likely that a man can go quite a long way by himself, seeking only his own salvation, not in an egoistic sense, but on the contrary, wishing to throw out all egoism, truly wishing his only concern to be with God. But sooner or later it is shown to him that if his concern is with God, he must not forget that God's concern is with the world and not just with him alone.

You know that certain Eastern doctrines place Nirvana as the summit and the goal of man's spiritual achievement. Nirvana is a state of pure creativity from which all outward forms have disappeared; but where there also is no involvement in the demands of the spiritual world. In other words, Nirvana is a point of stillness, a point of infinite freedom, an unconditioned state which can be mistaken for the goal. In that state, man can create for himself whatever he will: but it is a complete illusion to suppose that this is the goal of man's striving. Anyone who succumbs to this illusion cuts himself off from God. The truth is that Nirvana is the gateway to reality, it is not reality itself.

Q. When the prodigal son has returned to his Father's House and is given shoes, he is not permanently with his Father, but goes forth again. Does this not show that the aim of evolution is that the soul should go forth on the other side of Nirvana?

J.G.B. Yes, I am sure it is so. When I say the world of reality is the world of act, I think it is no doubt true that this is no world to sit down and do nothing. There is contact with the problems created by the difference between spirit and matter, between quantity and quality, between the form and the formless. All that has to be endured, and that is what makes the act possible. If one were to repudiate all that, then one would be stuck at that central point, and nothing would be realized. The notion that the goal of existence is liberation, to be free from this endless incompatibility of the spiritual and the material, to be able to get out of it all, is an illusion; there is something much more significant than that in human destiny.

Q. I have been wanting to formulate a question about the two acts of will which you call affirmation and receptivity. Would you say that these are active and passive states of the 'I'? Are they equally valuable for us or is one to be preferred to the other? This seems to be connected with the question of 'submission' versus 'effort'. Some people say that without effort we cannot be saved. Others say that effort is useless and that with submission we get all we need. This seems to have turned into a kind of dispute between 'Subud' people and 'Gurdjieff' people, and I would like to get at the bottom of it.

J.G.B. The first part of your question is easy to answer. The distinction of affirmation and receptivity is not the same as that of active and passive. Active and passive can be applied to energies: sensitivity is more active than automatism, desire is more active than sensitivity, creative energy is the most active energy there can be in man. Heat is the most passive form of energy. The distinction of affirmation and receptivity applies to will and not to energy.

Now let us come to the main question. My own belief in the matter is quite definite. Both the affirmative and the receptive will are necessary for salvation. But there is a third will that I have not spoken of before; it is the reconciling will that is the Will of God. This does not come into our scheme because we have no power over it. Nevertheless nothing could happen without it. It is through this third will that the Divine Omnipotence is manifested. Man can only affirm or accept; he can neither make laws nor set himself free from them. Those powers are reserved by God; but it seems that at moments God allows man to exercise them. That is the real secret of freedom.[1] I am saying this so that you will remember that man is never alone. His 'I' can affirm or it can accept, but nothing whatever can happen without God, for there can be no act without the third or Reconciling Will.

Now let us return to the two modes of willing that are allowed to us men. You ask about *effort* and *submission*. First we must see what effort means. It is the action of one energy upon another. For example, the energy of consciousness can act upon the sensitive energy. In psychological language, we can say that a desire can repress a reaction. Again, sensitive energy can act upon the automatic energy of the organism. This is happening all the time as we use our bodies to sense, to feel, to move, to think, to remember. Now, by exercising my power of affirmation—that is, the affirmative will—'I'— can bring the more passive energy into contact with the more active. I can, for example, choose to bring my reactions under the influence of a desire—say the desire to be admired and esteemed by others. This is an 'act of will' and it will result in the suppression of a particular reaction—say, the habit of

---

1   This was said very succinctly, as I did not wish to go into long explanations. The six chapters on Will and the Triad in *The Dramatic Universe*, Vol. II, deal with the subject in a thorough but abstract manner. I hope to be able at some time to show how these notions can be applied to the solution of most problems connected with will.

wasting time. As I do this, I experience a tension and I call this 'effort'. It is still easier to see this in the case of what we call 'physical effort', where 'I' bring the automatic energy under the influence of the sensitivity. If l am running a race, I put my attention on winning, and my sensitive energy draws on the automatic until it is exhausted. If I then mobilize the animal energy of desire, I can get a 'second wind'. If l can bring the creative energy of my True Self to bear, I can even kill my body. That is effort, super-effort and super-super-effort.

You will certainly have noticed that effort can come from egoism as well as from 'I'. There is even a special danger for the affirmative will of being entangled in egoism, just because it is able to exercise the powers of the self to satisfy its needs and desires. But it certainly does not follow from this that the affirmative will is a 'bad' will. The first chapter of Genesis brings this out beautifully. Adam was endowed by God with power over all other creatures on the earth and he was to exercise this power in God's service. God the Reconciling Will—'walked with him'. All would have been well, but for the evil suggestion; coming, not from the material, but from the spiritual world—for Satan is a spiritual essence—that man could himself become 'like God knowing good and evil'. The affirmative will became evil only when it sought to usurp a power to which it was not entitled. Moreover, it was not Adam alone that was at fault. The initial step was taken by Eve, who 'accepted' the bait offered by the serpent. In this way both the male and the female will were equally tainted—that is the Original Sin.

It must be perfectly clear to you that there is nothing inherently evil in the receptive Will either. Eve was made as pure as Adam. This is emphasized in the Christian religion by the figure of the Blessed Virgin Mary who is the pure receptive will untainted by sin. This supremely important doctrine resolves many questions—even in philosophy. For example, philosophers have recently been discussing the question whether there is a logical contradiction in God's creating a free being who would never sin—the point being that it is usual to say that sin is the *inevitable* consequence of freedom. The question is answered very simply for Christians, because the Blessed Virgin is precisely such a creature, who by her free acceptance of the Annunciation made the Incarnation possible.

The question remains whether effort is *necessary* for the perfecting of the soul, or whether acceptance alone will bring about the transformation.

I would be inclined to answer that acceptance is *necessary*, but that effort is *obligatory*. This is illustrated in the parable of the steward who owed a thousand talents and was forgiven; but, because he would not forgive a small debt, ended in outer darkness. What can be achieved by effort is small, but it is in our power and therefore it is an obligation. Acceptance is another matter. We cannot act upon a power that is greater than our own. There is nothing in man that can overcome egoism. That would be the Prince of Devils, casting out devils. There is no way except to submit the selfhood to the action of a higher spiritual power. We have already seen how this appears to work in the latihan, when the personal spirit—the *Roh Rohani*—acts through the various levels of the selfhood.

Only, I must say that my experience has shown me that if what we receive in the latihan is not complemented by the fulfillment of our obligation to act, we shall be no better off. Indeed we may be very much worse off. The parables of Jesus several times refer to the situation of the man who is *freely given* the action that will cleanse him, but fails to do his part.[1]

Q. There comes a time in one's work when one can sense what is possible, and yet knows one has not the necessary strength, and to me this seems a time for prayer. Then strength seems to be given.

J.G.B. I think that the real mystery of 'I' is the secret of separation and union. This cannot be brought within the grasp of our reason. 'I am I'. Therefore alone. And yet I am not alone, because God is 'I', and God is great enough for me to be within God's power. Therefore I am I and yet not alone. Somehow or other, there is an act which transforms this condition of separateness without destroying it. That is what I think is prayer. Prayer is

---

1   There are the parables of the Wedding Garment, of the Ungrateful Steward, and of the man out of whom a devil was cast. Each brings out an important aspect of the reciprocity of receptivity and affirmation.

really and truly an act of the 'I'. It is the special act concerned
with this dilemma of separateness and union. Evidently we are
separated. This is so tremendous that every 'I' has at a certain
moment to experience this isolation; even as Jesus experienced it
on the Cross. But, at the same time, this is all within the 'I' of God.

Q. The 'I' must be, for each of us, the creation of God. Would
the creative power that flows through the latihan give my 'I' more
possibilities?

J.G.B. This is a theological question that I cannot answer. It
does seem to me that 'I' is not created in the way that matter and
spirit are created. 'I' is different from everything else. It is more
as if it were given to us than created. In 'I', resides a power that
we associate with God—that is the power to act. But the 'I' can
act only if it is enabled to do so by *Grace*. Grace alone makes it
possible for the 'I' to perform these real acts which bring us into
the world of reality.

Every one of us has an I-nature. It is neither spiritual nor
material, but concerned with acts. Its power lies in choosing and
willing. This is not reserved for 'special people'. If we begin to
think: 'Can I reach such and such a level? Can I become a Man
No. 4, or Man No. 5, or even Man No. 6?—we miss the point. We
do not know why we were brought here. What is in our power is
to be *real* and in that we are all equal. It does not matter if our
destiny seems to have no significance at all and we just seem to
be sitting and watching what is going on. This is not our business.
Our business is to become real and to establish our own 'I'. We all
know very humble people whose reality we can feel.

Q. There was one change of understanding I had during the
day. St. Francis said "Lord, what are Thou, and what am I?", and
I had thought that what he meant was 'Lord, as Thou art in all Thy
Glory, then I am nothing', but now I wonder whether he had not
meant 'Lord, since Thou art, then how am I allowed to be?'

J.G.B. Yes, I think it can be understood in this way also. 'How
is it that I am allowed to be? For what? Why should I be there at
all? I cannot be needed. If I am there, then it must be for some
purpose of Thine. But why should it be I? Why should I be there?'
Why should God have any need for 'I' other than His own 'I'?' This
question is the very heart of what we are concerned with here. Only

God Himself can reveal the answer, and if He has ever done so, no man has been able to convey it to others. Here we can only accept.

Q. Would you then say that the latihan is a purely spiritual action in which the will plays no part?

J.G.B. I think it is clear enough to everyone that the working of the latihan is a descent into us of a spiritual power that is present within us all. When we enter the latihan we do so because we believe that this spiritual power is good, and that it will have a cleansing and strengthening effect upon our own body and psyche. Pak Subuh has been very careful to say that this power is not God—that is the Holy Spirit—but a 'power that comes from God'. Every good gift comes from God and I believe that Subud is truly a 'good gift' and that it is therefore right to say that Subud comes from God. But this is not the same as to say that 'God works on us in the latihan'. Pak Subuh has never said that. As I said the other day, he has said that the immediate action is through the spiritual power of the fifth order—the *Roh Rohani*. In a more general sense, he speaks of the Great Life Force—the *Daja Hidup Besar*.

We can trace the different stages of the working of the latihan on our Symbol. Each of the lines represents one of the seven conditions or states of the soul.

Q. Where does the Great Life Force fit in?

J.G.B. That same question was put to Bapak by a group of Benedictine monks who were interested in Subud. They wanted to know whether he meant by this the same as the Holy Spirit in our Christian belief. Bapak was very clear in his answer. He said that the Great Life Force is certainly not God but a created power that comes from God. He said that it is universal and can enter into everything. Perhaps we should be right to connect it with the universal spiritual power on the sixth level of our symbol; but I cannot say. We do not have in our Western schemes, the idea of universal, natural powers or energies—except those on the gross material level like of gravitation or electricity. My own view is that all the energies I have spoken of in these talks, are universal like gravitation—but of course totally different in their nature and action. The Great Life Force would then be an energy that has the properties that we see working in the latihan. There is nothing that Pak Subuh has said which suggests that the Great Force of Life is not a part of the natural order. Therefore, however we may take it, there is no suggestion that in the latihan it is God the Holy Spirit that acts upon the soul. In more theological language, the action of the latihan is natural, not supernatural.

Now, we cannot be sure that a natural action will free us from egoism. If egoism is the consequence in man of the original sin, then only God Himself can remove it. This is our Christian belief that God, incarnating in Jesus Christ and dying for mankind upon the Cross, liberated men from the otherwise inevitable consequences of the Fall. If this is correct, then it would follow that the latihan can take us a certain distance, but it cannot take us all the way. Whatever we may do to prepare ourselves, and there is much we can and must do, in the end it is God alone—directly and without the mediation of any created power, spiritual or material— who can set us free. Do not think that I am decrying the latihan, or diminishing the immense value that I see in Subud. I know what I myself have gained from it. I have seen what hundreds of others have gained from it. I am certain that the latihan, sincerely practised, will open in us a channel through which spiritual influences can penetrate into all the different levels of the self. It will transform our bodily condition, our sensitivity, our consciousness and our understanding. But I believe that sooner or later everyone who wishes to be free from egoism will have to turn to Him who alone can accomplish that supreme act in the soul of man.

Once again, I am afraid of misleading you. I do believe that there is such a state as being a Christian and not knowing it. I know people who say: "I cannot accept Christianity, but I do believe in God and I do know that only by submitting to the Will of God can I be saved from my present wretched condition". Such people are afraid of words; they will not call themselves Christians, but they live as Christians: by which I mean that they are humble, loving their fellow men, and wanting above all to know and to do God's Will. In such people, we can recognize the act of will, both to receive and to affirm. The rest depends solely upon the Reconciling Will of God which alone is omnipotent.

Before I leave this subject—and I am afraid that I have already trespassed too far into theology—I must speak about death and resurrection. In a very true sense, every transformation is a death and a resurrection. To be liberated from material forces, means to die to the material self and be born again to the reactional self. When this is done, material forces have no more power over the soul. To pass to the next stage, we must die to our likes and dislikes, to all slavery to our reactions. Then we are born again on the level of consciousness and understanding; but not yet free from desires. To reach the True Self and be able to live as a real man, we must die to all other desires except the desire to be. Hard and bitter though each of these deaths is bound to be, they are nothing to the final death of egoism. Then we share the Passion of Christ. If you look again at our symbol, you can see it was the self upon the cross. There it must die. But that dying is our very own death; it is not the death of a lower self, of automatic manifestations, of sensitive reactions, of desires, but the death of our own self. In no other way can egoism be taken out of us. But as we die in Christ, so do we rise again in Christ. The soul in whom egoism has died rises as the bride of Christ. The supreme encounter of the bride and the bridegroom takes place there in the centre of the soul. From that the true 'I' is born—the 'I' that is one with Christ, and being one with Christ is also being the Son of God.

Now let me see if I have answered your question about Subud and Gurdjieff. I would say that these represent the two aspects of the will. One is necessary and the other is an obligation. I know many who feel like that about it and are convinced, as I am, that both must be developed by practice. But neither of them separately nor both together, is the whole story. The crown of a spiritual psychology is the soul's encounter with Christ. For that our receptive will must take the Virgin Mary as its model: "Behold the handmaid of the Lord, be it done unto me according to Thy word". The affirming will must take Christ as its model: "I came not to do my own will but the will of Him who sent me". With these two, we shall find our own 'I' ready to meet Christ in the holy of holies; that is, the purified human soul. Then, and only then, will we know the answer to the question: "Who am I?" We may guess the answer and we shall certainly guess wrong: for it is only when I meet God that "I shall know even as I am known."

EPILOGUE: WORK AND NOT WORK

Looking back over the events of my life since I wrote *Witness* and the experience of the Institute Summer School of 1962; it becomes more than ever clear to me that our understanding of man turns upon the problem of Reality. If the aim of existence is Self-Realization and if this is identical with God-Realization, then the connecting link that makes them one and the same is to be found in the meaning of the word 'Reality'. If all were equally real, realization would have no meaning. If all is not equally real, then realization means the process of transformation that leads from unreality or imperfect reality towards Reality in the fullest sense.

The theme of this book is that there are both. degrees and distinctive modes of Reality and that there is a process that leads from the Unreal to the Real. This, in its turn, requires that there should be a means of effecting the transformation. This 'means' is what we call by the name of WORK. In the book, there are few references to Work, either in the absolute sense as the process of universal realization, or in the relative sense of personal transformation. This is because those who participated in the discussions started from the premise that Work is a reality in both senses: absolute and relative. We were not concerned to discuss the authenticity of the process of transformation, but to understand it better.

The obligation to work for Reality is the Categorical Imperative from which life derives its meaning. It is, as Kant showed in the *Grundlage*, the ultimate, irreducible, moral certainty from which are derived our notions of God, Immortality and Ethic. I have never been satisfied, nor I believe was Kant himself, with the *Critique of Practical Reason*. It does not convey the sense of urgency which we experience in contemplating life based on Work and life without Work.

I was impelled to write this Epilogue by the impact of a vision or vivid dream that woke me from sleep a few nights ago.

I found myself in some remote, antipodean place where

people were living ordinary lives. I recognized not a few of them as people I knew or had read about and noticed with a sense of wonder rather than surprise that some were still living, and others were dead. They did not notice this difference because in any case they were all ghosts. But they were all aware of being ghosts and wanted to turn into real people. From time to time, an aeroplane arrived with others who joined them and among the new arrivals were both living ghosts and dead ghosts. I was made aware that all was well with these people because eventually they would cease to be ghosts.

Then I found myself back again nearer home; but this time I was taken to some kind of underground place. Here also were people more or less happily occupied with their daily lives and some of them were now living and others were dead. These also were ghosts but these ghosts were neither able to distinguish between life and death, nor did they understand that they were no more than ghosts.

I knew that I must tell them about their condition and about the other place where ghosts were being transformed into real beings. When I spoke to them of aeroplanes that could take them over, they said that they would go only if an aeroplane would come back and assure them that there was a place for them over there.

I remember very clearly explaining that once an aeroplane had gone over, it would never return. This seemed to them illogical and unreasonable and they took no more notice of what I said.

Then I found myself in a kind of lift being taken back to the surface. I looked at the lift-man and said to myself, "If I were not colour blind I should see that his face is grey". Somehow, this observation brought home to me the terror of being a ghost and immense pity filled me for these people who had lost the possibility of becoming real.

As I began to wake up, I said to myself: "What does it really matter that they are only ghosts? They are good, decent people, living good, decent lives and if they are satisfied with unreality why should they be disturbed? Their ghostly existence is also necessary."

At that moment I awakened completely and saw, in a flash, the infinite significance of Work. It is the imperative of all imperatives, the source from which all life takes its meaning, the way to Reality and even Reality itself. Work takes many forms: but all forms have one common character: the Will to Reality. Whether active or passive, whether in solitude or in society, work is always one and the same: it is the dedication of the will to the realization of Reality. This dedication carries with it the obligation to share understanding with others and to serve the Work in its universal significance. That is why those who have seen the difference between ghost-life and real-life are compelled to speak of what they have seen—even to those who do not wish to hear.

I am more than ever aware of the imperfections and even the errors in what I have written. I am ashamed to offer it as a "Spiritual Psychology" to those who are seeking for the Reality that is Work. Let it be taken as an essay and an attempt to share an understanding that is still in the process of being born.

J.G. Bennett.

January, 1964

INDEX

Made in the USA
Columbia, SC
18 November 2024